Columbia University

Contributions to Education

Teachers College Series

No. 195

AMS PRESS
NEW YORK

LEGISLATIVE CONTROL OF THE ELEMENTARY CURRICULUM

BY

JESSE KNOWLTON FLANDERS, Ph. D.

Teachers College, Columbia University
Contributions to Education, No. 195

Bureau of Publications
Teachers College, Columbia University
New York City
1925

Library of Congress Cataloging in Publication Data

Flanders, Jesse Knowlton, 1878-
Legislative control of the elementary curriculum.

Reprint of the 1925 ed., issued in series: Teachers College, Columbia University. Contributions to education, no. 195.
Originally presented as the author's thesis, Columbia.
Bibliography: p.
1. Educational law and legislation--United States. --States. 2. Education, Elementary--United States--States--Curricula. I. Title. II. Series: Columbia University. Teachers College. Contributions to education, no. 195.

KF4201.Z95F56 1972 344'.73'077 75-176777
ISBN 0-404-55195-5

Reprinted by Special Arrangement with Teachers College Press, New York, New York

From the edition of 1925, New York
First AMS edition published in 1972
Manufactured in the United States

AMS PRESS, INC.
NEW YORK, N. Y. 10003

FOREWORD

In his current annual report Dean James E. Russell of Teachers College has called attention to the importance of the problem of legislative enactments affecting "the freedom of teaching." He characterizes this issue as one of the most important in the development of our system of public education. The seriousness of the situation is portrayed in the following paragraph from Dean Russell's report:

> The trend of public opinion in matters educational is part and parcel of the tendency of the times to shape conduct by legal enactment. Whether we like it or not, some school boards will sit in judgment on history texts and some will bar out modern science. The war taught us that German could be eliminated from our schools. Who knows what labor unionists, or chambers of commerce, or Biblical fundamentalists will insist on next? I foresee trouble enough to keep us from stagnation. Once a homogeneous group, bent on having its own way, gets the notion that the schools can be used to promote its particular tenets, that group will surely seek to shape educational procedure. As soon as one group succeeds in influencing school affairs, some other group will rise in opposition and demand to be heard. This is no idle speculation: parties and sects and unions are even now contending for preferment in a way embarrassing to those who look to the larger good. The most hopeful sign is that contending groups may neutralize each other, thus giving the teacher a chance to work out his own salvation.

For one who would study the distance which we have already gone in the direction of controlling the curriculum of our schools by legislation this pioneer piece of work by Dr. Flanders is indispensable. He has brought together here without prejudice the provisions of the state constitutions and of the statute law as they affect the curriculum of the elementary school. He has raised many searching questions without dogmatizing concerning the answers which may be developed.

For the student of the problems of the curriculum Dr. Flanders' list of references will prove most helpful. The well selected quotations included in the study, together with the bibliography, will prove invaluable to the scientific student of the curriculum.

GEORGE D. STRAYER.

ACKNOWLEDGEMENTS

The study here reported is the result of nearly two years of intensive research. For the accuracy of the findings the author alone is responsible; the errors and the omissions are his. But for whatever of merit it contains his debt of obligation is large. First of all to Dr. George D. Strayer and Dr. N. L. Engelhardt who jointly pointed out the need for investigation to discover the extent to which the public school curriculum is controlled by state legislatures. This study is a direct outgrowth of their suggestion and the writer has enjoyed their criticism throughout. Thanks are due also to Dr. Edward S. Evenden and Dr. Fletcher Harper Swift for many helpful suggestions and for their patient and thoughtful guidance. Dr. Robert J. Leonard, Dr. William A. McCall and Dr. Carter Alexander each gave timely constructive advice. To Dr. William Heard Kilpatrick I acknowledge a special debt of gratitude for his painstaking reading of the first and final chapters. These were greatly improved by his kindly criticism. I am not unmindful of the encouragement which I received from many who are not here specifically mentioned as well as from those just enumerated. Dr. Frederick C. Hicks and Lawrence H. Schmehl gave valuable aid in locating and making available necessary books in the law library. Several of the state superintendents of public instruction generously furnished copies of their compilation of the school law, which not only served as a convenient check upon my independent search but also greatly reduced the labor of making a transcript of the statutes. Assistance was also rendered by the Research Division of the National Education Association through the courtesy of its director, Dr. John K. Norton. Most of all, I am under obligation to one who, although in no way directly concerned with the conduct of this study, was a constant source of inspiration. From Dr. Ellwood P. Cubberley as teacher, counsellor, and friend, I have caught, I hope, something of the spirit of his gospel of service to humanity through education.

November 26, 1925 J. K. F.

CONTENTS

TABLES

LEGISLATIVE CONTROL OF THE ELEMENTARY CURRICULUM

CHAPTER I

INTRODUCTION—THE PROBLEM

The problems involved in curriculum construction and reconstruction are perennial. Each generation has to meet them. In the life of each youth they must, for him, receive an answer. And yet as problems they ever remain with us. They are manifold, intricate, and interdependent. They are being studied today as never before. Books and articles are being written, surveys and investigations are being conducted, schoolmen and other public-minded citizens are trying to find something more objective and reliable than personal opinion, imitation, and hoary custom in accordance with which to determine what the child should learn and what the school should teach.

Since that which the child really learns will so completely control the habits and ideals of the future citizen, it would be difficult to over-estimate the importance of these problems. An adequate public school curriculum must conform to an educational philosophy which is in harmony with an acceptable social and political philosophy. We no longer question the right of a people to decide the form of government under which they shall themselves live. Have they the right to decide the form of government under which others after them shall live? More specifically, have they the right, through the child's curriculum, to limit the thoughts which future citizens shall think? If so, what becomes of progress? These and many other questions are, as a matter of fact, in some degree being answered, consciously or unconsciously, whenever a curriculum is established.

Moreover, in any actual instance of instruction, matter cannot be divorced from method. There are some educators who would subordinate the curriculum to the educative process. They hold it to be less important that the child should be exposed to particular facts than that he should acquire skill in using facts.

They put greater emphasis upon developing ability to think and ability to find reliable information when needed, along with an interest in and a disposition to seek pertinent facts. They regard teaching "how to study" as a greater objective of education than the acquisition of predetermined knowledges and skills. They feel that there has been, and still is, altogether too much stress put upon memorizing; not because memorizing is bad but because there is no assurance that that which is merely memorized will, in fact, influence conduct. From this standpoint, the main consideration of the school should be to establish desirable habits of thought and action; the subject-matter used for the purpose is of secondary importance. While these views are not universally accepted in theory and are even less generally followed in practice, there is an unmistakable tendency away from indoctrination toward development of ability to think independently.

Many of the complex problems associated with curriculum-making can be solved only when we know very much more than we do now about the learning process and about the sort of citizens we wish to develop. In the meantime, education must go on. Just as we may not stop living in order to learn how to live but must, while learning to live better, continue to live somehow, so it is with the instruction of the young. Some kind of school must be maintained; and that which is maintained will make or mar human lives.

Public schools have been established and their support and direction have been authorized by state law. The political representatives of the general public have exercised an important influence in determining the present curriculum and in making the public schools what they are. The nature and extent of this influence is far from adequately known. It seems never to have received the consideration it deserves. Changes in the curriculum may come about through the initiative of teachers and other school officials; they may also come about through the initiative of those who are not directly connected with the schools. In the latter case, the changes may be made voluntarily by school authorities who have been convinced of their desirability, or they may be made under the coercion of public opinion or legal mandate. Legal mandates, however, need not effect any change in the curriculum; they may merely embody present practice. Moreover, when they do effect a change it may not be in opposition to established school authority; sometimes schoolmen seek legislation in order to bring about a desired change.

Students of education commonly assume that the making of a curriculum is a professional undertaking; and that the limiting factors are the nature and the needs of the child. Books dealing with the principles of curriculum construction usually take no account of legal prescriptions; surveys in their recommendations for changes in the course of study seldom, if ever, provide for meeting such requirements. Nevertheless, in any actual situation the curriculum must conform to the existing laws of the state and to any new laws which may from time to time be adopted. These laws may or may not be in harmony with approved educational theory and practice. There is always the possibility that a desirable change may be unlawful while a condemned practice may by law be required. For educators to assume that they can solve their problems without reference to the action of legislators is obviously unwarranted. For legislators to dictate the course of study may seriously impair the effectiveness of the schools.

We need to know the extent to which state legislatures are controlling the curriculum; not only directly by specific mandate but indirectly through prescribed textbooks, through teacher certification, through organization and support which together frequently determine both equipment and personnel. We need to know the effect of various laws as revealed in the habits and ideals which are actually being developed by the schools. With most of these problems we are not now directly concerned. They are mentioned because it is hoped that the facts which are made available through this investigation may contribute to the eventual solution of some of them.

THE PROBLEM

The purpose of this study has been to discover the subject-matter of instruction which is prescribed by legislative enactment for the public elementary school. What subjects must be taught, in each of the forty-eight states, because of a direct and specific mandate in the statutes or the constitution? The aim has included also the getting of similar information for two earlier periods, at intervals of ten years, so that comparisons could be made and trends noted. How does the present practice of law-makers regarding direct control of the curriculum of the common school compare with former practice?

SOURCE OF MATERIAL

The facts for each state have been obtained directly from the session laws, the compiled laws, and the constitutions on file in the law library at Columbia University.

METHOD

The year 1923 was selected because, at the time the search was started, it was the latest year for which all of the session laws were available; accordingly 1903 and 1913 were taken in order to give two consecutive ten-year periods. A careful search was made of all books necessary to determine the laws in force in each of these years in each of the forty-eight states. The latest compilation prior to each of the above dates was made the starting point of the search in each instance; all subsequent session laws were examined to and including those for the year in question. References to all pertinent laws, including amendments and repeals, were noted. In this manner a list was obtained of the subjects prescribed to be taught in each state by laws which were in force in each of the three years 1903, 1913, and 1923. The subjects so obtained were then classified and the various laws regarding each subject were further analyzed and compared.

CLASSIFICATION

The subjects and activities concerning which "prescriptions" were found have been listed under sixty titles which have been classified into the following eight groups:

1. Nationalism
2. Health and "Prohibition"
3. Conservation of Life and Property
4. Practical and Cultural Subjects
5. Humaneness
6. "Fundamental" Subjects
7. Religious and Ethical Subjects
8. Miscellaneous Subjects

The captions used throughout the classification are such as have appeared to the writer to be appropriate. They are not mutually exclusive; there is much overlapping. On the basis of the law alone no rigid classification is possible unless such general terms are used as would obscure important existing differences. On the other hand, if all of the variations in nomenclature were preserved comparisons would be difficult if not impossible. The attempt has been made to follow a middle course. In reducing the list to sixty items many minor differences have been ignored which are, however, pointed out in the text. At the same time sufficient detail has, it is believed, been preserved to enable those interested to form for themselves other classifications of the material if that here presented does not meet their need.

USE OF TERMS

Among the sixty items are Flag Display and Placards which were considered of sufficient general interest and direct bearing upon the curriculum to justify their inclusion. The word "subject" and the phrase "subject matter of instruction" will each be used to embrace these items. "Prescription" will be used as a general term to include not only positive mandates and direct prohibitions but also permissive legislation in a few instances where such legislation has been regarded as of special significance; for example, Bible Reading and Foreign Language.

LIMITATIONS AND DIFFICULTIES

No effort has been spared to make the search exhaustive. The size of the undertaking and its tedious and perplexing character will be fully appreciated only by those who, through a similar investigation, have become familiar with the idiosyncrasies of law-makers and law-compilers. Many of the provisions are of doubtful meaning. Some arbitrary decisions were necessary in order that the results might be classified. It is not to be expected that these decisions have always been such as would have been made by other investigators. It is hoped that they may be found not inconsistent with one another. It should be remembered that this study has been limited to legislative enactments: to session laws, compilations, and constitutional provisions. It has not included either court decisions or state board requirements.

PRESENTATION OF THE FINDINGS

A high percentage of the approximately twenty-two hundred prescriptions embody some sort of unique or exceptional provision. It would be impracticable to reproduce here all the pertinent law in order to reveal these differentiations. Generous quotations are presented in the following eight chapters for the purpose of supplying sufficient detail to give a fairly accurate impression of the real conditions. A list of references has been included in the Appendix which will enable those interested to locate the law regarding any given prescription.

CHAPTER II

LEGISLATIVE PROVISIONS CONCERNING THE TEACHING OF NATIONALISM

The term Nationalism has been used to denote a group of subjects whose promotion may be assumed to have been prompted chiefly by a desire to increase a knowledge of and devotion to our country and its institutions. A few closely related subjects which are local rather than national in viewpoint are also included, such as the history and the government of a particular state. In all, seventeen subjects are here classified. Table I shows the states having prescriptions regarding each of these subjects for each of the three years 1903, 1913, and 1923; these facts are summarized in Table III. Details regarding the provisions for each subject will be presented in the following order:

1. Flag Display
2. Flag Exercises
3. Patriotic Songs
4. Patriotism
5. All Instruction in English
6. Foreign Language
7. German
8. History of the United States
9. History of the State
10. Government of the United States
11. Government of the State
12. Civil Government
13. Citizenship
14. Constitution of the United States
15. Constitution of the State
16. Declaration of Independence
17. Days of Special Observance

FLAG DISPLAY

The legislative requirement that a flag of the United States be procured and displayed in, on or near every public school in the state is the item classified under the heading, Flag Display.

TABLE I CURRICULAR PRESCRIPTIONS IN NATIONALISM FOR THE PUBLIC

Year	Subject or Activity		Alabama	Arizona	Arkansas	California	Colorado	Connecticut	Delaware	Florida	Georgia	Idaho	Illinois	Indiana	Iowa	Kansas	Kentucky	Louisiana	Maine	Maryland
1903	Days of Special Observance	1		M			M	M			M	M								
	Flag Display	2		M				M	M			M	M							
	History of the United States	3	M	M		M	M	M		M			M	M	M	M	M	M		M
	All Instruction in English	4		M		M								M	M	M				
	History of the State	5	M							M						M	M			M
	Civil Government	6				M	M				M						M			M
	Constitution of the United States	7	M				M													M
	Foreign Language	8					P							P	P			P		
	Constitution of the State	9	M				M													M
	Citizenship	10						M												
	Patriotism	11																		
	Flag Exercises	12		M																
	Government of the State	13								M										
	Government of the United States	14								M										
	Patriotic Songs	15																		
	Declaration of Independence	16																		
	German	17					P							P						P
1913	Days of Special Observance	1		M	M		M	M		M	M	M		M		M		M	M	M
	Flag Display	2		M		M		M	M			M	M		M	M			M	
	History of the United States	3	M			M	M	M		M	M		M	M	M	M	M	M		M
	All Instruction in English	4		M		M								M	M	M				
	History of the State	5	M							M	M		M			M	M			M
	Civil Government	6				M	M			M	M		M				M			M
	Constitution of the United States	7	M				M				M									M
	Foreign Language	8					P							P	P			P		
	Constitution of the State	9	M				M		M		M									M
	Citizenship	10						M												
	Patriotism	11																	M	
	Flag Exercises	12		M												M				
	Government of the State	13								M										
	Government of the United States	14								M										
	Patriotic Songs	15												M						
	Declaration of Independence	16																		
	German	17					P							P						
1923	Days of Special Observance	1		M	M	M	M	M		M	M	M		M	M	M	M	M	M	M
	Flag Display	2	M	M	M	M		M	M	M		M	M		M	M			M	M
	History of the United States	3	M		M[T]	M		M		M	M			M	M	M	M	M	M	M
	All Instruction in English	4	M	M	M	M	M	M	M		M	M	M	M	M	M		M	M	
	History of the State	5	M		M	M	M			M	M					M	M			M
	Civil Government	6				M		M		M	M		M[T]			M	M	M	M	
	Constitution of the United States	7	M			M			M		M	M			M					
	Foreign Language	8	F				F	P				P							P	
	Constitution of the State	9							M		M				M					
	Citizenship	10	M			M		M							M	M		M		M
	Patriotism	11			M								M[T]			M			M	M
	Flag Exercises	12		M			M								M	M				M
	Government of the State	13			M		M			M										
	Government of the United States	14			M					M										
	Patriotic Songs	15												M			M			M
	Declaration of Independence	16																		
	German	17												F						

M = Mandatory. P = Permissive. F = Forbidden. M[T] = Mandatory with a time specification

Elementary Schools in Each of the Forty-eight States, 1903, 1913, 1923

	Massachusetts	Michigan	Minnesota	Mississippi	Missouri	Montana	Nebraska	Nevada	New Hampshire	New Jersey	New Mexico	New York	North Carolina	North Dakota	Ohio	Oklahoma	Oregon	Pennsylvania	Rhode Island	South Carolina	South Dakota	Tennessee	Texas	Utah	Vermont	Virginia	Washington	West Virginia	Wisconsin	Wyoming	
1	M					M		M	M	M	M	M			M	M	M		M	M		M			M					M	20
2	M	M				M			M	M		M		M	M				M								M		M	M	17
3	M			M		M		M			M		M	M	M					M	M	M	M		M	M	M	M	M		30
4		M				M								M		M					M		M	M			M		M		14
5						M							M							M		M	M		M	M		M			13
6													M	M	M						M	M	M			M		M			13
7									M				M							M		M			M				M		9
8	P		P					P									P						P		P				P		11
9									M				M							M		M			M				M		9
10																															1
11																															–
12												M							M												3
13																									M						2
14																															1
15																															–
16																															–
17															P																4
																															147
1	M	M	M			M	M	M	M	M	M	M		M	M	M	M		M	M		M		M	M			M		M	33
2	M	M				M		M	M	M	M	M		M	M	M	M	M	M		M			M	M		M		M	M	29
3	M			M		M		M			M		M	M	M			M		M	M	M	M		M	M	M	M	M	M	32
4		M				M						M		M	M	M		M			M		M	M			M		M		17
5						M					M		M					M		M	M	M	M		M	M		M	M	M	20
6						M							M	M	M			M			M	M	M			M		M			17
7									M				M							M		M			M						9
8	P		P	P			P										P						P						P		11
9									M				M							M		M			M						10
10																															1
11																															1
12												M							M												4
13											M														M				M	M	5
14											M																		M		3
15																															1
16																															–
17															P																3
																															196
1	M	M	M		M	M	M	M	M	M	M	M	M	M	M	M	M	M	M	M	M	M		M	M		M	M	M	M	42
2	M	M	M	M		M	M	M	M	M	M	M		M	M	M	M	M	M		M	M	M	M	M		M	M	M	M	39
3	M			M		M	M	M			M	M	M	M	M	M[T]		M		M	M	M	M		M	M	M	M	M	M	35
4		M	M			M	M	M	M	M		M	M	M	M	M	M	M			M		M				M	M	M		34
5				M		M		M		M	M		M					M	M	M	M	M	M[T]		M	M			M	M	25
6				M		M	M	M			M	M		M	M	M		M	M		M		M			M		M			24
7	M	M	M					M	M	M	M		M		M[T]		M	M		M	M	M		M	M			M			23
8			P	P			F	P	P		M					F	P	P											P		15
9		M						M	M		M		M		M[T]					M	M	M			M			M			14
10	M									M		M			M										M	M[T]			M		14
11			M					M[T]				M	M			M					M[T]		M[T]								12
12							M					M				M			M								M				10
13																			M						M				M	M	7
14																													M		3
15																															3
16			M								M																				2
17															F																2
																															304

(minimum number of minutes or periods). *Days of Special Observance,*—One or more; see Table II.

While not a subject of instruction it is considered of sufficient interest to justify the isolation. Seventeen states had such a prescription in 1903, twenty-nine in 1913 and thirty-nine in 1923. The following had the requirement in all three years:

Arizona	Michigan	Ohio
Connecticut	Montana	Rhode Island
Delaware	New Hampshire	Washington
Idaho	New Jersey	Wisconsin
Illinois	New York	Wyoming
Massachusetts	North Dakota	

The following had the requirement in 1913 and 1923:

California	Nevada	Pennsylvania
Iowa	New Mexico	South Dakota
Kansas	Oklahoma	Utah
Maine	Oregon	Vermont

The following had the requirement in 1923 only:

Alabama	Minnesota	Tennessee
Arkansas	Mississippi	West Virginia
Florida	Nebraska	
Maryland	Texas	

No legal provision for a flag, in any of the three years under consideration, was found in the five states, Georgia, Kentucky, Louisiana, Missouri, and North Carolina. There was a permissive law in Colorado in all three years. The law in South Carolina pertained only to the state flag which in 1913 had to be displayed "upon every public school building" and in 1923 "upon the inside of every public school building." In Indiana in 1913 and 1923 and Virginia in 1923 the provision became mandatory in any district upon the petition of a majority of the patrons of that district. The flag of the "Commonwealth of Virginia" likewise became mandatory upon petition. In Alabama both the state and national flags were required.

Commonly it is stipulated that the flag must be displayed, weather permitting, during the hours when school is in session either over the schoolhouse or upon a suitable flagstaff in the yard. In stormy weather it must be displayed inside the building. Sometimes the size and material of the flag and even the height of the pole are specified. Sometimes there must also be a small flag in every schoolroom. Sometimes the law requires the flag to be flown on legal holidays and other special occasions. Sometimes entire discretion as to when, where and how it shall be displayed is left to school authorities. Not infrequently there is a penalty for failure either to provide or display the flag. In Arizona,

> It shall be the duty of the school authorities of every public school in the several districts of the State of Arizona to purchase a United States flag, flagstaff, and the necessary appliances therefor, and to display such flag upon or near the public school building during school hours, and at such other times as such school authorities may direct.

In West Virginia,

> Every board of education shall, out of the building fund, purchase United States flags, four by six feet, of regulation bunting, for schoolhouses in their district, and require same to be displayed from the schoolhouse during the time the school is in session, except in inclement weather. And it shall be the duty of the teacher, custodian or other person in charge of said building during the session to see that this flag is displayed on the schoolhouse as herein provided, and for failure to comply with this duty, such person in charge shall forfeit the sum of fifty cents per day for each day such failure shall continue, payable from the salary of such person to the building fund.

In Connecticut,

> The selectmen shall provide every schoolhouse in which a school is maintained within their respective towns with a United States flag of silk or bunting, not less than four feet in length, and a suitable flagstaff, or other arrangement whereby such flag may be displayed on the schoolhouse grounds every school day when the weather will permit, and on the inside of the schoolhouse on other school days, and renew such flag and apparatus when necessary.

In Alabama,

> All schools in this state that are supported in whole or in part by public funds are hereby required to display every day on which school is in session, at some suitable place about the school building the flag of the United States and the flag of the State of Alabama. Teachers in making their monthly reports shall show on the same that the provisions of this Act have been complied with and superintendents of city schools in drawing public money, or monies, shall

certify that each school under this supervision has complied with this Act. Teachers in the State subject to the provisions of this Act shall not be allowed to draw public funds unless the provisions of this Act are complied with and the State Superintendent of Education is charged with the enforcement of the provisions hereof. The flags provided for in this Act shall be paid for by local school boards in localities where local school boards exist and in localities where there are no local school boards such flags shall be paid for by the County Boards of Education.

FLAG EXERCISES

There were three states in 1903 which required flag exercises in the public schools, four in 1913 and ten in 1923. Arizona, New York, and Rhode Island required them in all three years; Kansas, in 1913 and 1923 and Colorado, Iowa, Maryland, Nebraska, Oklahoma, and Washington in 1923. The law in Rhode Island has remained unchanged since enacted in 1901. It directs that the Commissioner of Education shall

> prepare for the use of the schools a printed programme providing for a uniform salute to the flag to be used daily during the session of the school.

In New York a law was enacted in 1898, on the day following the declaration of war with Spain, making it the duty of the State Superintendent of Public Instruction to

> prepare, for the use of the public schools of the State, a program providing for a salute to the flag at the opening of each day of school and such other patriotic exercises as may be deemed by him to be expedient, under such regulations and instructions as may best meet the varied requirements of the different grades in such schools.

This same law, expressed in the same language, was enacted in Arizona in 1903 and in Kansas in 1907; it was still in force in Kansas in 1923. The law was amended in Arizona and New York previous to 1913 by omitting the phrase "at the opening of each school day," and in this amended form was still in force in 1923.[1]

A law exactly similar to this as amended was enacted in Maryland in 1918 with the following added:

[1] The title of the chief educational officer in New York was changed to Commissioner of Education in 1904.

> all to the end that the love of liberty and democracy, signified in the devotion of all true and patriotic Americans to their flag and to their country, shall be instilled in the hearts and minds of the youth of America.

Iowa had a permissive law in 1913 which was amended in 1923 by changing the "may" to "shall." In Washington the obligation is placed upon the board of directors in each school district to cause

> appropriate flag exercises to be held in every school at least once in each week at which exercises the pupils shall recite the salute to the Flag.

In Oklahoma,

> The pupils of every public, private, parochial and denominational school in the State of Oklahoma shall by appropriate ceremonial, to be formulated by the State Superintendent of Public Instruction, be taught the proper reverence and respect for the American Flag.

In Colorado the Superintendent of Public Schools must provide the necessary information and the teachers must instruct the pupils in

> the proper respect of the Flag of the United States, to honor and properly salute the Flag when passing in parade and to properly use the Flag in decorating and displaying.

The law in Nebraska has this wording:

> A program providing for a salute to the flag and such other patriotic exercises as may be deemed best adapted to the requirements of whatever grades in such schools shall be carried out by each teacher on Lincoln's Birthday, Washington's Birthday, Memorial Day, Flag Day, and upon such other special occasions as may be required by law or rule of the school board.

There may be ground for disagreement as to the mandatory character of some of the provisions just quoted. For instance, in Arizona, Kansas, Maryland, and New York it might be contended that the only obligation is the one resting upon the chief educational officer of the state to prepare a program; that it is not obligatory upon teachers that they should use this program. For the present purpose it has seemed futile to make any such distinction; it has therefore been assumed that the legislators expected this program to be used.

On the other hand, the following resolution, passed by the Thirty-sixth Texas Legislature, has not been considered mandatory:

> It is the wish of the people of Texas, through their Representatives in the Texas Legislature, that the State Superintendent of Public Instruction shall include, in instructions to city and county superintendents, provisions requiring the flag of each schoolhouse to be kept within doors, to be displayed on the exterior of the building only in good weather, on suitable occasions, and at such regular intervals as may be desirable, at the same time providing for such regular use of the flag in patriotic exercises as may inspire in the children of the State the proper reverence and enthusiasm for the Star Spangled Banner of the greatest republic in the world.

PATRIOTIC SONGS

A law was in force in Indiana in both 1913 and 1923 that

> The State Board of Education shall require the singing of the "Star-Spangled Banner," in its entirety in the schools of the State of Indiana, upon all patriotic occasions.

In Kentucky in 1923 there was a law requiring

> that singing be included in the curriculum of the State for the opening and recreational exercises. That the minimum requirement shall include the State song and two National airs. That singing be regarded as a subject in the public schools of the State for the purpose of instilling into the minds of youth patriotic feeling and a deeper love for their country.

Maryland in 1923 made it obligatory upon the one in charge of any grammar school, preparatory school or private school which has morning, afternoon or evening exercises or other gatherings, to open such exercises or gatherings on at least one day of each school week

> with the singing of the Star Spangled Banner.

Apparently, if no such general exercises are held, the singing is not required.

PATRIOTISM

Without attempting to define patriotism or to set forth what elements have been included in, or excluded from, it, the provisions will here be presented which have been interpreted as requiring that patriotism be taught. There was one such requirement in 1913 and twelve in 1923. Some of the provisions also contain other items which are elsewhere classified.

In 1913 there was in force in Maine a law which provided that flags should be furnished to all schools and that

> These flags are to be used in all schools for the education of the youth of our state to teach them the cost, the object and the principles of our government, the great sacrifices of our forefathers, the important part taken by the Union army in 1861 to 1865 and to teach them to love, honor and respect the flag of our country that cost so much and is so dear to every true American citizen.

This provision was amended in 1915 by striking out the words preceding the first "to teach" and substituting therefor the following:

> It shall be the duty of instructors to impress upon the youth by suitable references and observances the significance of the flag.

In Illinois, in the seventh and eighth grammar grades, not less than one hour of each school week shall be devoted to the study of

> American patriotism and the principles of representative government as enunciated in the American Declaration of Independence, the Constitution of the United States of America and the Constitution of the State of Illinois.

In Kansas,

> All schools, public, private, or parochial, shall provide and give a complete course of instruction to all pupils, in civil government, and United States history, and in patriotism and the duties of a citizen, suitable to the elementary grades.

In Maryland the required flag exercises must be given

> all to the end that the love of liberty and democracy, signified in the devotion of all true and patriotic Americans to their flag and to their country, shall be instilled in the hearts and minds of the youth of America.

In Minnesota,

> In all of the common, graded and high schools of this state it shall be the duty of the superintendent or teachers in charge of such schools to teach and require the teaching therein, on at least one day out of each week, of subjects and exercises tending and calculated to encourage and inculcate a spirit of patriotism in the pupils and students. Such exercises shall consist of the singing of patriotic songs, readings from American history and from the biographies of American statesmen and patriots and such other patriotic exercises as the superintendent or teachers of such schools may determine. The time to be spent thereon on each of said days shall not exceed one-half hour.

In Nevada,

> There shall be at least one hour set aside each school week in the graded schools and high schools in the State of Nevada for the purpose of holding patriotic exercises.

In Oklahoma and Arkansas at least one hour in every scholastic week must be devoted to the teaching of American History.

> The instilling into the hearts of the various pupils of an understanding of the United States and of a love of country and devotion to the principles of American Government shall be the primary object of such instruction, which shall avoid, as far as possible, being a mere recital of dates and events.

In Texas,

> The daily program of every school in this State shall be so formulated by teacher, principal, or superintendent as to include at least ten minutes for the teaching of intelligent patriotism, including the needs of the State and Federal governments, the duty of citizens to the State, and the obligation of the State to the citizens.

In North Carolina,

> There shall be taught in the public schools of North Carolina a course of instruction which shall be known as Americanism. There shall be included in the term herein called Americanism the following general items of instruction:
>
> (*a*) Respect for law and order.
> (*b*) Character and ideals of the founders of our country.
> (*c*) Duties of good citizenship.
> (*d*) Respect for the national anthem and the flag.

> (*e*) A standard of good government.
> (*f*) Constitution of North Carolina.
> (*g*) Constitution of the United States.
>
> Said course of instruction shall be taught not less than thirty hours during each and every school year and shall not be optional in the grade or grades in which said course is taught. The State Board of Education shall, as soon as convenient, adopt some suitable and proper textbook which shall conform as near as possible and practicable to the carrying out of the general items of instruction as herein contained in section two of this act and the State Superintendent shall prepare or have prepared such outline courses of study and shall distribute the same among the teachers of the State which will give them proper direction in carrying out the provisions of this act.
>
> The State Board of Education shall, before the beginning of the next school year, adopt such suitable rules and regulations as may be necessary as to the time, manner, grade, or grades in which said course of Americanism shall be taught.

In New York,

> In order to promote a spirit of patriotic and civic service and obligation and to foster in the children of the State moral and intellectual qualities which are essential in preparing to meet the obligations of citizenship in peace or in war, the Regents of the University of the State of New York shall prescribe courses of instruction in patriotism and citizenship, to be maintained and followed in all the schools of the State. The boards of education and school trustees of the several cities and school districts of the State shall require instruction to be given in such courses, by the teachers employed in the schools therein. All pupils attending such schools, over the age of eight years, shall attend upon such instruction.
>
> The Regents of the University of the State of New York shall determine the subjects to be included in such courses of instruction in patriotism and citizenship, and the period of instruction in each of the grades in such subjects. They shall adopt rules providing for attendance upon such instruction and for such other matters as are required for carrying into effect the objects and purposes of this article. The Commissioner of Education shall be responsible for the enforcement of this article and shall cause to be inspected and supervise the instruction to be given in such subjects. The Commissioner may, in his discretion, cause all or a portion of the public school money to be apportioned to a district or city to be withheld for failure of the school author-

> ities of such district or city to provide instruction in such courses and to compel attendance upon such instructions, as herein prescribed, and for a noncompliance with the rules of the Regents adopted as herein provided.

In South Dakota,

> In every educational institution in this state, whether public or private, one hour each week in the aggregate shall be devoted to the teaching of patriotism, the singing of patriotic songs, the reading of patriotic addresses, and a study of the lives and history of American patriots. It shall be the duty of all instructors, and of all school officers and superintendents, to enforce the provisions of this section and any person who shall fail, neglect or refuse to enforce its provisions shall be deemed guilty of a misdemeanor, and upon conviction thereof shall be punished by a fine of not less than five nor more than one hundred dollars, or by imprisonment in the county jail not less than five nor more than thirty days, or by both such fine and imprisonment. It shall be the duty of the superintendent of public instruction to revoke the certificate of any instructor in any school in this state, who shall fail, neglect or refuse to enforce the provisions of this section.

ALL INSTRUCTION IN ENGLISH

In 1903 there were fourteen states which had some sort of provision requiring that instruction in the elementary schools should be in English. There were seventeen such states in 1913 and thirty-four in 1923. The following had the requirement in all three years:

Arizona	Michigan	Texas
California	Montana	Washington
Indiana	North Dakota	Wisconsin
Iowa	Oklahoma	
Kansas	South Dakota	

Utah had such a provision in 1903 and 1913; New York, Ohio, and Pennsylvania, in 1913 and 1923; and the following in 1923:

Alabama	Idaho	Nevada
Arkansas	Illinois	New Hampshire
Colorado	Louisiana	New Jersey
Connecticut	Maine	North Carolina
Delaware	Minnesota	Oregon
Georgia	Nebraska	West Virginia

In the following states no provision regarding the use of English was found in any of the three years:

Florida
Kentucky
Maryland
Massachusetts
Mississippi
Missouri
New Mexico
Rhode Island
South Carolina
Tennessee
Vermont
Virginia
Wyoming

Probably the remarkable increase, from seventeen to thirty-four in the last ten years, is due largely to the pronounced enthusiasm for Americanism which developed during the period of the World War. There is a marked lack of uniformity in the language of the law which possibly connotes a widespread interest in and popular demand for such a provision. There is no set verbal formula commonly used; hardly any two are alike; but the same intent is quite universal. No essential difference is to be noted in the character of the provisions in the different years. "All schools must be taught in the English language"; "all the elementary school subjects must be taught in the English language"; "the instruction given shall be in the English language"; "the medium of instruction shall be the English language"; "the basic language of instruction shall be the English language only"; "unlawful to teach any subject in any language other than the English language," or some such equivalent expression is usually found. In a majority of the states the provision applies to all of the elementary schools in the state; but in a few, Colorado, Louisiana, Minnesota, Montana, and Texas, it applies only to public schools. This is probably also true of Georgia, Kansas, and North Dakota. In Alabama the provision refers only to the first six grades of the public schools. In Georgia there is a provision that a

> uniform series of books shall be in use in all the common schools of the State and shall include the . . . elements of an English education only.

Also, in its constitution we find

> the powers of taxation over the whole State shall be exercised by the General Assembly for the following purposes only: . . . instruction children in the elements of an English education only.

period covered by this study. By itself, it was not considered as
This constitutional provision has been in force throughout the

definitely prescribing that all instruction should be given in English. It is a definite limitation upon the taxing power. The mandate regarding the exclusive use of English in Illinois does not apply to

> vacational schools where the pupils have already received the required instruction in English during the current school year.

In Iowa,

> The medium of instruction in all secular subjects taught in all of the schools, public and private, within the state of Iowa, shall be the English language, and the use of any language other than English in secular subjects in said schools is hereby prohibited.

The provision in Louisiana is that

> the general exercises in the public schools shall be conducted in the English language.

Michigan has a constitutional provision that all instruction in the primary schools "shall be conducted in the English language," and a statutory provision that

> all instruction from the first to the eighth grade, inclusive, in those subjects required for an eight grade diploma, in all the schools of this state, public, private, parochial, or in connection with any state institution . . . shall be conducted in the English language.

In Minnesota,

> The books used and the instruction given in public schools shall be in the English language, but any other language may be used by teacher in explaining to pupils who understand such language the meaning of English words.

Also

> A school, to satisfy the requirements of compulsory attendance, must be one in which all the common branches are taught, in the English language, from textbooks written in the English language and taught by teachers qualified to teach in the English language.

North Dakota provides that

> if any money belonging to any district shall be expended in supporting a school in which the English language is not

> the medium of instruction, exclusively, the county superintendent or any taxpayer of the school corporation may in a civil action in the name of the corporation recover for such corporation all such money from the officer expending it or voting for its expenditure.

In South Dakota,

> It is the civic right of every child of school age to receive instruction in the subjects outlined in the State course of study and mentioned in Chapter 168, Laws of 1919, in the English language, for a term provided in the State course of Study and in the laws of the State, until such child shall have completed the eighth grade; and it shall be unlawful for any person or persons to act, aid, assist, advise or be instrumental in abridging or attempting to abridge the privilege of any child to receive such instruction by submitting therefor instruction in some foreign language either by shortening the course of instruction in English in any school or by coercing, requiring or inducing any child to withdraw from a school in which instruction is given in English to attend a school in which instruction is given in any foreign language, or to establish a school in which instruction is given in any foreign language as a substitute for a school in which English is the sole medium of instruction.
>
> It shall be unlawful at any time during the months from September to May, both inclusive, for any person or persons or corporation to occupy or use any public school room or other public building in this State for the purpose of giving instruction in any foreign or ancient language or for teaching any subject, or subjects, in any excepting the English language except as permitted by the State Course of Study and in conformity with the provisions of Chapter 168 of the Session Law of 1919; and it shall be unlawful during the time above specified for any school board or officer to authorize or permit the use of any public school room or other public building within this State for the purpose of teaching any foreign or ancient language or for the purpose of teaching any subject in such language contrary to the provisions of this section and of the laws herein before referred to. Provided, that nothing herein contained shall be construed to interfere with religious exercises on days other than school days. Any person who shall violate any of the provisions of this Act shall be guilty of a misdemeanor, and shall be punished by a fine of not less than fifty dollars and not exceeding five hundred dollars, or by imprisonment in the county jail for a period not less than thirty days nor more than ninety days, or both such fine and imprisonment.

In Oklahoma,

> The English language is hereby declared to be the language of the people of the State of Oklahoma. And it shall be unlawful to teach or instruct in any other language in any Public, Parochial, Denominational or Private School or other institution of learning within the State of Oklahoma except pupils receiving such instructions shall have completed the eighth grade of common school curriculum.

New York, New Jersey, and New Hampshire enumerate particular subjects in the teaching of which English must be used. New Jersey places the obligation upon every parent or guardian of a child of school age to cause such child to attend a day school in which

> at least reading, writing, spelling, English grammar, arithmetic and geography are taught in the English language.

New York requires instruction

> at a public elementary school in which at least the nine common school branches of reading, spelling, writing, arithmetic, English language, geography, United States history, civics and hygiene are taught in English.

In 1913 New York had a similar provision covering the teaching of

> at least the six common school branches of reading, spelling, writing, arithmetic, English language and geography.

New Hampshire has this provision:

> In the instruction of children in all schools, including private schools, in reading, writing, spelling, arithmetic, grammar, geography, physiology, history, civil government, music and drawing, the English language shall be used exclusively, both for the purposes of instruction therein and for purposes of general administration.

There may be some question as to the all-inclusiveness of the provision in each of these three states, particularly in the case of New York and New Jersey. New Hampshire has this further provision:

> The exclusive use of English for purposes of instruction and administration is not intended to prohibit the conduct of devotional exercises in private schools in a language other than English.

In Nebraska,

> No person, individually or as a teacher, shall, in any private, denominational, or parochial or public school, teach any subject to any person in any language other than the English language.

This requirement does not apply to

> schools held on Sunday or on some other day of the week which those having the custody and care of the pupils attending same conscientiously observe as the Sabbath, where the object and purpose of such schools is the giving of religious instruction, but shall apply to all other schools and to schools held at all other times.

FOREIGN LANGUAGE

Aside from German, which will be considered separately, there were eleven prescriptions in 1903, eleven in 1913, and fifteen in 1923. These figures, however, give slight indication of the change which has taken place in the period which we are studying. Only four states had prescriptions in all three years, Colorado, Minnesota, Oregon, and Wisconsin. Five states had prescriptions in 1903 and 1913, Indiana, Iowa, Louisiana, Massachusetts, and Texas. Two states had prescriptions in 1913 and 1923, Mississippi and Nebraska. Nevada had a prescription in 1903 and 1923; Vermont, in 1903 only. There were eight states with prescriptions in 1923 which had not had them previously, Alabama, Connecticut, Idaho, Maine, New Hampshire, New Mexico, Oklahoma, and Pennsylvania. All the prescriptions in 1903 and 1913 were permissive; four of the prescriptions in 1923 were prohibitions, those in Alabama, Colorado, Nebraska, and Oklahoma; one, that of Spanish in New Mexico, was mandatory. In addition to these direct provisions foreign languages would doubtless also be permitted or forbidden in some states by reason of interpretations, by a court or by the state department of education, regarding all instruction being given in English. Such interpretations are not included in this study.

In 1903 and 1913 the law in Colorado permitted the school board of any district, upon demand of twenty or more parents or guardians, to introduce Spanish as a branch of study and also to teach the subjects of the required course of study in Spanish. In 1923, after specifying that the common branches of study shall be conducted through the medium of the English language only, the law continues,

> nor shall any other than the English language be taught as a separate and distinct branch of itself.

In Indiana, in 1903 and 1913, certain enumerated subjects were prescribed,

> and such other branches of learning and other languages as the advancement of pupils may require and the Trustees from time to time direct.

In Iowa, in 1903 and 1913,

> the voters assembled at the annual meeting shall have power . . . to determine upon added branches that shall be taught but instruction in all branches except foreign languages shall be in English.

In Louisiana, in 1903 and 1913, there was a constitutional provision that the French language might be taught in those parishes or localities where the French language predominated if no additional expense was incurred thereby. A Session Law of 1902 provided that the required elementary branches

> may also be taught in the French language in those localities where the French language is spoken; but no additional expense shall be incurred for this cause.

In Massachusetts, in 1903 and 1913,

> one or more foreign languages . . . and such other subjects as the school committee considers expedient may be taught in the public schools.

In Minnesota, in 1903,

> teachers able to speak any other language that is the vernacular to any pupil may use that language to aid in teaching the meaning of English words, and may also give instruction in such language not to exceed one hour in each day; but no such instruction shall be given unless the trustees of such district have expressed themselves unanimously in favor thereof.

Essentially this same law was in effect in 1913 and 1923. There was also an additional law in 1923 which provided that

> A foreign language may be taught when such language is an elective or a prescribed subject of the curriculum, but not to exceed one hour in each day.

In Nevada, in 1903, provision was made for the issuance of special certificates authorizing those duly qualified to teach

> any of the foreign languages in the public schools of this state when employed by the Trustees of any school district for that purpose.

In 1923,

> It shall be unlawful for any board of school trustees, regents, or board of education, or for any teacher or other person teaching in the public or private schools of the State of Nevada, to cause to be taught or to teach any subject or subjects, other than foreign languages, in the public or private schools in the State of Nevada in any language except English.

This same law was in force in Oregon in 1923, and in addition the following was in force in all three years:

> The district schoolboard of any school district of the first class may, upon the petition of not less than one hundred qualified electors of such school district, provide that in one or more of the common schools, to be kept in such district, any one modern language may be taught as a branch study, and a teacher employed in such school shall be educated in such language and qualified to teach the same.

In Texas, in 1903 and 1913,

> It shall be the duty of every teacher in the public free schools of this State to use the English language exclusively, and to conduct all recitations and school exercises exclusively in the English language; provided, that this provision shall not prevent the teaching of any other language as a branch of study, but when any other language is so taught, the use of said language shall be limited to the recitations and exercises devoted to the teaching of said language as a branch of study.

No direct repeal of the foregoing law was found, but the following law which was in force in 1923 would, apparently, not permit the teaching of a foreign language.

> Every teacher, principal, and superintendent employed in the public free schools of this State shall use the English language exclusively in the conduct of the work of the

> schools, and all recitations and exercises of the school shall be conducted in the English language, and the trustees shall not prescribe any textbooks for elementary grades not printed in the English language.

In Vermont, in 1903,

> a district maintaining a school taught by three or more teachers may direct the teaching of foreign languages, ancient or modern, therein.

This law was enacted in 1888 and may refer to high school subjects rather than elementary. In Wisconsin, in 1903, 1913, and 1923, it was provided that any foreign language might be

> taught by a competent teacher to such pupils as desire it, not to exceed one hour each day.

In Alabama, in 1923,

> English shall be the only language employed and taught in the first six grades of the elementary school.

In Connecticut, in 1923,

> The medium of instruction and administration in all public and private elementary schools in this state shall be the English language and not more than one hour in any school day may be given to instruction in any one language other than English. A person who shall violate any provision of this act shall be fined not less than fifty dollars nor more than five hundred dollars or imprisoned not more than six months or both.

In Idaho, in 1923, the mandate regarding the use of English

> shall not apply to instructions in any particular language for the purpose of teaching said language, nor to the use of foreign words and phrases in designating scientific terms.

In Maine, in 1923, the section of the law making English the basic language of instruction in the common school branches contains this provision:

> Nothing in this section shall be construed to prohibit the teaching in elementary schools of any language as such.

The present law in Mississippi was enacted in 1904 and is a part of the section regulating the adoption of textbooks. It prescribes that

> all textbooks adopted for use in the public schools of the state shall be printed in English except such books as shall be adopted as textbooks in the study of a foreign language.

Apparently this recognizes the possibility of such foreign languages being taught. In Nebraska, in 1913,

> In every high school, city school or metropolitan school in this state the proper authorities of such school districts shall upon the written request, when made at least three months before the opening of the fall term of such school, by the parents or guardians of fifty pupils above the fourth grade then attending such school, employ competent teachers and provide for the teaching therein, above the fourth grade, as an elective course of study, of such modern European language as may be designated in such request. Provided, not more than five hours each week and not less than one period each day shall be devoted to the teaching of any such modern European language in any elementary or grade school.

In 1923,

> Languages other than the English language may be taught as languages only after a pupil shall have attained and successfully passed the eighth grade as evidenced by a certificate of graduation issued by the county superintendent of the county or the city superintendent of the city in which the child resides. . . . Provided that nothing in this act shall prohibit any person from teaching his own children in his own house any foreign language.

In New Hampshire, in 1923,

> a foreign language may be taught in the elementary schools provided the course of study outlined by the State Board of Education in the common English branches . . . . be not abridged.

In New Mexico, in 1923, Spanish is one of the subjects in the prescribed course of study. The provision in Oklahoma prohibiting the teaching of any language other than English in the first eight grades has been quoted above under "All Instruction in English." In Pennsylvania, in 1923, all subjects in the public elementary schools

> except foreign languages shall be taught in the English language and from English texts.

GERMAN

There is, of course, no logical reason for tabulating German separately from the other foreign languages. It has been done because of the special interest in the subject which developed during the World War. German was specifically mentioned in Colorado, Indiana, Maryland and Ohio in 1903; in Colorado, Indiana and Ohio in 1913; and in Indiana and Ohio in 1923. The provisions in 1903 and 1913 were permissive; those in 1923 were prohibitive. This does not tell the whole story, because the teaching of German would be permissible in all those states which permit the teaching of "foreign languages" and would be forbidden in those which prohibit the teaching of these. An act was adopted in Louisiana in 1918 prohibiting the teaching of German in public or private elementary, high or higher schools.[2] This law was repealed in 1921.[3] In Colorado, in 1903 and 1913, the provision was as follows:

> Whenever the parents or guardians of twenty or more children of school age shall so demand, the board of such school district may procure efficient instructors and introduce the German and Spanish languages, or either of them, and gymnastics, as a branch of study into said school, and said district board may, upon like demand of the parents and guardians of children of school age, procure efficient instructors to teach the branches specified in said section fifteen[4] in the German and Spanish languages, or in either of said languages, as said board may direct.

In Indiana, in 1903 and 1913,

> The common schools of the state shall be taught in the English language; . . . and whenever the parents or guardians of twenty-five or more children in attendance at any school of a township, town or city shall so demand, it shall be the duty of the School Trustee or Trustees of said township, town or city to procure efficient teachers, and introduce the German language, as a branch of study into such schools; and the tuition in said schools shall be without charge; *Provided,* Such demand is made before the teacher for said district is employed.

[2] Acts of 1918, p. 188, Act No. 114.

[3] Acts of 1921 (Special Session), p. 102, Act No. 71.

[4] Section fifteen names the subjects in which an applicant was to be examined or a certificate to teach in the elementary school.

In 1923,

> The German language shall not be taught in any of the elementary schools of this state.

In Maryland, in 1903,

> in districts where there is considerable German population the Board of County School Commissioners are authorized to cause the German language to be taught if they think proper to do so.

In Ohio, the following provisions were found in 1903:

> The board of any district shall cause the German language to be taught in any school under its control, during any school year, when a demand therefor is made, in writing, by seventy-five freeholders resident of the district, representing not less than forty pupils who are entitled to attend such school, and who, in good faith, desire and intend to study the German and English languages together; but such demand shall be made at a regular meeting of the board, and prior to the beginning of the school year, and any board may cause the German or other language to be taught in any school under its control without such demand.

In 1913,

> Boards of Education may provide for the teaching of the German language in the elementary and high schools of the District over which they have control but it shall only be taught in addition and as auxiliary to the English language. All the common branches in the public schools must be taught in the English language.

In 1923,

> the German language shall not be taught below the eighth grade in any of the elementary schools of this state.

HISTORY OF THE UNITED STATES

There has been a slight increase in the number of states requiring the teaching of United States history. It was prescribed in thirty states in 1903, thirty-two in 1913, and thirty-five in 1923. In the following twenty-seven states it was required in all three years:

Alabama	Maryland	South Carolina
California	Massachusetts	South Dakota
Connecticut	Mississippi	Tennessee
Florida	Montana	Texas
Indiana	Nevada	Vermont
Iowa	New Mexico	Virginia
Kansas	North Carolina	Washington
Kentucky	North Dakota	West Virginia
Louisiana	Ohio	Wisconsin

It was prescribed in Arizona in 1903; in Colorado and Illinois in 1903 and 1913; in Georgia, Pennsylvania, and Wyoming in 1913 and 1923; and in Arkansas, Maine, Nebraska, New York, and Oklahoma in 1923.

In Georgia in 1913 and 1923, and in Alabama and Nevada in 1903 and 1913, the subject is not directly specified in the course of study; but textbooks in the subject are required which must be used. In Colorado in 1903, and in Illinois and Mississippi in 1903 and 1913, the obligation is established by including the qualification to teach this subject among the requirements for a teacher's certificate, and then specifying that all branches so included must be taught. In Iowa the obligation to teach the subject was not placed directly upon the school but apparently it amounts to the same thing.

> Any person having control of any child of the age of seven to sixteen years inclusive,[5] in proper physical and mental condition to attend school, shall cause such child to attend some public, private, or parochial school, where the common school branches of reading, writing, spelling, arithmetic, grammar, geography, physiology, and United States history are taught.

In most instances the prescription for teaching the history of the United States is found in the same section with the other fundamental subjects and no special emphasis is given to it. This was uniformly true in 1903 and 1913, and in a majority of the cases in 1923. However, in a number of states in 1923 supplementary laws are found and the prescription is more detailed and specific. Quite often the prescription regarding history is joined with some other subject, such as "the history and civil government of the United States" or "American history and civics" or "history of the United States containing the constitu-

[5] In 1903, "child of the age of seven to fourteen inclusive."

tion of the United States." In California in 1923 instruction must be given in the

> history of the United States with special reference to the history of the constitution of the United States and the history of the reasons for the adoption of each of its provisions.

In Florida, in all three years, the history of the United States must be taught in the seventh and eighth grades. In the third, fourth, fifth and sixth grades, such lessons in history must be given as may be provided for in the course of study.

Following are some of the provisions in force in 1923. Arkansas and Oklahoma have identical laws and require that the subject be taught one hour per week. They are the only states with a time specification in this subject.

> The teaching of American history in the primary grades of all the schools, both public and private, of this State shall be compulsory. Such teaching shall commence in the lowest primary grade of each of said schools and shall be continued through all the primary grades; provided that the teaching of the Arkansas [Oklahoma] history, as now provided by law, may be substituted for American history, in one of the said grades. At least one hour in every scholastic week shall be devoted to such instruction. The instilling into the hearts of the various pupils of an understanding of the United States and of a love of country and of a devotion to the principles of American Government, shall be the primary object of such instruction, which shall avoid, as far as possible, being a mere recital of dates and events.

In Kansas,

> All schools, public, private, or parochial, shall provide and give a complete course of instruction to all pupils, in civil government and United States history, and in patriotism and the duties of a citizen, suitable to the elementary grades.

Maine provides that

> American history and civil government shall be taught in all common schools of elementary and high school grades, both public and private, and American history and civil government shall be required for graduation from all grammar schools, both public and private.

In Massachusetts,

> In all public elementary and high schools American history and civics, including the constitution of the United States,

shall be taught as required subjects for the purpose of promoting civic service and a greater knowledge thereof, and of fitting the pupils, morally and intellectually, for the duties of citizenship.

Nebraska provided that

> All public, private, denominational, and parochial schools shall give in the proper grades such courses in American history and in civil government, both state and national, as will give the pupils therein a thorough knowledge of the history of our country and its institutions and of our form of government, and shall conduct such patriotic exercises as may be prescribed from time to time by the state superintendent.

In Texas a textbook must be adopted in the

> history of the United States in which the construction placed on the Federal constitution by the fathers of the Confederacy shall be fairly represented.[6]

In Wisconsin, in addition to the law requiring the teaching of the history of the United States which has been in force throughout the period of this study, the following, enacted in 1923, provides for the censorship of history textbooks:

> No history or other textbook shall be adopted for use or be used in any district school, city school, vocational school or high school which falsifies the facts regarding the war of independence, or the war of 1812, or which defames our nation's founders, or misrepresents the ideals and causes for which they struggled and sacrificed, or which contains propaganda favorable to any foreign government.[7]

Upon complaint of any five citizens, filed with the state superintendent of public instruction, that any history or other textbook contains any matter prohibited by the foregoing subsection, that official must arrange for a public hearing within thirty days; and within ten days after the hearing must make a finding upon the complaint. Any textbook found to contain prohibited matter shall be removed from the list of adopted textbooks and withdrawn from use prior to the opening of the following school year. State aid shall not be

> paid for the support of any district school, city school, vocational school or high school during any year in which

[6] Complete Statutes 1920, p. 498, Art. 2909*bb*.

[7] Statutes 1923, p. 432, Sec. 40.36.

> any such textbook is used in such school after the finding of the state superintendent.

The following law, adopted in Oregon in 1923, has not been considered as making mandatory the teaching of the history of the United States:

> It shall be the duty of every board, commission, committee or officer charged with the selection of textbooks for use in the public schools to select and install textbooks on American history and civil government which adequately stress the services rendered by the men who achieved our national independence, who established our form of constitutional government, and who preserved our federal union. No textbook shall be used in our schools which speaks slightingly of the founders of the republic, or of the men who preserved the union, or which belittles or undervalues their work.[8]

HISTORY OF THE STATE

The history of an individual state is not as frequently prescribed as is the history of the United States but the subject has shown more of an increase, from thirteen in 1903 to twenty-five in 1923. It was required in the following states in all three years:

Alabama	Maryland	Tennessee
Florida	Montana	Texas
Kansas	North Carolina	Vermont
Kentucky	South Carolina	Virginia

It was prescribed in West Virginia in 1903 and 1913; in Illinois in 1913; in Georgia, New Mexico, Pennsylvania, South Dakota, Wisconsin, and Wyoming in 1913 and 1923; and in Arkansas, California, Colorado, Mississippi, Nevada, New Jersey, and Rhode Island in 1923. In Alabama in 1903 and 1913 and in Georgia in 1913 and 1923 it was required through the compulsory use of textbooks.

Texas, in 1923, was the only instance of a time requirement in this subject.

> The history of Texas shall be taught in all public schools of this State, which history shall be taught in the history course of all public schools in this State and in this course only. The said history course shall be not less than two

[8] General Laws 1923, p. 60, Ch. 39.

> hours in any one week and as much more time as the State Superintendent of Public Instruction, in his discretion, thinks it necessary.

The Textbook Commission of Mississippi is directed to select and adopt for use in the public schools of the state a series of books including a history of the State of Mississippi. The law provides that

> no history in relation to the late civil war between the states shall be used in the schools of this state, unless it be fair and impartial.[9]

A law enacted in 1901, which was still in force in 1923, in Wyoming empowered but did not command the school directors

> to purchase, as a book of reference for use in their schools, the History of Wyoming, in three volumes, of which C. G. Coutant is the author, and "The Sabbath as an American War Day," in one volume, of which W. P. Carroll is the author; Provided, That the price paid for the said work shall not exceed the price paid therefor by subscribers generally.[10]

These laws are exceptional; the typical situation is for the subject to be mentioned along with the history of the United States among the required branches, without further comment. Colorado, New Jersey and Rhode Island were the only states in 1923 which required the history of the State which did not also require the history of the United States; in 1903 and 1913 no such instances were found.

GOVERNMENT OF THE UNITED STATES

No clear-cut line of demarcation can be drawn between the various subjects dealing with the form of government and the duties of citizenship. When one state requires "civil government" to be taught and another the "government of the United States and of this State" the mandate in each case can be fully met by courses which are exactly alike or by those which have very little in common. A course in "civics" may stress governmental forms or just ordinary neighborliness; the same is true of "citizenship." It is manifestly impossible, on the basis of the law alone, to establish a classification which will avoid all

[9] The Annotated Code, 1917, Vol. II, p. 3127, Sec. 7838.
[10] Compiled Statutes 1920, p. 486, Sec. 2315.

overlapping. The terms here used for the purpose of tabulation are not mutually exclusive. The provisions in most of the states fall clearly under the headings where they are placed but in a few instances arbitrary decisions had to be made; they will be given in full.

The Government of the United States was specifically prescribed as a subject of study in the elementary school in one state in 1903, in three states in 1913, and in three states in 1923. Florida, in 1903, 1913, and 1923, included among the required subjects of its course of study "history and civil government of Florida and of the United States." In New Mexico, in 1913,

> It shall be the duty of the teachers in the public schools in the State to give such instruction as is practicable in the History and Civics of the United States with special reference to the History and Civics of the State of New Mexico which said instruction may be given orally or by study of textbooks covering the subject and which said textbooks shall have been adopted by the State Board of Education. The said History and Civics of the State of New Mexico shall be prepared by a known historian of the State and shall be sold at a price to be fixed by the State Board of Education not to exceed one dollar per volume.

Wisconsin in 1913 and 1923 required

> history and civil government of the United States and of the state of Wisconsin.

Arkansas in 1923 prescribed

> civil government of the United States and the State of Arkansas.

GOVERNMENT OF THE STATE

The teaching of the government of the state was required in two states in 1903, in five in 1913, and in seven in 1923. It was joined in each instance with some other subject, either the government of the United States or the history of the individual state. It was provided for in connection with the government of the United States in Florida in 1903, 1913, and 1923; in New Mexico in 1913; in Wisconsin in 1913 and 1923; and in Arkansas in 1923.

The prescription in Vermont in 1903, 1913, and 1923 includes

> special instruction in the geography, history, constitution and principles of government of Vermont.

The prescription in Wyoming in 1913 and 1923 is for "history and civil government of Wyoming."

In Colorado in 1923,

> history and civil government of the State of Colorado shall be taught in all the public schools.

In Rhode Island, in 1923,

> In every class of the seventh or eighth year in elementary schools instruction shall be given in the history and government of Rhode Island.

CIVIL GOVERNMENT

Civil government was required in thirteen states in 1903, seventeen in 1913, and twenty-four in 1923. It was prescribed in the following states in all three years:

California	North Dakota	Texas
Georgia	Ohio	Virginia
Kentucky	South Dakota	West Virginia

In 1903 and 1913 it was also required in Colorado, Maryland, North Carolina, and Tennessee; in 1913 and 1923, in Florida, Illinois, Montana, and Pennsylvania; and in the following states in 1923:

Connecticut	Mississippi	New York
Kansas	Nebraska	Oklahoma
Louisiana	Nevada	Rhode Island
Maine	New Mexico	

In approximately half of the cases the prescription is for "civil government" without further qualification.

In California, in 1903 and 1913, the provision is for "history of the United States and civil government"; in 1923 it is for

> the duties of citizenship together with instruction in local civil government;

also, in connection with the course in the Constitution of the United States, there is to be included the "study of American institutions and ideals."

In Nevada in 1923,

> American civil government shall be taught in all of the graded schools.

It is also provided, in connection with the instruction in the constitution of the United States and the constitution of the State of Nevada, that there shall be

> the study of and devotion to American institutions and ideals.

In New Mexico in 1923 the provision is for "local civil government." In Florida in 1913 and 1923, and in North Carolina and Tennessee in 1903 and 1913, the provision is for "the elements of civil government."

In Connecticut in 1923,

> The duties of citizenship, including the knowledge of the form of national, state and local government, shall be taught in all elementary schools, both public and private, as a regular branch of study to pupils above the fourth grade.

In Illinois in 1923,

> American patriotism and the principles of representative government as enunciated in the American Declaration of Independence, the Constitution of the United States of America and the Constitution of the State of Illinois shall . . . be taught in all the public schools of this State . . . not less than one hour of each school week.

Louisiana in 1923 had a constitutional provision for instruction, in the elementary schools, in

> the constitutional system of state and national government and the duties of citizenship.

Maine in 1923 provided

> that American history and civil government shall be taught in all common schools of elementary and high school grades, both public and private, and that American history and civil government shall be required for graduation from all grammar schools, both public and private.

Maryland in 1903 provided that

> Civil government shall be taught to and studied by all pupils whose capacity will admit of it in all departments of the public schools of this state.

Mississippi in 1923 had

> civil government with special reference to local and state government;

and Montana, in 1913 and 1923, required "civics (state and federal)." Illinois in 1913 and Nebraska, New York, Oklahoma, and West Virginia in 1923 prescribed the teaching of "civics." Pennsylvania in 1923 had

> civics including loyalty to the state and national government.

Ohio, in 1903, 1913, and 1923, had

> history of the United States including civil government;

and in 1923, also, "American government and citizenship" in the seventh and eighth grades.

In Rhode Island in 1923,

> The principles of popular and representative government as enunciated in the constitution of Rhode Island and the constitution of the United States shall be taught in all the public schools of this state.

CITIZENSHIP

This was a required subject in one state, Connecticut, in 1903 and 1913; in the following states in 1923:

Alabama	Louisiana	Ohio
California	Maryland	Vermont
Connecticut	Massachusetts	Virginia
Iowa	New Jersey	Wisconsin
Kansas	New York	

In Connecticut in 1903 and 1913 the provision was,

> The duties of citizenship shall be taught in the public schools. The state board of education shall prepare and distribute to every school an outline of questions and suggestions relating to said subject, and said outline may be used in said schools.

In 1923,

> The duties of citizenship, including the knowledge of the form of national, state and local government, shall be taught in all elementary schools, both public and private,

> as a regular branch of study to pupils above the fourth grade. The provisions of this section shall apply to classes in ungraded schools corresponding to the grades designated herein.

The provisions in Vermont and Wisconsin were for "citizenship," and in Alabama and Maryland for "community civics."

In Ohio a course of study was required which

> shall include American government and citizenship in the seventh and eighth grades.

In Kansas, a course in

> the duties of a citizen suitable for the elementary grades

must be given.

In California, the requirement was for

> the duties of citizenship together with instruction in local government.

In Massachusetts, instruction and training were required in "the duties of citizenship." It is also provided that

> In all public elementary and high schools American history and civics shall be taught as required subjects for the purpose of promoting civic service and a greater knowledge thereof, and of fitting the pupils, morally and intellectually, for the duties of citizenship.

In Iowa,

> All public and private schools located within the state of Iowa shall be required to teach the subject of American citizenship. The Superintendent of Public Instruction shall prepare and distribute to all elementary schools an outline of American citizenship for all grades from one to eight, inclusive.

The constitution in Louisiana provides for instruction in "the duties of citizenship."

In New Jersey,

> For the elementary grades, a course in the geography, history and civics of New Jersey shall be provided, which course shall be prescribed by the Commissioner of Education, with the approval of the State Board of Education; and the course thus prescribed shall be required in all public elementary schools and shall be taken by all pupils in the grade in which it is given.

It is provided that the course

> shall be given together with instruction as to the privileges and responsibilities of citizenship as they relate to community and national welfare with the object of producing the highest type of patriotic citizenship.

In New York, courses of instruction in patriotism and citizenship, prescribed by the Regents of the University of the State of New York, must be maintained and followed in all the schools of the state

> in order to promote a spirit of patriotic and civic service and obligation and to foster in the children of the state moral and intellectual qualities which are essential in preparing to meet the obligations of citizenship in peace or war.

All pupils over eight years of age shall attend upon such instruction. In Virginia the language of the law is somewhat confused.

> Each teacher shall devote not less than thirty minutes in each month of the school session instructing the pupils therein as to ways and means of proper observations in connection with the course in civics and citizenship, so as to prevent accidents and in connection with the same course, and may devote not less than one hour in each month of the school session in instructing the pupils in the ways and means of preventing loss and damage to lives and property through preventable fires.

CONSTITUTION OF THE UNITED STATES

The constitution of the United States was a required subject in nine states in 1903, nine in 1913 and twenty-three in 1923. Only six states required the subject in all three of these years, Alabama, New Hampshire, North Carolina, South Carolina, Tennessee, and Vermont. It was prescribed in Wisconsin in 1903; in Colorado and Maryland in 1903 and 1913; in Georgia in 1913 and 1923; and in the following states in 1923:

California	Minnesota	Pennsylvania
Delaware	Nevada	South Dakota
Idaho	New Jersey	Utah
Iowa	New Mexico	West Virginia
Massachusetts	Ohio	
Michigan	Oregon	

The provisions in 1903 and 1913 were, in the main, merely a statement that this subject must be taught.

In Alabama, in both 1903 and 1913, the duty is placed upon the Superintendent of Education to

> make provision for instructing all pupils in all schools and colleges supported, in whole or in part, by public money, or under state control, in the constitution of the United States and the constitution of the State of Alabama.

In Colorado, in 1903 and also in 1913, there was a provision that those subjects should be taught in the public schools of the state upon which an applicant was required by law to pass an examination in order to teach in such schools. Among the subjects so required were the "constitution of the United States and constitution of Colorado."

In North Carolina in 1903, among the branches to be taught in the public school were

> history of North Carolina and the constitution of the state,

and

> history of the United States including the constitution of the United States.

In 1913 the wording was

> the elements of civil government containing the constitution of North Carolina and of the United States.

In Tennessee, in 1903 and 1913, in both the primary school and the secondary school it was provided that the

> history of the United States containing the constitution of the United States

should be taught.

In South Carolina, in both 1903 and 1913 "the principles of the constitution of the United States and of this State" were to be taught "as far as practicable."

In Maryland, in every school district, there must be taught

> the constitution of the United States and the constitution and history of the State of Maryland.

In New Hampshire, in 1903 and 1913, it was prescribed that

> the constitution of the United States and of the State

> of New Hampshire be read aloud by the scholars at least once during the last year of the course below the high school.

In Vermont, in 1903 and 1913,

> all pupils shall be thoroughly instructed in . . . the history and constitution of the United States;

and shall also receive

> special instruction in the geography, history, constitution and principles of government of Vermont.

In Wisconsin in 1903,

> the constitution of the United States and the constitution of this State shall be taught in every district school.

Georgia in 1913 directed the adoption of a textbook in the

> history of the United States containing the constitution of the United States

and specified that it should be in use in all the common schools of the state.

The provisions just quoted are, in the main, merely items in a list of required subjects. In 1923 we find not only a marked increase in the number of states requiring the teaching of the constitution of the United States, but also a larger number of laws devoted exclusively to this subject. A number of these laws quite obviously follow a common pattern. The eleven states,

Alabama	Michigan	Pennsylvania
Delaware	New Hampshire	South Dakota
Idaho	New Jersey	Utah
Iowa	Oregon	

embody the same provisions which are similarly expressed. All of these eleven laws, excepting those of Iowa and Michigan, were enacted in 1923.

The law in Alabama reads:

> In all public and private schools located within the State of Alabama, commencing with the school year, next ensuing after the passage of this Act, there shall be given regular courses of instruction in the Constitution of the United States. Such instruction in the Constitution of the United States shall begin not later than the opening of the Eighth

> Grade and shall continue in the High School course and in courses in state colleges, universities and the educational departments of state and municipal institutions to an extent to be determined by the Superintendent of Public Instruction.

The same law was enacted in Pennsylvania and Oregon. It was the same, also, in Delaware, Iowa, Michigan, and South Dakota, but these states include, in addition, provision for instruction in the constitution of the individual state.

New Hampshire provides for the teaching of the state constitution and places the obligation upon the local school board to see that the studies prescribed by the State Board of Education are thoroughly taught, adding that

> any member of the Board who neglects or refuses to comply with the provisions of this section shall forfeit $200.

New Jersey provides that the instruction in this subject shall begin

> not later than the opening of the seventh grade, or in private schools a grade equivalent thereto.

Idaho has the instruction begin in the elementary course in the sixth grade and provides that it shall also be given as a grammar grade course in the eighth grade. In Utah, the instruction

> shall be given at such time and be pursued to such an extent in the public and private schools as shall be determined by the State Board of Education.

The following was enacted in Georgia in 1923:

> All schools and colleges in this State that are sustained or in any manner supported by public funds shall give instruction in the essentials of the United States Constitution and the Constitution of Georgia including the study of and devotion to American institutions and ideals. And no student in said schools and colleges shall receive a certificate of graduation without previously passing a satisfactory examination upon the provisions and principles of the United States Constitution and the Constitution of the State of Georgia.

Laws were enacted in Nevada and California in 1923 which have many elements in common but they will be quoted in full.

In Nevada,

> Section 1. In all the public and private schools, colleges and universities, including the Nevada school of industry, located within this state, commencing with the school year next ensuing after the passage and approval of this act, there shall be given instruction in the essentials of the constitution of the United States and the constitution of the State of Nevada, including the origin and history of said constitution and the study of and devotion to American institutions and ideals; and no student in said schools and colleges shall receive a certificate or diploma of graduation without previously having passed a satisfactory examination upon the said constitutions.
>
> Sec. 2. The instruction provided for in section 1 of this act shall be given during at least one year each of the elementary, the high-school, and the college grades.
>
> Sec. 3. Hereafter any person who is granted a certificate to teach in the Nevada public schools or who is granted a renewal of his certificate, or anyone in any of the institutions named in section 1 of this act charged with the duty of giving instruction in the said constitutions shall be required to show, by examination or credentials showing college, university or normal-school study, satisfactory evidence of adequate knowledge of the origin, history, provisions and principles of the said constitutions; *provided, however,* that the state board of education may grant a reasonable time for compliance with the terms of this section.
>
> Sec. 4. The wilful neglect or failure on the part of any public-school superintendent, principal, or teacher, or any officer in charge of any of the other schools named in this act, to observe and carry out the requirements of this act, shall be sufficient cause for the dismissal or removal of such party from his or her position.
>
> Sec. 5. It shall be the duty of the state board of education, the board of regents of the University of Nevada, the superintendent of the Nevada school of industry, and those having charge of any other schools or institutions named in this act, to make due arrangements for carrying out the provisions of this act as regards the schools under their respective control or administration.

In California,

> Section 1. In all public and private schools located within the State of California, commencing with the school year next ensuing after the passage of this act, there shall be

given regular courses of instruction in the constitution of the United States, including the study of American institutions and ideals.

Sec. 2. Such instruction in the constitution of the United States shall begin not later than the opening of the eighth grade and shall continue in the high school course and in courses in state colleges, universities and educational institutions, to an extent to be determined by the superintendent of public instruction. No pupil shall receive a certificate of graduation from any such school unless he has satisfactorily passed an examination on the provisions and principles of the United States constitution.

Sec. 3. All persons granted regular certificates authorizing them to teach in the public schools of this state, shall, in addition to existing requirements, be required to pass a satisfactory examination upon the provisions and principles of the constitution of the United States or complete a course therein in a teachers' training institution in the State of California; *provided,* that a limited certificate, not exceeding one year in term, may be granted without the passing of such examination or the completion of such course.

Sec. 4. The wilful neglect or failure on the part of any superintendent, principal or teacher, to observe and carry out the requirements of this act, shall be sufficient cause for the dismissal or removal of such party from his or her position.

Sec. 5. It shall be the duty of the superintendent of public instruction to make arrangements for carrying out the provisions of this act and prescribe a list of suitable texts adapted to the needs of the school and college grades, as specified in this act.

Sec. 6. All acts or parts of acts inconsistent herewith are hereby repealed.

In West Virginia,

Section 9-a. In all the public, private, parochial and denominational schools located within the state of West Virginia there shall be given regular courses of instruction in history of the United States, in civics and the constitutions of the United States and the state of West Virginia, for the purpose of teaching, fostering and perpetuating the ideals, principles and spirit of Americanism, and increasing the knowledge of the organization and machinery of the government of the United States and of the state of West Virginia. The state board of education shall prescribe, with and on the advice of the state superintendent of schools, the courses of study covering these subjects for the public elementary and grammar schools, public high schools and the state normal schools.

Sec. 9-b. It shall be the duty of the officials or boards having authority over the respective private, parochial and denominational schools to prescribe similar courses of study for the school under their control and supervision, as is required by the preceding section for the public schools.

Sec. 9-c. Any person or persons violating the provisions of sections 9-a and 9-b, shall be guilty of a misdemeanor, and on conviction thereof shall be fined not exceeding ten dollars for each violation, and each week during which there is a violation shall constitute a separate offense. If the person or persons so convicted occupy a position in connection with the public schools, he or she or they shall also automatically be removed from said position or positions and be ineligible for reappointment to that or a similar position for the period of one year.

Sec. 9-d. The holding of any of the provisions of sections nine-a, nine-b, and nine-c to be void, ineffective or unconstitutional for any cause, shall not be deemed to affect the validity of any of the other provisions thereof.

In Tennessee,

All students in the State Normal Schools and public high schools, and all pupils in the senior classes of the public grammar schools in the State of Tennessee, shall receive instruction and be required to study the Constitution of the United States, and no student or pupil of any of said public schools shall receive a certificate of graduation without previously passing a satisfactory examination upon the provisions and principles of said Constitution. *Provided,* that the above mentioned course is taught in connection with United States History; and that all examinations on the Constitution be given along with that in the history course. Wilful neglect or failure on the part of any public school Superintendent, public school principal or public school teacher, to observe and carry out the requirements of this Act, shall be sufficient cause for the dismissal or removal of such party from his or her position as such Superintendent, principal or teacher.

In Minnesota,

In the eighth grade and in the high school grades of all public schools, and in the corresponding grades in all other

> schools within the State of Minnesota, and in the educational departments of state and municipal institutions there shall be given regular courses of instruction in the Declaration of Independence and the Constitution of the United States, to an extent to be determined by the State Commissioner of Education.

In Ohio,

> It shall be the duty of the board of education of each school district to provide for the study of the United States constitution and the constitution of Ohio, either in the seventh or eighth grade for a period of equivalent to one recitation period each week for the full school year. . . It shall be the duty of the director of education to compile, publish and distribute to the various school boards of the state prior to September 1, 1923, a pamphlet containing the United States constitution and the constitution of Ohio together with such explanatory matter as he may deem advisable.

In Vermont there is provided a nine-year elementary course which shall include

> an additional year of review and advanced work in . . . the history and constitution of the United States . . . and shall also include special instruction in the geography, history, constitution and principles of government of Vermont.

In Massachusetts the provision is for "the history and constitution of the United States" and

> American history and civics including the constitution of the United States.

In New Mexico it is

> United States history including the Declaration of Independence and the constitution of the United States and of New Mexico.

In North Carolina, a law enacted in 1923 enumerated the Constitution of the United States and the Constitution of North Carolina as general items in a required course of instruction known as "Americanism." In South Carolina the law is the same as it was in 1903 and 1913. The law in Louisiana and in Rhode Island has been regarded, for the purpose of classification in this study, as prescribing the teaching of "civil government" rather than "constitution."

Louisiana provides

> instruction upon the constitutional system of state and national government and the duties of citizenship.

In Rhode Island,

> The principles of popular and representative government as enunciated in the constitution of Rhode Island and the constitution of the United States shall be taught in all the public schools of this state.

Seventeen of the mandatory provisions for teaching the constitution of the United States, as given above, were enacted in the year 1923. These enactments were in the following states:

Alabama	Minnesota	Oregon
California	Nevada	Pennsylvania
Delaware	New Hampshire	South Dakota
Georgia	New Jersey	Tennessee
Idaho	North Carolina	Utah
Massachusetts	Ohio	

CONSTITUTION OF THE STATE

The teaching of the constitution of the individual state was required in nine states in 1903, in ten in 1913, and in fourteen in 1923. Delaware in 1913 is the only instance in which this subject is required and the teaching of the Constitution of the United States is not also required. Commonly the provision is to be found in the same section with that which requires the teaching of the constitution of the United States. In no case is the prescription elaborated and all variations of phraseology have been presented along with the Constitution of the United States. There were only five states which required this subject in all three of the years under discussion, New Hampshire, North Carolina, South Carolina, Tennessee, and Vermont.

New Hampshire in 1903 and 1913 merely provided that the Constitution

> be read aloud by the scholars at least once during the last year of the course below the high school.

DECLARATION OF INDEPENDENCE

The teaching of the Declaration of Independence was specifically provided for in two states in 1923. In Minnesota,

> there shall be given regular courses of instruction in the Declaration of Independence and the Constitution of the United States, to an extent to be determined by the State Commissioner of Education.

In New Mexico,

> In such grades as the State Board of Education shall prescribe, the following subjects shall be taught in the public schools of the state . . . United States history including the Declaration of Independence and the Constitution of the United States and of New Mexico.

In Michigan in 1915 the following provision was enacted regarding the observance of the twelfth of February, the twenty-second of February and the twelfth of October:

> It shall be the duty of every teacher in the public schools of this State to cause the Declaration of Independence to be read to his or her pupils above the fifth grade on said days. Any teacher neglecting to perform the duty hereby imposed shall be liable to have his or her certificate revoked by the county commissioner of schools or by the Superintendent of Public Instruction. Hereafter in all examinations for eighth grade diplomas, all applicants shall be required as a part of said examination to write from memory the first verse of the Star-Spangled Banner and the words of America.[11]

In 1919 this law was amended and the provision regarding the reading of the Declaration of Independence was omitted.[12]

DAYS OF SPECIAL OBSERVANCE

Only those days have been included among the days of special observance which the law requires the schools to observe with special exercises. School holidays, upon which no sessions are held, would affect the amount of available schooling but would not necessarily have any influence upon the content of the curriculum. Table II shows the days for which special observance is prescribed in the different states in the three years 1903, 1913, and 1923.

[11] Public Acts of Michigan 1915, p. 376, No. 223.
[12] Public Acts of Michigan 1919, p. 134, No. 72.

TABLE II REQUIRED DAYS OF SPECIAL OBSERVANCE IN THE PUBLIC ELE

Year	Day Observed		Alabama	Arizona	Arkansas	California	Colorado	Connecticut	Delaware	Florida	Georgia	Idaho	Illinois	Indiana	Iowa	Kansas	Kentucky	Louisiana	Maine	Maryland
	Lincoln's Birthday	1		M																
	Washington's Birthday	2		M																
	Columbus Day	3																		
	Lee's Birthday	4																		
	Roosevelt's Birthday	5																		
	Carleton Day	6																		
	Memorial Day	7		M																
	Armistice Day	8																		
	Maine Memorial Day	9																		
	September Seventeenth	10																		
1903	Flag Day	11		M				M												
	Thanksgiving Day	12																		
	Labor Day	13																		
	Mother's Day	14																		
	State Day	15																		
	Temperance Day	16																		
	Arbor Day	17		M			M	M			M	M								
	Bird Day	18																		
	Fire Prevention Day	19																		
	State Fire Day	20																		
	Good Roads Day	21																		
	Lincoln's Birthday	1		M												M			M	
	Washington's Birthday	2		M												M				M
	Columbus Day	3																M		
	Lee's Birthday	4			M															
	Roosevelt's Birthday	5																		
	Carleton Day	6																		
	Memorial Day	7		M												M				
	Armistice Day	8																		
	Maine Memorial Day	9																		
	September Seventeenth	10																		
1913	Flag Day	11		M				M								M				
	Thanksgiving Day	12																		
	Labor Day	13																		
	Mother's Day	14								M										
	State Day	15									M									M
	Temperance Day	16																		
	Arbor Day	17		M			M	M			M	M		M				M		
	Bird Day	18																M		
	Fire Prevention Day	19																		
	State Fire Day	20																		
	Good Roads Day	21					M													
	Lincoln's Birthday	1		M		M										M			M	
	Washington's Birthday	2		M		M						M				M				M
	Columbus Day	3				M						M						M		
	Lee's Birthday	4			M															
	Roosevelt's Birthday	5																		
	Carleton Day	6																		
	Memorial Day	7		M												M				M
	Armistice Day	8				M		M												M
	Maine Memorial Day	9						M												
	September Seventeenth	10																		
1923	Flag Day	11		M				M								M				
	Thanksgiving Day	12																		
	Labor Day	13				M						M								
	Mother's Day	14								M										
	State Day	15										M								M
	Temperance Day	16								M	M					M	M		M	
	Arbor Day	17		M		M	M	M				M		M				M		M
	Bird Day	18													M			M		
	Fire Prevention Day	19						M												
	State Fire Day	20																		
	Good Roads Day	21					M													

M = Mandatory.

MENTARY SCHOOLS IN EACH OF THE FORTY-EIGHT STATES, 1903, 1913, 1923

	Massachusetts	Michigan	Minnesota	Mississippi	Missouri	Montana	Nebraska	Nevada	New Hampshire	New Jersey	New Mexico	New York	North Carolina	North Dakota	Ohio	Oklahoma	Oregon	Pennsylvania	Rhode Island	South Carolina	South Dakota	Tennessee	Texas	Utah	Vermont	Virginia	Washington	West Virginia	Wisconsin	Wyoming	
1										M		M							M												**4**
2										M		M																			**3**
3																															
4																															
5																															
6																															
7	M								M	M		M													M						**6**
8																															
9																															
10																															**3**
11												M																			
12										M																					**1**
13																															
14																															
15						M																									**1**
16																															
17						M		M		M	M	M			M	M	M			M		M								M	**16**
18																															
19																															
20																															
21																															
																															34
1		M						M		M	M	M		M			M		M									M			**12**
2		M						M		M		M		M			M														**9**
3		M															M											M			**4**
4																															**1**
5																															
6																															
7	M								M	M		M		M											M						**8**
8																															
9																															
10																															
11										M		M																			**5**
12										M																					**1**
13																															
14																															**1**
15			M			M		M											M	M											**7**
16																															
17						M		M		M	M	M			M	M	M			M		M								M	**18**
18																								M							**2**
19																															
20							M																								**1**
21																															**1**
																															70
1		M				M	M	M		M		M		M			M		M						M			M	M		**16**
2		M				M	M	M		M		M		M			M											M	M		**15**
3		M				M								M			M											M			**8**
4																															**1**
5		M																													**1**
6		M																													**1**
7	M						M		M	M		M													M						**9**
8		M				M								M													M				**7**
9																															**1**
10		M																													**1**
11						M	M			M		M																			**7**
12										M																					**1**
13														M			M														**4**
14																															**1**
15			M		M	M		M											M	M											**8**
16					M			M					M	M	M		M			M	M	M					M				**15**
17						M		M		M	M	M	M		M	M	M		M	M		M								M	**21**
18																		M						M							**4**
19																															**1**
20							M																								**1**
21																															**1**
																															124

LINCOLN'S BIRTHDAY

Exercises in commemoration of the birthday of Abraham Lincoln were required in four states in 1903, in twelve in 1913, and in sixteen in 1923. They were required in Arizona, New Jersey, New York, and Rhode Island in all three years; in Kansas, Maine, Michigan, Nevada, North Dakota, Oregon, and West Virginia in 1913 and 1923; in California, Montana, Nebraska, Vermont, and Wisconsin in 1923, and in New Mexico in 1913. The requirement is usually briefly expressed and is frequently joined with that for some other day, especially Washington's Birthday. In Arizona, Kansas, and New York it was made the duty of the state superintendent of public instruction or the commissioner of education to make special provision for the observance of the day in the public schools. In California, the public schools "shall hold proper exercises commemorating the day."

In Maine,

> Lincoln day shall be observed by devoting some part of the day to the study of the life and character of Abraham Lincoln.

In Michigan the day must be observed "by proper and appropriate commemorative exercises." In New Jersey,

> In all public schools there shall be held on the last school day preceding the following holidays, namely, Lincoln's Birthday, Washington's Birthday, Decoration or Memorial Day and Thanksgiving Day, and on such other patriotic holidays as shall be established by law, appropriate exercises for the development of a higher spirit of patriotism.

In North Dakota in 1913, all schools

> shall assemble for a portion of the day and devote the same to patriotic exercises consistent with the day.

In 1923 this was changed to

> excepting in those communities where community celebrations are held on that day . . . the schools shall be in session as usual and at least one hour of the day shall be devoted to patriotic exercises consistent with the day.

In Rhode Island, in all three years, special observance of the twelfth of February as Grand Army Flag Day "in honor of the birthday of Abraham Lincoln" was required.

> It shall be the duty of the commissioner of education to prepare a programme of patriotic exercises for the proper observance of Grand Army Flag Day, and to furnish printed copies of the same to the school committees of the several cities and towns at least four weeks previous to the twelfth day of February in each year.

In Vermont,

> Exercises in commemoration of the birth, life and services of Abraham Lincoln shall be conducted in all public, private and parochial schools on the twelfth day of February, annually, and if such date is not a school day, such exercises shall be conducted on the last school day before such date.

In Wisconsin, exercises appropriate to commemorate the memory of Abraham Lincoln must be held in the public schools at some time in the afternoon. In Montana, Nebraska, Nevada, Oregon, and West Virginia "appropriate exercises" must be held. In New Mexico in 1913 the day was to "be observed with patriotic exercises."

WASHINGTON'S BIRTHDAY

The law regarding the observance of the birthday of George Washington is similar to that of Abraham Lincoln. Three states had the requirement in 1903, nine in 1913, and fifteen in 1923. As a rule, provision for the observance of the birthdays of Lincoln and Washington is made by the same states and is found in the same section of the law. This was the case in

Arizona	Montana	New York
California	Nebraska	North Dakota
Kansas	Nevada	Oregon
Michigan	New Jersey	Wisconsin

Observance of the day was also required in Idaho and West Virginia in 1923 and in Maryland in 1913 and 1923. In Idaho the day was to "be observed with appropriate exercises."

In Maryland,

> On Washington's Birthday the schools shall devote a portion of the day to exercises bearing on the life and services of "The Father of our Country."

In Oregon,

> The twenty-second day of February shall be a school holiday except that not less than one and one-half hours of the forenoon of such day shall be set apart and observed in the public schools of the state by appropriate exercises and the afternoon of such day shall be a holiday.

In West Virginia,

> schools shall be assembled for instruction on Washington's Birthday and shall devote a portion of the day to exercises commemorating the life and services of the "Father of Our Country."

COLUMBUS DAY

Observance by the public schools of the anniversary of the discovery of America by Christopher Columbus was mandatory in four states in 1913 and in eight in 1923; in Louisiana, Michigan, Oregon, and West Virginia in both of these years and in California, Idaho, Montana, and North Dakota in 1923. Usually it is prescribed in the same section as that for the national heroes, Lincoln and Washington. In North Dakota, the twelfth of October (Discovery Day) must be observed.

In Louisiana,

> The several school boards of the State of Louisiana shall annually authorize, direct and instruct the parish superintendent of education, or other proper authority to observe the anniversary of the date of the discovery of America by Christopher Columbus, October 12, by such fitting and appropriate exercises as the said various and several school boards may determine upon and select. Any failure upon the part of the said several and various school boards and parish superintendents to comply with the provisions of this Act, shall subject said school boards and members thereof, and the parish superintendent to charges of non-feasance, and neglect of duty, which may be preferred by any person, before the proper authority.

LEE'S BIRTHDAY

In Arkansas in 1913 and 1923,

> The nineteenth of January, the birthday of Robert E. Lee, shall be observed in all the public schools of this State as a day for patriotic exercises and the study of the history and achievements of Arkansas men.

ROOSEVELT'S BIRTHDAY

The observance of the twenty-seventh day of October, the birthday of Theodore Roosevelt, by proper and appropriate commemorative exercises was prescribed by Michigan in 1923.

CARLETON DAY

In Michigan in 1923,

> The twenty-first day of October in each year shall be observed with appropriate exercises in the schools of Michigan as "Carleton Day" in memory of Will Carleton, Michigan's pioneer poet. Whenever said twenty-first day of October shall fall on other than a school day, the superintendent of public instruction shall designate the day nearest such twenty-first day of October as "Carleton Day." On such day it shall be the duty of each teacher in any grade above the fifth grade to read, or cause to be read, to his or her pupils at least one of the poems of Will Carleton and may, in addition, provide such other proper and fitting observance of such Carleton Day as they may desire.

MEMORIAL DAY

Special commemorative exercises on or near the thirtieth of May of each year was prescribed for the public schools in six states in 1903, eight in 1913 and nine in 1923. In Arizona, Kansas, Nebraska, New Jersey, and New York the provision is found in the same section of the law as that for Lincoln's Birthday and Washington's Birthday. This was the case also in North Dakota in 1913. In Maryland in 1923,

> Memorial Day shall be observed at such time and in such manner as the State Board of Education may direct.

In Massachusetts, in all three years,

> In all the public schools the last regular session, or a portion thereof, prior to May thirtieth, known as Memorial Day, shall be devoted to patriotic exercises.

In New Hampshire, in all three years,

> In all public schools of the state one session, or a portion thereof, during the week in which Memorial Day falls, shall be devoted to exercises of a patriotic nature.

In Vermont, in all three years,

> The last half-day's session of the public schools before Memorial Day shall be devoted to exercises commemorative of the history of the nation during the War of the Rebellion and to patriotic instruction in the principles of liberty and the equal rights of man.

ARMISTICE DAY

There were seven states in 1923 which required in the schools special observance of November the eleventh as Armistice Day: California, Connecticut, Maryland, Michigan, Montana, North Dakota, and Washington. In Michigan the day is referred to as "Liberty Day" and in Washington as "Victory and Admission Day." In Connecticut,

> suitable exercises having reference to the historical event to be commemorated thereby shall be held in the public schools.

In Maryland,

> the schools shall devote a portion of the day to exercises bearing on the World War and the participation of the United States and the State of Maryland in said war.

In North Dakota the day is apparently to be observed in the schools

> Excepting in those communities where community celebrations are held on that day.

In Washington, Victory and Admission Day must be observed on the eleventh of November each year or the Friday preceding when the day falls on a non-school day.

> For the proper observance of this day, it shall be the duty of each teacher in the public schools of this state, or principal in charge of the school buildings, to prepare and, in coöperation with the pupils in his charge, present a program of exercises of at least sixty minutes in length, setting forth the part taken by the United States and the state of Washington in the world war for the years 1917 and 1918, and the principles for which the allied nations fought, and the heroic deeds of American soldiers and sailors, the leading events in the history of our state and of Washington territory, the character and struggles of the pioneer settlers and other topics

tending to instill a loyalty and devotion to the institutions and laws of our state.

MAINE MEMORIAL DAY

In Connecticut in 1923, the fifteenth of February, Maine Memorial Day, must be commemorated by suitable exercises.

SEPTEMBER SEVENTEENTH

In Michigan in 1923, the seventeenth day of September, being the date of the adoption of the federal constitution, shall be observed by proper and appropriate commemorative exercises.

FLAG DAY

Special observance of Flag Day was required in three states in 1903, five in 1913, and seven in 1923. Suitable exercises for this day were prescribed in the same section of the law as those for other holidays with no especial comment in Arizona and New York in all three years; in Kansas in 1913 and 1923, and in Montana and Nebraska in 1923. In Connecticut in all three years,

> The governor shall, annually, in the spring, designate by official proclamation the fourteenth day of June as Flag Day, and suitable exercises, having reference to the adoption of the national flag, shall be held in the public schools on that day, or, in case that day shall not be a school day, on the school day preceding, or on such other day as the school visitors, board of education or town school committee may prescribe.

In New Jersey in 1913 and 1923,

> It shall be the duty of the principals and teachers in the public schools of this State to make suitable arrangements for the celebration, by appropriate exercises among the pupils in said schools, on the fourteenth day of June, in each year, as the day of the adoption of the American flag by the Continental Congress.

Rhode Island in all three years required special observance of Grand Army Flag Day on the twelfth of February "in honor of the birthday of Abraham Lincoln."

THANKSGIVING DAY

In New Jersey, in all three years, appropriate exercises for the development of a higher spirit of patriotism were required to be held in all public schools on the last school day preceding Thanksgiving Day.

LABOR DAY

Special observance of Labor Day was required in the public schools in 1923 in California, Idaho, North Dakota, and Oregon. An exception was made in North Dakota in those communities where community celebrations of the day were held.

MOTHER'S DAY

In Florida in 1913 and 1923,

> The first Friday in November of each and every year shall be set apart and known as Mother's Day in the State of Florida. It shall be the duty of all teachers in the State of Florida to commemorate Mother's Day with appropriate exercises.

STATE DAY

A day with special local significance was observed in one state in 1903, seven in 1913, and eight in 1923. In Montana, in all three years,

> The first Monday of November of each year shall be designated and known as Pioneer day in the state of Montana. On said Pioneer day in the public schools the afternoon thereof shall be devoted to the study and discussion of pioneers and pioneer history of the region and country now comprising the state of Montana.
>
> The state board of education is hereby authorized to award annually its pioneer medal to the student of the public schools or state institutions who shall on said day deliver the best essay on such subject of pioneer history, having regard to historical research and literary merit.
>
> Copies of such essays shall be filed by the said state board of education with the librarian of the historical and miscellaneous department of the state library.
>
> The superintendent of public instruction shall have power and it shall be his duty to prescribe from year to year a

> suitable course of exercises to be observed in the public schools of the state on Pioneer day.

In Maryland in 1913 and 1923,

> Maryland Day shall be observed at such a time and in such manner as the State Board of Education may direct.

In Minnesota in 1913 and 1923,

> There shall be designated annually by proclamation by the superintendent of public instruction of this state, by and with the consent of the governor, a day between October 1st and May 1st to be designated and known as "Minnesota Day." On that day all the public schools of this state shall give special attention to exercises devoted to matters of interest appertaining to the State of Minnesota and its geography, history, industries and resources.

In Nevada, in 1913 and 1923, the thirty-first day of October, which is Nevada's admission day, was required to be observed with appropriate exercises. In Rhode Island, in 1913 and 1923,

> The fourth day of May in each and every year hereafter is hereby established, in this state, as "Rhode Island Independence Day";—being a just tribute to the memory of the members of our general assembly, who, on the fourth day of May, 1776—in the state house at Providence, passed an act renouncing allegiance of the colony to the British crown and by the provisions of that act declaring it sovereign and independent;—the first official act of its kind by any of the thirteen American colonies.
>
> The fourth day of May in each and every year hereafter is hereby established in the annual school calendar to be known as "Rhode Island Independence Day," and shall be observed with patriotic exercises in all public schools of the state.
>
> The commissioner of education shall annually prepare a programme of patriotic exercises for the proper observance of "Rhode Island Independence Day" in the schools, and shall furnish printed copies of the same to the school committees of the several cities and towns of the state at least four weeks previous to the fourth of May in each year.

In South Carolina in 1913 and 1923,

> The public schools of this State shall observe Calhoun's birthday, the 18th of March, of each year, as "South Carolina Day," and on that day the school officers and teachers shall conduct such exercises as will conduce to a more gen-

> eral knowledge and appreciation of the history, resources and possibilities of the State.

In Idaho in 1923, June 15th, as Pioneer Day, was to be observed with appropriate exercises. In Missouri in 1923,

> The first Monday of October of each and every year shall be known and designated as Missouri Day and shall be, and is hereby, set apart as a day commemorative of Missouri history, to be observed by the teachers and pupils of schools with appropriate exercises.
> That the people of the state of Missouri, and the educational, commercial, political, civic, religious and fraternal organizations of the state of Missouri be requested to devote some part of the day to the methodical consideration of the products of the mine, field and forest of the state and to the consideration of the achievements of the sons and daughters of Missouri in commerce, literature, statesmanship, science and art and in other departments of activity in which the state has rendered service to mankind.

In Georgia in 1913,

> The twelfth of February in each year shall be observed in the public schools of this State, under the name of "Georgia Day," as the anniversary of the landing of the first colonists in Georgia under Oglethorpe; and it shall be the duty of the State School Commissioner, through the county School Commissioners, annually to cause the teachers of the schools under their supervision to conduct on that day exercises in which the pupils shall take part, consisting of written compositions, readings, recitations, addresses or other exercises, relating to this State and its history and to the lives of distinguished Georgians.

In 1923 the following days must be "observed either by holidays or appropriate exercises": Thanksgiving Day, Uncle Remus Day (December 9), Lee's Birthday, Georgia Day, Washington's Birthday, Arbor and Bird Day, and Memorial Day (April 26). Washington in 1923 required the observance of admission day on November eleventh as a part of Victory and Admission Day.

TEMPERANCE AND CONSERVATION DAYS

Six other special days have been classified here so that all of the days of special observance could be shown together in Table II. The descriptions of the provisions regarding these days have been presented in other chapters. Temperance Day is presented in the chapter on Health and "Prohibition." Arbor Day, Bird Day, Fire Prevention Day, State Fire Day, and Good Roads Day are presented in the chapter on Conservation of Life and Property.

In 1903 there were twenty states which prescribed one or more days of special observance; there were thirty-three such states in 1913, and forty-two in 1923. In 1903 there were a total of thirty-four days prescribed in twenty states; in 1913 there were seventy days in thirty-three states, and in 1923 there were one hundred twenty-four days in forty-two states. Practice varies widely in different states. Michigan and Montana in 1923 each required the observance of seven different days. Alabama, Delaware, Illinois, Mississippi, Texas, and Virginia did not require the observance of any days during the period of this study.

If we separate the fifteen days, which are chiefly commemorative of the birthdays of national heroes and memorial days for national events, from the six temperance and conservation days, we find that the former type increased in twenty years from a total of eighteen days in eight states to eighty-one days in twenty-eight states. Temperance Day has developed entirely during the last decade and is now found in fifteen states. The five conservation days have increased from a total of sixteen in as many states to twenty-eight days in twenty-five states.

SUMMARY

This group of subjects whose obvious tendency is to foster local, provincial and national pride has shown a marked growth, especially in the last decade. By adding together the number of states which prescribed each of the seventeen items listed under Nationalism we obtain a total of one hundred forty-seven prescriptions in 1903, one hundred ninety-six in 1913, and three hundred four in 1923. This is an increase of forty-nine prescriptions from 1903 to 1913 and of one hundred eight prescriptions from 1913 to 1923; a total increase of one hundred fifty-seven prescriptions in twenty years. The items showing the largest increase are flag display, days of special observance, all instruction in English, Constitution of the United States, citizenship, patriotism, and history of the state. These facts are summarized in Table III. No quantitative statement, however, will reveal that which is doubtless far more significant, the change in the character of the legislative provisions. The recent enactments are, on the whole, more definite and restrictive. They embody more detail. Recent legislation reveals an increase in assurance on the part of law-makers. Apparently they are more conscious of their authority and more determined to insure the realization of their will. Eight states, Arkansas, Illinois, Nevada, Ohio, Oklahoma, South Dakota, Texas, and Virginia had, in 1923, provisions which required that a definite minimum time allotment be devoted to certain specified subjects within this group. There has been a decided increase in the number of provisions imposing a penalty for failure to carry out a particular mandate. Responsibility is more definitely fixed. It is much more frequent than formerly

TABLE III

SUMMARY OF CURRICULAR PRESCRIPTIONS IN NATIONALISM SHOWING INCREASE 1903–1923

Item	Number of States in Which Prescribed			Increase		
	1903	1913	1923	1903 to 1913	1913 to 1923	1903 to 1923
Days of Special Observance	20	33	42	13	9	22
Flag Display	17	29	39	12	10	22
History of the United States	30	32	35	2	3	5
All Instruction in English	14	17	34	3	17	20
History of the State	13	20	25	7	5	12
Civil Government	13	17	24	4	7	11
Constitution of the United States	9	9	23	--	14	14
Foreign Language	11	11	15	--	4	4
Constitution of the State	9	10	14	1	4	5
Citizenship	1	1	14	--	13	13
Patriotism	--	1	12	1	11	12
Flag Exercises	3	4	10	1	6	7
Government of the State	2	5	7	3	2	5
Government of the United States	1	3	3	2	--	2
Patriotic Songs	--	1	3	1	2	3
Declaration of Independence	--	--	2	--	2	2
German	4	3	2	(−1)	(−1)	(−2)
Total Number of Prescriptions	147	196	304	49	108	157

This table is based upon Table I.

The items are arranged according to the number of states which had the prescription in 1923.

Foreign Language.—The "prescriptions" in 1903 and 1913 were all permissive; of those in 1923 one was mandatory, ten were permissive and four were prohibitive.

German.—The "prescriptions" in 1903 and 1913 were permissive; those in 1923 were prohibitive.

to specify that an approved textbook must be used and that the teacher shall have special training to enable her to perform the imposed task.

Provisions in different states regarding a given subject are not infrequently similarly phrased. This suggests that some of the laws may not represent a popular demand but may have been promoted by special organizations. From other sources we know that this is sometimes the case.

CHAPTER III

LEGISLATIVE PROVISIONS CONCERNING THE TEACHING OF HEALTH AND "PROHIBITION"

Under the caption Health and "Prohibition" the following subjects have been classified:

1. Stimulants and Narcotics	6. Communicable Diseases
2. Physiology and Hygiene	7. Sanitation
3. Physical Education	8. Accident Prevention
4. Physical Examination	9. Tobacco
5. Personal Hygiene	10. Placards

Next to Nationalism, this group shows the largest increase during the twenty-year period which we are considering. From Table IV (pp 66-67) it will be observed that there were one hundred two prescriptions in 1903, one hundred thirty-one in 1913, and one hundred seventy-one in 1923. This shows a net gain of sixty-nine prescriptions during the interval. It will be observed that the gain is in those subjects which deal with physical well-being; with personal and community hygiene. If Temperance Day had been tabulated with this group intead of with the other days of special observance the number of prescriptions in Health and "Prohibition" in 1923 would have been increased to one hundred eighty-six. The reader is reminded that, while the amount of the increase is significant, the actual figures should not be given too great emphasis; the number of prescriptions would be larger if physiology and hygiene were listed separately; likewise, if the various items which have here been grouped under the heading "Stimulants and Narcotics" had been isolated. On the other hand, there would be no misrepresentation if physiology and hygiene, stimulants and narcotics were regarded as a single subject; as a matter of fact they are joined in a single statement in the great majority of instances. Because they are so closely associated they will here be presented together.

PHYSIOLOGY AND HYGIENE, STIMULANTS AND NARCOTICS

Various expressions are used in different states to designate the subject matter which we shall refer to as Stimulants and Narcotics.

Stimulants and narcotics
Alcohol and narcotics
Alcoholic stimulants and narcotics
Alcoholic drinks and narcotics
Alcoholic beverages and narcotics
Alcoholic drinks, stimulants and narcotics

"Tobacco" is included in Alabama and California; "nicotine" in Indiana; "smoking cigarettes" in Tennessee; "habit-forming drugs" in South Dakota; "poisonous substances" in Iowa. The language in nearly every case directs that "the effect upon the human system" is to be emphasized. Several states provide for the teaching of "the nature" as well as "the effect." These various expressions are, in most instances, joined with provision for the teaching of "Physiology and Hygiene." Georgia had

> Health and hygiene and special instruction as to the nature of alcoholic drinks and narcotics;

North Carolina,

> Health education including the evil effects of alcohol and narcotics;

Connecticut,

> Hygiene including the effects of alcohol and narcotics on health and character;

Colorado,

> the nature of alcoholic drinks and narcotics and special instruction as to their effects upon the human system, in connection with the several divisions of the subject of physiology and hygiene.

It is probably safe to say that no other subject of the curriculum has received so much legislative attention as the composite one which we are here considering. "Stimulants and narcotics" was required in forty-seven states in 1903, in forty-five states in 1913, and in forty-three states in 1923. Physiology and hygiene was required in forty-six states in 1903, forty-five states in

TABLE IV CURRICULAR PRESCRIPTIONS IN HEALTH AND "PROHIBITION" 1903, 1913,

Year	Subject or Activity		Alabama	Arizona	Arkansas	California	Colorado	Connecticut	Delaware	Florida	Georgia	Idaho	Illinois	Indiana	Iowa	Kansas	Kentucky	Louisiana	Maine	Maryland
1903	Stimulants and Narcotics	1	M	M	M	M	M	M	M	M	M		M^T	M	M	M	M	M	M	M
	Physiology and Hygiene	2	M	M	M	M	M	M	M	M	M		M^T	M	M	M	M	M	M	M
	Physical Education	3				M														
	Physical Examination	4						M												
	Personal Hygiene	5																		M
	Communicable Diseases	6																		
	Sanitation	7																		
	Accident Prevention	8																		
	Tobacco	9																		
	Placards	10																		
1913	Stimulants and Narcotics	1	M		M	M	M	M	M	M		M	M^T	M	M	M	M	M	M	M
	Physiology and Hygiene	2	M		M	M	M	M	M	M	M	M	M^T	M	M	M	M	M	M	M
	Physical Education	3				M														
	Physical Examination	4					M	M										M	M	
	Personal Hygiene	5												M						M
	Communicable Diseases	6												M						
	Sanitation	7												M						
	Accident Prevention	8																		
	Tobacco	9	M			M								M						
	Placards	10	M																	
1923	Stimulants and Narcotics	1	M			M	M	M		M	M	M	M	M	M	M	M	M	M	M
	Physiology and Hygiene	2			M	M	M	M		M	M	M	M	M	M	M	M	M	M	M
	Physical Education	3	M			M^T		M^T			M^T	M	M^T				M^T		M	M^T
	Physical Examination	4	M				M	M		M		M						M	M	
	Personal Hygiene	5	M					M^T						M					M	M
	Communicable Diseases	6												M						
	Sanitation	7	M											M					M	M
	Accident Prevention	8																		
	Tobacco	9	M			M								M						
	Placards	10															M			

M=Mandatory. M^T=Mandatory with a time specification. (Minimum number of minutes or periods)

FOR THE PUBLIC ELEMENTARY SCHOOLS IN EACH OF THE FORTY-EIGHT STATES
1923

	Massachusetts	Michigan	Minnesota	Mississippi	Missouri	Montana	Nebraska	Nevada	New Hampshire	New Jersey	New Mexico	New York	North Carolina	North Dakota	Ohio	Oklahoma	Oregon	Pennsylvania	Rhode Island	South Carolina	South Dakota	Tennessee	Texas	Utah	Vermont	Virginia	Washington	West Virginia	Wisconsin	Wyoming	
1	M	M	M	M	M	M	M	M	M	M	M	M	M	M^T	M	M	M	M	M	M	M	M	M	M	M	M	M	M	M	M	**47**
2	M	M	M	M	M	M	M	M	M		M	M	M	M^T	M	M	M	M	M	M	M	M	M	M	M	M	M	M	M	M	**46**
3														M^T	M		M^T	M													**5**
4																															**1**
5																															**1**
6		M																													**1**
7																															**–**
8																															**–**
9																						M									**1**
10																															**–**
																															102
1	M	M	M	M	M	M	M	M	M	M	M	M	M	M^T	M		M	M	M	M	M	M	M	M	M	M	M	M	M	M	**45**
2	M	M	M	M	M	M	M	M	M		M	M	M	M^T	M		M	M	M	M	M	M	M	M	M	M	M	M	M	M	**45**
3		M												M^T	M		M^T	M											M		**7**
4	M									M		M						M	M					M	M	M		M			**13**
5																															**2**
6	M	M			M	M								M^T				M						M							**8**
7																								M							**2**
8										M^T					M^T														M^T		**3**
9																						M									**4**
10				M																											**2**
																															131
1	M	M	M	M	M	M	M	M	M	M		M	M	M	M	M	M	M	M	M	M	M	M	M	M	M	M		M	M	**43**
2	**M**	**M**	M	M	M	M	M	M	M		M	M	M	M	M	M	M	M	M	M	M	M	M	M	M	M	M		M	M	**43**
3	M	**M**	M		M					M^T	M	M^T		M^T	M^T		M^T	M	M^T			M				M	M^T		M^T		**25**
4	M					M	M			M		M	M		M			M	M	M				M	M	M				M	**21**
5			M		M					**M**	M							M								**M**			**M**		**12**
6	M	M			M	M								M				M						**M**					**M**		**9**
7				M																				**M**					**M**		**7**
8										M^T					M^T			M								M^T			M^T		**5**
9																						M									**4**
10				M																											**2**
																															171

1913, and forty-three states in 1923. From the various enactments one might infer that "stimulants and narcotics" is regarded as our most important branch of learning; not only is it more widely prescribed but it has received more extensive and more specific legislation than any other. It is our nearest approach to a national subject of instruction; it might be called our one minimum essential. In practically every state in the Union some sort of law was in force in 1903. Although the earlier history of these laws was not traced, it appears that most of them had their origin during the middle 80's. They had already undergone many changes in several of the states prior to 1903 and there have been more changes since. In some states the law has been abridged, in others it has been elaborated and reinforced; in some it has undergone both of these changes in succession; there is almost no end to the variety of the provisions; no two laws will be found exactly alike, although there are many similar provisions and much identical phraseology. In a few states the law is still essentially the same as when originally passed. It would be tedious, and for our present purpose profitless, to reproduce here all the various laws now in force; this is even more true of those which have been in force at intervals during the period of this study. Regardless of the particular language used, they are of similar import. The law whose provision is stated in a single line and the law which is spread over three printed pages alike require that the subject shall be taught. No typical law can be given, and no significant trend is discernible in the changes which have taken place aside from the slight decrease in the number of prescriptions. In 1903 Oklahoma, New Mexico, and Arizona were still territories and were required by a national law to teach stimulants and narcotics. Idaho was then the only state where it was not specifically prescribed. We find there that

> physiology and hygiene with particular reference to the effect of alcoholic drinks, stimulants and narcotics upon the human system [1]

was included among the subjects upon which an applicant to teach in Idaho, in all grades above the fourth, was required to pass a satisfactory examination before being granted a certificate. Moreover, Idaho as a territory had been required to teach this subject. In 1913 Arizona, Georgia, and Oklahoma did not pre-

[1] Political Code 1901, p. 311, Sec. 1028.

scribe "stimulants and narcotics" and in 1923 it was not required in Arizona, Arkansas, Delaware, New Mexico, and West Virginia. Physiology and Hygiene was not required in Idaho and New Jersey in 1903; in Arizona, New Jersey, and Oklahoma in 1913; or in Alabama, Arizona, Delaware, New Jersey, and West Virginia in 1923.

The law which was in force in the territories of Arizona, New Mexico, and Oklahoma regarding these subjects in 1903 was enacted in 1886; and since it illustrates also the kind of provisions that were to be found in several of the states its substance is here given.

> *Section 1.* The nature of alcoholic drinks and narcotics, and special instruction as to their effects upon the human system, in connection with the several divisions of the subject of physiology and hygiene, shall be included in the branches of study taught in the common or public schools, and in the Military and Naval Schools, and shall be studied and taught as thoroughly and in the same manner as other like required branches are in said schools, by the use of textbooks in the hands of pupils where other branches are thus studied in said schools, and by all pupils in all said schools throughout the territories, in the Military and Naval Academies of the United States, and in the District of Columbia, and in all Indian and colored schools in the Territories of the United States.
>
> *Section 2.* It shall be the duty of the proper officers in control of any school described in the foregoing section to enforce the provisions of this act; and any such officer, school director, committee, superintendent, or teacher who shall refuse or neglect to comply with the requirements of this act, or shall neglect or fail to make proper provision for the instruction required and in the manner by the first section of this act, for all pupils in each and every school under his jurisdiction, shall be removed from office, and the vacancy filled as in other cases.
>
> *Section 3.* No certificate shall be granted to any person to teach in the public schools of the District of Columbia or territories, after the first day of January, anno domini eighteen hundred and eighty-eight, who has not passed a satisfactory examination in physiology and hygiene, with special reference to the nature and the effects of alcoholic drinks and other narcotics upon the human system.[2]

[2] Statutes At Large of the United States, Volume XXIV, p. 69, Ch. 362 (Forty-ninth Congress, 1885–1887, Session I).

Alabama will serve to illustrate the sort of transformation which legislation regarding this subject has undergone. An act approved February 10, 1885, required

> that provision be made by the Superintendent of Education for instructing all pupils in all schools and colleges supported in whole or in part by public money, or under state control, in hygiene and physiology with special reference to the effects of alcoholic drinks, stimulants and narcotics upon the human system.

This act also provides that no certificate of first or second grade shall be granted to one who has not passed a satisfactory examination on the subject. Another act, approved February 4, 1891, directed

> that in addition to the branches in which instruction is now given in the public schools instruction shall also be given as to the nature of alcoholic drinks and narcotics, and special instruction as to their effects upon the human system, in connection with the several divisions of relative physiology and hygiene, and such subjects shall be taught as regularly as other branches are taught in said schools. Such instruction shall be given orally from a text-book in the hands of a teacher to the pupils who are not able to read; and shall be given by the use of text-books in the hands of the pupils in case of those who are able to read, and such instruction shall be given as aforesaid to all pupils in all public schools in the state to all the grades until completed in the high school. No certificate shall be granted hereafter to any new applicant to teach in the public schools of Alabama who has not passed a satisfactory examination in the study of the nature of alcoholic drinks and narcotics, and of their effects upon the human system, in connection with the several divisions of the subject of physiology and hygiene.

The phraseology of the two acts just quoted was condensed in the codes of 1896 and 1907 and in the school code of 1919 became

> County and city boards of education shall require that regular instruction be given in all schools under their direction as to the nature of alcoholic drinks, tobacco and other narcotics, and their effect upon the human system.

This law was approved September 26, 1919. Four days later, September 30, 1919, the following law was approved.

> *Section 1.* The county and city boards of education, and the county superintendent and superintendents of city schools,

and all boards of directors and presidents of all schools and colleges, supported in whole or in part by public money, or under state control, shall, respectively, require and provide that regular instruction shall be given in all grades of all said schools and colleges under their supervision, direction or control as to the nature of alcoholic drinks, tobacco and other narcotics, and their effect upon the human system; and they shall, from time to time, as they may be called upon by the governor or State superintendent of education, report to the governor or State superintendent, respectively, what they have done to comply with the duty hereby imposed upon them; to the end that such subjects shall be taught in the schools and colleges of the State as regularly as any other subjects of instruction.

Section 2. The board of directors and president of every normal school or college in this State shall require and provide that all students therein shall have regular instruction in the subjects mentioned in the preceding section; to the end that such students, when authorized to teach in the schools of the State, shall be qualified to give the like instruction therein. The president of said schools shall report to the governor at the end of each scholastic year to what extent such instruction has been provided for in the said schools and colleges during the preceding scholastic year.

Section 3. In the examination of applicants for certificates of the 1st, 2nd and 3rd grades, or of applicants for the life certificates, whether such examination be held by the State board of examiners or whether the examination be held in the county, in the cases provided for by law, such applicants shall be examined upon the subjects or branches referred to in Section 1 of this act, and the subjects referred to in Section 1 of this act shall be embraced in the branches of learning, upon which the said applicants are required to be examined in writing, and such examination shall include questions on those subjects as on others.

Section 4. The board of directors of the State normal schools shall arrange with the president of the Woman's Christian Temperance Union to have a trained scientific temperance institute worker to visit each normal school of the State at least once a year, and to be allowed one hour per day on not less than three days to lecture before the student body upon the subjects mentioned in Section 1 of this act; and that the reasonable expense of the services of such institute worker shall be agreed upon by the presidents of the school with the worker, and the expenses of the services of such institute worker while she is in attendance upon the

> school for the purposes aforesaid, shall be paid out of the treasury of the State upon a warrant issued by the auditor to the president of the school, upon a statement of the account presented under affidavit by the president, and approved by the governor; and the proceeds of such warrant shall be used either to pay the said worker for services and entertainment, or to reimburse the president of the school, if he has paid the worker for such services and entertainment.
>
> *Section 5.* The program for the exercises of temperance day to be observed in the public schools of the State one day in each scholastic term, as provided by law, may be prepared and furnished to the State superintendent of education by the Alabama Woman's Christian Temperance Union, or by a committee of said Union, named for that purpose, and the programme may be so prepared, either in collaboration with the State superintendent of education, or under the supervision of such superintendent, and it shall be the duty of the State superintendent of education to have the said programme printed and to have the same sent out to the schools or heads thereof from his office at the expense of the State, and the expense of printing and distributing said programme shall be paid upon a warrant issued by the auditor, upon an account under oath, made out by the State superintendent of education and approved by the governor; and the said warrant shall be issued to the State superintendent and the proceeds thereof used by him to pay the expenses of such printing and distribution, or to reimburse him therefor, if he has already advanced such payment.

Section 6 provides that in his annual report to the governor the State superintendent of education shall set forth the extent to which the instruction in this particular field has been given in the public schools and colleges of the State. The following law was enacted in 1909:

> It shall be the duty of the State superintendent of education of the State of Alabama to have prepared and furnished to the teachers in the public schools placards printed in large type upon which shall be set forth in attractive style statistics, epigrams and mottoes showing the evils of intemperance especially from the use of intoxicating liquors.
>
> It shall be the duty of the said State superintendent of education to make changes in the matter printed on the said placards from time to time as he may deem proper and that he shall at all times keep the public schools of Alabama provided with a sufficient number of said placards to post one of them in every schoolroom of Alabama.

> The expenses of printing and expressing the said placards shall be paid out of the State treasury on an account made out by the said State superintendent of education and approved by the governor and the auditor shall draw his warrant for the same.
> It shall be the duty of every public school teacher in the State to keep one of the said placards posted in a conspicuous place in the schoolroom occupied by such teacher.
> It shall be the duty of the county superintendent of education and the district trustees to assist in the carrying out of the provisions of this act.
> There shall be one day in each scholastic term of the public schools set apart to be known as Temperance Day when a suitable program shall be prepared to the end that the children of Alabama may be taught the evils of intemperance.

The foregoing law was in force in 1913. No evidence was found to show either that it was in force in 1923 or that it had been repealed unless it was repealed by implication when the school code was adopted in 1919.

To illustrate further the situation in 1923 selected provisions from several states will be given and the laws of Florida and New York will be quoted in full. The local school board in Iowa

> shall require all teachers to give and all scholars to receive instruction in physiology and hygiene which study in every division of the subject shall include the effects upon the human system of alcoholic stimulants, narcotics and poisonous substances. The instruction in this branch shall of its kind be as direct and specific as that given in other essential branches and each scholar shall be required to complete the part of such study in his class or grade before being advanced to the next higher and before being credited with having completed the study of the subject.

In Ohio,

> the same tests for promotion shall be required in this as in other branches.

In South Dakota,

> such subjects shall be taught as thoroughly as arithmetic and geography are taught.

In Maryland these subjects

> shall be taught to and studied by all pupils whose capacity will admit it in all departments of the public schools of the state.

In Idaho this study is to be taught

> during such portion of each school term as may be necessary to enable all pupils to pass prescribed examinations in the textbooks on said study

and the boards of trustees are to provide

> the best authoritative textbooks that can be obtained on said study.

New Jersey directs,

> In the text-books on physiology and hygiene the space devoted to the consideration of the nature of alcoholic drinks and narcotics and their effects upon the human system shall be sufficient for a full and adequate treatment of the subject.

In Michigan,

> The textbooks to be used for such instruction shall give at least one-fourth of their space to the consideration of the nature and effects of alcoholic drinks and narcotics and the books used in the highest grade of graded schools shall contain at least twenty pages of matter relating to this subject.

Oklahoma provides that

> this subject shall be taught as a part of physiology and hygiene and that no additional text be employed.

In South Carolina these branches

> shall be studied and taught as thoroughly and in the same manner as other like required branches are in said schools, by the use of textbooks in the hands of pupils where other branches are thus studied in said schools, and orally in case of pupils unable to read, and shall be taught by all teachers and studied by all pupils in all said schools supported wholly or in part by public money.

In Missouri the instruction shall be given

> In all schools supported wholly or in part by public money or under state control.

California requires instruction in

> physiology and hygiene with special reference to the injurious effects of tobacco, alcohol and narcotics on the human system;

and also requires instruction in

> the nature of alcohol and narcotics and their effects upon the human system as determined by science.

In New Hampshire the state board, through the commissioner of education, shall

> investigate the condition and efficiency of public education with special reference to the instruction given in physiology in relation to the effects of alcohol and narcotics on the human system.

Numerous devices are resorted to in order to give force to the laws which require these subjects to be taught. Provisions are common regarding one or more of the following: the use of an approved textbook by the pupils; the teacher to pass an examination; the normal school to give special training; definite reports that all provisions of this particular law have been complied with; fines and forfeitures for neglect or failure.

The law in Florida is,

> *Section 1.* The evils of alcoholic beverages and narcotics shall be taught in the public schools of the State, and the State Superintendent of Public Instruction is hereby authorized and directed to encourage and put in execution an effective system for teaching the evils of alcoholic stimulants and narcotics in the public schools of the State to all children between the ages of six and twelve years.
>
> *Section 2.* It is hereby made the duty of the county superintendent and the county board of public instruction of each and every county to receive, promulgate and to require all instructions and directions of the State Superintendent of Public Instruction for the teaching of the effects of alcoholic beverages and narcotics to all youth between the ages of six and twelve years to be faithfully and efficiently executed, and to require such reports from teachers showing that such subjects are being faithfully taught by means of pictures and oral instructions to pupils not sufficiently advanced to use a text-book on the subject; and to see that properly graded text-books treating of the effects of alcoholic beverages and narcotics are provided all pupils under the age of twelve years that are prepared to use such text-books, and that the same are faithfully and efficiently taught.
>
> *Section 3.* It shall be the duty of the principal of every school to make report as may be required to the county board of public instruction, showing that the instruction

required in Section 1 is being efficiently given by competent teachers, and that the spirit of this law is being faithfully carried out.

Section 4. Any county board of public instruction may be enjoined from employing any teacher who does not make a faithful attempt to teach the subject directed in Section 1, and to make such report as may be required.

Section 5. It shall be the duty of every county superintendent to make, at least annually, and oftener when required, to the State Superintendent of Public Instruction, on blanks furnished, a full and complete report of the method of instruction, the time devoted to the teaching of the subject embraced in Section 1, and of such other matters as may be required in the several schools under his supervision. Refusal or neglect to make such reports shall subject any county superintendent to be reported to the Governor as negligent in the discharge of his duties.

Section 6. The annual appropriation for the contingent expenses of the office of State Superintendent of Public Instruction shall be sufficient to cover all necessary expenses in the proper execution of this law; and he shall make report of this matter in his biennial report to the Governor.

The law in New York reads as follows:

Section 690. (1) The nature of alcoholic drinks and other narcotics and their effects on the human system shall be taught in connection with the various divisions of physiology and hygiene, as thoroughly as are other branches in all schools under state control, or supported wholly or in part by public money of the State, and also in all schools connected with reformatory institutions.

(2) All pupils in the above-mentioned schools below the second year of the high school and above the third year of school work computing from the beginning of the lowest primary, not kindergarten, year, or in corresponding classes of ungraded schools, shall be taught and shall study this subject every year with suitable textbooks in the hands of all pupils, for not less than three lessons a week for ten or more weeks, or the equivalent of the same in each year, and must pass satisfactory tests in this as in other studies before promotion to the next succeeding year's work; except that, where there are nine or more school years below the high school, the study may be omitted in all years above the eighth year and below the high school, by such pupils as have passed the required tests of the eighth year.

(3) In all schools above-mentioned, all pupils in the lowest three primary, not kindergarten, school years or in corresponding classes in ungraded schools shall each year be instructed in this subject orally for not less than two lessons a week for ten weeks, or the equivalent of the same in each year, by teachers using textbooks adapted for such oral instruction as a guide and standard, and such pupils must pass such tests in this as may be required in other studies before promotion to the next succeeding year's work. Nothing in this article shall be construed as prohibiting or requiring the teaching of this subject in kindergarten schools.

(4) The local school authorities shall provide needed facilities and definite time and place for this branch in the regular courses of study.

(5) The textbooks in the pupils' hands shall be graded to the capacities of fourth year, intermediate, grammar and high school pupils, or to corresponding classes in ungraded schools. For students below high school grade, such textbooks shall give at least one-fifth their space, and for students of high school grade, shall give not less than twenty pages to the nature and effects of alcoholic drinks and other narcotics. This subject must be treated in the textbooks in connection with the various divisions of physiology and hygiene, and pages on this subject in a separate chapter at the end of the books shall not be counted in determining the minimum. No textbook on physiology not conforming to this article shall be used in the public schools.

(6) All Regents' examinations in physiology and hygiene shall include a due proportion of questions on the nature of alcoholic drinks and other narcotics and their effects on the human system.

Section 691. (1) In all normal schools, teachers' training classes and teachers' institutes, adequate time and attention shall be given to instruction in the best methods of teaching this branch, and no teacher shall be licensed who has not passed a satisfactory examination in the subject and the best methods of teaching it. On satisfactory evidence that any teacher has wilfully refused to teach this subject, as provided in this article, the Commissioner of Education shall revoke the license of such teacher.

(2) No public money of the State shall be apportioned by the Commissioner of Education or paid for the benefit of any city until the superintendent of schools therein shall have filed with the treasurer or chamberlain of such city an affidavit, and with the Commissioner of Education a dupli-

cate of such affidavit, that he has made thorough investigation as to the facts, and that to the best of his knowledge, information and belief, all the provisions of this article have been complied with in all the schools under his supervision in such city during the last preceding legal school year.

(3) Nor shall any public money of the State be apportioned by the Commissioner of Education or by school commissioners, or paid for the benefit of any school district, until the president of the board of trustees, or in the case of common school districts the trustee or some one member of the board of trustees, shall have filed with the school commissioner having jurisdiction an affidavit that he has made thorough investigation as to the facts and that to the best of his knowledge, information and belief, all the provisions of this article have been complied with in such district, which affidavit shall be included in the trustees' annual report.

(4) It shall be the duty of every school commissioner to file with the Commissioner of Education an affidavit in connection with his annual report, showing all districts in his jurisdiction that have and those that have not complied with all the provisions of this article, according to the best of his knowledge, information and belief, based upon a thorough investigation by him as to the facts.

(5) Nor shall any public money of the State be apportioned or paid for the benefit of any teachers' training class, teachers institute or other school mentioned herein until the officer having jurisdiction or supervision thereof shall have filed with the Commissioner of Education an affidavit that he has made thorough investigation as to the facts and that to the best of his knowledge, information and belief, all the provisions of this article relative thereto have been complied with.

(6) The principal of each normal school in the State shall at the close of each school year file with the Commissioner of Education an affidavit that all the provisions of this article applicable thereto have been complied with during the school year just terminated and until such affidavit shall be filed no warrant shall be issued by the Commissioner of Education for the payment by the treasurer of any part of the money appropriated for such school.

(7) It shall be the duty of the Commissioner of Education to provide blank forms of affidavit required herein· for use by the local school officers, and he shall include in his annual report a statement showing every school, city or district which has failed to comply with all the provisions of this article during the preceding school year.

(8) On complaint by appeal to the Commissioner of Education by any patron of the schools mentioned in the last preceding section or by any citizen that any provision of this article has not been complied with in any city or district, the Commissioner of Education shall make immediate investigation, and on satisfactory evidence of the truth of such complaint shall thereupon and thereafter, withhold all public money of the State to which such city or district would otherwise be entitled, until all the provisions of this article shall be complied with in said city or district, and shall exercise his power of reclamation and deduction under section 491 of this chapter.

TEMPERANCE DAY

A day of special observance has developed within the last decade which in five states is known as Temperance Day (Georgia, Kentucky, Maine, North Dakota, and Ohio); in five states as Frances Willard Day (Kansas, Missouri, Nevada, South Carolina, and South Dakota); in two as Frances E. Willard Day (Oregon and Tennessee); in Florida as Temperance and Health Day; in Washington as Temperance and Good Citizenship Day; and in North Carolina as Temperance or Law and Order Day. Of these fifteen laws, two were enacted in 1915, four in 1917, two in 1918, one in 1919, two in 1921, one in 1922, and three in 1923. The law in Kansas was approved March 8, 1915; that in Tennessee, May 17, 1915. The day set apart varies in the different states; it comes in January in four, in March in two, in September in four, and in October in five. January 16 is named in one state, September 28 in four. In the other ten states Friday is named; for example, in four states it is the fourth Friday of October. In nine states there is a time specification; "one-half of the school day" in Nevada; "one-quarter of the school day" in Kansas, Missouri, and South Dakota; "at least two hours" in Florida, Georgia, and Ohio; "not less than one hour" in North Dakota; "not less than forty-five minutes" in Maine. In Oregon,

> such portion of the afternoon of the fourth Friday in October of each year as may be deemed proper by the teacher in charge.

In eight of the states the duty is placed upon the state chief school executive to prepare a suitable program or suitable material; for example, in North Carolina

> The State Superintendent of Public Instruction shall have prepared and furnished in due time to every teacher of said public and high school for the State a suitable program to be used on said Temperance or Law and Order Day.

In Maine,

> It shall be the duty of the state superintendent of schools to prepare suitable material for the observance of Temperance Day.

Seven states have a clause similar to the following:

> It shall be the duty of all state, county, city and school-district officers, and of all public-school teachers in the state to carry out the provisions of this act.

The purpose of the required observance is variously expressed although several of the states follow a common pattern, at least in part.

In Kansas,

> for instruction and appropriate exercises relative to the history and benefits of the prohibitory amendment to the constitution and the prohibitory laws of the state of Kansas.

In Missouri,

> for instruction and appropriate exercises relative to the history and benefits of the prohibition of the manufacture and sale of intoxicating liquors in the United States.

In Nevada,

> for instruction and appropriate exercises relative to the history and benefits of prohibition of the manufacture of narcotics and sale of intoxicating liquors in the United States.

In North Dakota,

> for instruction and appropriate exercises relative to the history and benefits of prohibition and prohibitory laws of the State of North Dakota.

In Maine,

> for instruction and appropriate exercises relative to the history and benefits of prohibition and prohibitory laws.

In Oregon,

> for instruction and appropriate exercises in commemoration of the life, history and achievements of Frances E. Willard.

In South Dakota,

> for instruction and appropriate exercises in patriotism, civic improvement and the history and benefits of the prohibitory amendment to the constitution and the prohibitory laws of the state.

In Ohio,

> information relative to the history of the temperance movement and of the physiological value of temperance shall be given the pupils.

In Florida and Georgia,

> a program which shall be educational in nature, teaching the good of Temperance and prohibition, and the evils of intemperance and disobedience to law.

In South Carolina and Tennessee,

> to the end that the children of the State may be taught the evils of intemperance.

In Washington,

> The state superintendent of public instruction shall have prepared and published in due time in one or more educational journals or publications of general circulation among the teachers of the state, a suitable program to be used on "Temperance and Good Citizenship Day" presenting the advantages of temperance to the individual and to the nation, the biographies of great leaders in temperance and good citizenship, the effect of alcoholic and narcotic poisons and drugs upon the human system, and the necessity for, the duty of obedience to, and respect for the laws of our state and nation on the part of all citizens. The superintendent of public instruction may from year to year designate important laws for special observance.

PHYSICAL EDUCATION

Some sort of legislative requirement falling within the field of Physical Education was found in five states in 1903, in seven states in 1913, and in twenty-five states in 1923. The remarkable increase shown within the last few years is undoubtedly due in large measure to the special interest aroused during the period of the World War. The following law, in force in North Dakota in 1903, was also in force there in 1913 and 1923.

> Physical education, which shall aim to develop and discipline the body and promote health through systematic exercise, shall be included in the branches of study required by law to be taught in the common schools, and shall be introduced and taught as a regular branch to all pupils in all departments of the public schools of the state and in all educational institutions supported wholly or in part by money from the state. It shall be the duty of all boards of education and boards of educational institutions receiving money from the state, to make provision for daily instruction in all the schools and institutions under their respective jurisdiction, and to adopt such method or methods as will adapt progressive physical exercise to the development, health and discipline of the pupils in the various grades and classes of schools and institutions receiving aid from the state.

California in 1903 provided that

> Attention must be given to such physical exercises for the pupils as may be conducive to health and vigor of body, as well as mind, and to the ventilation and temperature of schoolrooms.

Oregon had this provision in force in 1903, 1913, and 1923;

> In all schools two exercises in free gymnastics and suitable voice and breathing exercises shall be given daily.

In addition to the provisions just given, Oregon in 1923 and California in 1913 and 1923 had other laws also operative.
Ohio in 1903 provided that

> physical culture which shall include calisthenics shall be included in the branches to be taught in the common schools in cities of the first and second class and in all educational institutions supported wholly or in part by money received from the state.

Pennsylvania in 1903 provided for

> physical culture by a regular and progressive course of calisthenics.

to be given daily in cities of the first and second class. In 1913 California required

> physical culture including the necessary elements of physiology and hygiene with special reference to the injurious effects of tobacco, alcohol and narcotics on the human system.

Michigan required that

> physical training shall be included in the branches to be regularly taught in public schools in city school districts having a population of more than 10,000 and in the state normal schools.

Ohio in 1913 required that

> physical training shall be included in the branches regularly to be taught in public schools in city school districts and in all educational institutions supported wholly or in part by money received from the state.

Pennsylvania in 1913 required physical training in cities of the first class. Wisconsin in 1903 had physical education in school districts embracing in whole or in part an incorporated city.

The provisions in 1923 are, on the whole, more comprehensive in scope than those which we have just presented for 1903 and 1913. California, by a law enacted in 1917, prescribes "suitable courses of physical education" for all pupils enrolled in the day elementary schools.

> The aims and purposes of the course of physical education established under the provisions of this act shall be as follows: (1) To develop organic vigor, provide neuro-muscular training, promote bodily and mental poise, correct postural defects, secure the more advanced forms of co-ordination, strength and endurance, and to promote such desirable moral and social qualities as appreciation of the value of co-operation, self-subordination and obedience to authority, and higher ideals, courage and wholesome interest in truly recreational activities; (2) to promote a hygienic school and home life, secure scientific supervision of the sanitation of school buildings, playgrounds and athletic fields, and the equipment thereof.

In Maryland,

> there shall be established and provided in all the public schools of this state, and in all schools maintained or aided by this state, physical education and training for pupils of both sexes.

A minimum amount of directed play is also provided.

In Connecticut a course in

> health instruction and physical education . . . shall be adapted to the ages, capabilities and state of health of the pupils in the several grades and departments and shall include exercises, calisthenics, formation drills, instruction in personal and community health and safety and in preventing and correcting bodily deficiency.

In New Jersey,

> A Course in Physical Training . . . shall be adapted to the ages and capabilities of the pupils in the several grades and departments, and shall include exercises, calisthenics, formation drills, instruction in personal and community health and safety and in correcting and preventing bodily deficiency, and such other features and details as may aid in carrying out these purposes, together with instruction as to the privileges and responsibilities of citizenship, as they relate to community and national welfare, with special reference to developing bodily strength and vigor, and producing the highest type of patriotic citizenship; and in addition, for female pupils, instruction in domestic hygiene, first aid and nursing. To further promote the aims of this course any additional requirements or regulations as to medical inspection of school children may be imposed.

Georgia and Kentucky adopted in 1920 laws which are essentially identical. In each case the

> State Board of Education shall prescribe a course of study in physical education for all common schools of the state and shall fix the time when said course shall go into effect. This course shall occupy not less than 30 minutes each school day which shall be devoted to instruction in health and safety, to physical exercises, and to recess play under proper supervision.

Missouri had

> To promote the physical development of boys and girls in our public schools, and the correction of their physical defects and impairments, to secure proper health habits and to secure scientific sanitation in the schools, the state superintendent of public schools is hereby authorized and directed to adopt and promulgate such rules and regulations as he may deem necessary to secure courses in physical education to all pupils and students in all public schools

> and in all educational institutions supported in whole or in part by the state.

Oregon in 1919 enacted a law which required,

> All male and female pupils in all elementary and secondary schools shall receive as part of the prescribed course of instruction therein such physical training as determined by the state superintendent of public instruction during periods which shall average at least twenty minutes in each school day, exclusive of recess periods . . . This course of instruction shall consist of such activities as will promote correct physical posture and bearing, mental and physical alertness, self-control, disciplined initiative, sense of patriotic duty and spirit of co-operation under leadership.

In Minnesota,

> There shall be established and provided in the public schools of this state physical and health education, training and instruction of pupils of both sexes and every pupil attending any such school, in so far as he or she is physically fit, and able to do so, shall take the course or courses therein as provided.

In Alabama,

> every public school and private or parochial school shall carry out a system of physical education the character of which shall conform to the program or course outlined by the State Department of Education.

Ohio had

> such physical education as may be prescribed or approved by the Director of Education;

Tennessee,

> such physical education as may be prescribed by the State Board of Education.

Washington had

> such courses in physical education as shall be prescribed by the State Board of Education;

Maine,

> physical education including recreational exercises;

Wisconsin,

> instruction in the theory and practice of the art of physical exercise and instruction in hygiene;

Virginia,

> such examination, health instruction and physical training as shall be prescribed by the State Board of Education and approved by the State Board of Health.

Illinois provided for

> physical education and training;

New York, for

> such physical training, under the direction of the Commissioner of Education, as the Regents may determine, for all male and female pupils above the age of eight years.

Michigan prescribed a course in physical training for pupils of both sexes.

Rhode Island prescribed

> instruction and practice in physical training under such regulations as the State board of education may prescribe or approve;

Pennsylvania,

> health, including physical training and physiology.

New Mexico includes "physical exercise" among the prescribed branches of the course of study. In Idaho the state board of education and the board of regents of the University of Idaho

> shall provide for an efficient system of health supervision, medical inspection, and physical development work in all public schools.

Massachusetts includes

> indoor and outdoor games and athletic exercise

among the branches in which instruction and training are to be given.

In 1923 thirteen states had specific time requirements ranging from one hour per week to two and one-half hours per week. In Illinois,

> not less than one hour of each week during the whole of the school year

shall be devoted to physical education and training. California, New York, Oregon, Rhode Island, and Washington require

> periods which shall average at least twenty minutes in each school day.

In Ohio, the physical education provided shall occupy

> not less than 100 minutes per school week.

In Georgia and Kentucky the course shall occupy

> periods totaling not less than thirty minutes each school day.

The time devoted to such courses in Connecticut, New Jersey and Wisconsin shall aggregate

> at least two and one-half hours in each school week.

In Connecticut,

> four-fifths of such time shall be given to physical education and one-fifth to the teaching of health.

Maryland provided in the elementary public schools a minimum period of

> at least fifteen minutes each school day and also at least one hour of directed play outside of regular classroom work in each school week.

North Dakota has the less definite provision for "daily" instruction.

Tennessee directs that the

> program of physical education provided by the State Board of Education shall occupy periods totalling as many minutes each day and as many hours each week throughout each and every school term as may be determined upon by said Board of Education.

In seven states a state director or supervisor of physical education is required: California, Maryland, Michigan, Minnesota, Missouri, Virginia, Wisconsin. In Virginia the supervisor is appointed by the state board of education with the approval of the state board of health. In Michigan and Minnesota the salary of the state director is limited to $3000.

In New Jersey and Tennessee,

> the conduct and attainment of the pupils shall be marked as in other courses or subjects and shall form part of the requirements for promotion or graduation.

In Connecticut,

> such course shall be a part of the curriculum prescribed for the several grades. The standing of the pupil in connec-

> tion therewith shall form a part of the requirements for promotion or graduation.

In Ohio credits and penalties are to be applied for success or failure in physical education courses as in other school subjects.

In the following fourteen states special work in physical education is required to be given in all state teacher-training institutions:

California	Michigan	Tennessee
Connecticut	Minnesota	Virginia
Georgia	Missouri	Washington
Illinois	New Jersey	Wisconsin
Kentucky	Ohio	

Minnesota had

> suitable modified courses shall be provided for students physically or mentally unable or unfit to take the course or courses prescribed for normal pupils.

Similar modified courses are required in Ohio and Tennessee.

In Ohio,

> It is provided that this act shall not be construed to require any school child to receive a medical examination or receive medical treatment whose parent or guardian objects thereto.

In Minnesota it is

> provided that nothing in this act shall be held or construed to require any pupil to undergo a physical or medical examination or treatment if the parent or legal guardian of the person of such pupil shall in writing notify the teacher or principal or other person in charge of such pupil that he objects to such physical or medical examination or treatment.

In Michigan it is

> provided that nothing in this act shall be construed or operated to authorize compulsory physical examination or compulsory medical treatment of school children nor to allow the teaching of sex hygiene and kindred subjects in the public schools of this state.

In Washington it is provided

> that individual pupils or students may be excused on account of physical disability or religious belief.

In Ohio,

> At the close of each school month a report of the amount of time devoted to physical education shall be included in the report of every school.

Tennessee has this concluding provision:

> Nothing in this act shall require the said school officials to make any expenditures for said physical training in the elementary or secondary schools.

Mississippi in 1920 enacted a law making instruction in physical education mandatory and extending to the state board of education authority to prescribe a fairly comprehensive program of health education; the law, however, to become effective

> only upon condition that the federal government provide funds dollar for dollar with the state of Mississippi for carrying out the provisions.[3]

PHYSICAL EXAMINATION

One state in 1903 made provision for the physical examination of pupils in the public schools, thirteen states in 1913, and twenty-one in 1923. The provision in most cases was not comprehensive. Sometimes it applied only to the larger cities; sometimes it required an examination only every second or third year; frequently the examination was limited to tests of sight and hearing but several states included an examination for physical defects; usually the examination was to be made annually. Probably the requirements would not, in a single state, meet standards which would be regarded as adequate by experts in school health work. Nevertheless, the showing is remarkable. An increase of twenty states was exceeded in only three items: "flag display," "days of special observance," and "fire drill." Quite obviously there has been a wide-spread interest in this field due, doubtless, to a growing realization that a child's mental need cannot be met while his physical need is ignored. There are a number of provisions which are common to several states and there is evidence that the law-makers have, to some extent, copied from one another or from a common pattern; and yet the

[3] Laws of 1920, p. 225, Ch. 161.

law in each state is unique. We need not consider all the details of the variations but a few may prove of interest.

West Virginia in 1913 required each independent school district to appoint medical inspectors to test each child separately and carefully once during each school year

> to ascertain if the pupil is suffering from any defect or disability that would prevent the pupil receiving the full benefit of the school work or if some modification of the school work should be made that the pupil might receive the best educational results.

A similar provision was in force in 1913 and 1923 in Connecticut, Maine, Massachusetts, and New York. A few states included diseases of nose and throat; for example, Wyoming and South Carolina; a few "diseased teeth" and breathing "through the mouth," as Utah and Nebraska. Vermont required a test of the sight and hearing of every pupil "seven years of age and older" to be made in "September of every even year." North Carolina required that every child should be examined "at least once in three years." South Carolina required annually a "medical and dental inspection" of all pupils attending the public schools

> during the first three months of attendance, to ascertain the presence of any contagious or infectious disease or any disease or defect of the eye, nose, mouth, throat, lungs or skin, detrimental to the welfare of any child,

and provided that "not over ten cents per child" should be used for the purpose. Massachusetts, New Jersey, and New York require that competent physicians be employed as medical inspectors. Several states specify that suitable

> test cards, blanks, record books and other useful appliances

are to be furnished each school district. Idaho requires

> an efficient system of health supervision, medical inspection and physical development work in all public schools.

Montana directs every school board to

> employ a physician to make an examination into the sanitary conditions of the school and the general health conditions of each pupil.

Florida provides that

> all school children shall be examined as to their physical condition at least once during each school year.

In Ohio,

> Boards of education shall, in the institution and conduct of physical education, take due knowledge of the health supervision of school children maintained by boards of health or by boards of education and shall provide for the proper co-ordination of such work with the work in physical education. Where the board of education has not employed a school physician, the board of health shall conduct the health examination of all school children in the health district.

In North Dakota,

> Upon being petitioned in writing by a majority of the school directors of the County the Board of County Commissioners shall employ one or more licensed physicians or graduate nurses, duly registered and licensed to practice nursing under the laws of this state, whose duty it shall be to visit the schools in the county and to inspect and examine the pupils attending said schools.[4]

The law in Alabama is given in full.

> *Section 1.* The State Department of Education and the State Board of Health shall in conjunction arrange for the examination of each and every child attending the public schools of this State, both male and female, for any physical defects of any kind embracing mental deficiency, diseases of the ear, eye, nose and throat, mouth and teeth, and any deformity or dislocation of the hip-joints or spinal disease, phymosis, hook-worm disease, and any other disease requiring medical or surgical aid in developing the child into a strong and healthy individual. The several county boards of education and county boards of health shall co-operate fully with the State Board of Education and State Board of Health in the promotion of this work. The County Superintendent of Education shall arrange with the county health officer a schedule of dates for this examination of the children in the public schools under his supervision and the city superintendent of schools shall make like schedule for the schools under his supervision.
>
> *Section 2.* Each and every child shall be examined before October 1st in each and every year by the county health

[4] Laws of 1919, p. 391, Ch. 200.

> officer, and the State Superintendent of Education is hereby required to have blanks printed to be furnished by the county superintendent of education to the various school districts. The county health officer of each county shall make such physical examinations of the school children and he shall secure such assistance from the county board of health as is necessary. All examinations held under this Act shall be without charge to the child or its parents.
>
> *Section 3.* Every public school and private or parochial school shall carry out a system of physical education, the character of which shall conform to the program or course outlined by the State Department of Education.
>
> *Section 4.* Each child shall be furnished with a certificate of examination, which shall be recorded by the teacher in a record kept for that purpose, the certificate to be returned to the parent or guardian of the child.
>
> *Section 5.* The State Board of Health shall supply the county health officers with glass slides and tubes, if necessary, for the taking of specimens, for making blood tests and hook-worm tests.
>
> *Section 6.* The State Board of Health shall have all necessary tests made at the State Laboratory upon the request of the county health officer.
>
> *Section 7.* To the end that the objects and purposes of this Act may be fully carried into effect, and the health of the school children of Alabama may be materially improved, the co-operation of the county board of health in various counties of Alabama, in conjunction with the county health officers, is expected without charge to the parent or the child.

In Colorado and Wyoming the examination must be made by observation "without using drugs or instruments and without coming in contact with" the child. Ohio provides that the law

> shall not be construed to require any school child to receive a medical examination or receive medical treatment whose parent or guardian objects.

In North Carolina no pupil

> shall be compelled to submit to medical examination or treatment whose parent or guardian objects.

Nebraska provides that

> no child shall be compelled to submit to a physical examination by other than the teacher, over the written

> objection of his parent or guardian, delivered to the child's teacher, provided, however, that such objection shall not exempt the child from the quarantine laws of the state nor prohibit an examination for infectious or contagious diseases.

One can but wonder at the solicitude shown for the wishes of the parent regarding the body of his child; we find no such tender consideration regarding the child's mind except in connection with Bible reading and morals.

PERSONAL HYGIENE

No hard and fast line can be drawn between what is here called personal hygiene and the hygiene which is included with, and has been considered as a part of, physiology and hygiene. That something substantially different was in the minds of the lawmakers is indicated by the fact that, in the majority of cases, that which we are here considering is in addition to the hygiene which is joined with the provision for stimulants and narcotics. Personal hygiene was required in one state in 1903, in two in 1913, and in twelve in 1923. Maryland in 1903 and 1913 included "the laws of health" among the required branches. In 1923 the subjects to be taught in Maryland included "hygiene and sanitation."

In 1913 and also in 1923 Indiana had

> there shall be taught in each year in the fifth grade of every public school in Indiana the primary principles of hygiene and sanitary science.

Alabama in 1923 included "hygiene and sanitation" in its course of study and New Mexico included "the laws of health." Pennsylvania required the teaching of "health including physical training and physiology." Wisconsin, in connection with physiology and hygiene, required specifically that attention be given to health, sanitation and "the proper care of the body." The provision for personal hygiene in the five states, Virginia, New Jersey, Minnesota, Maine, and Connecticut is included in a law providing for physical education. In Virginia it is stipulated that all pupils in the public elementary schools shall receive such health instruction

> as shall be prescribed by the state board of education and approved by the state board of health.

In New Jersey,

> instruction in personal and community health and safety shall be given in connection with the course in physical training.

In Minnesota, provision shall be made in all the public schools of the state for

> health education, training and instruction of pupils of both sexes.

In Maine, instruction must be given

> to pupils in all public schools in personal hygiene, community sanitation and physical education.

In Connecticut, a course in health instruction and physical education shall include "instruction in personal and community health and safety." At least two and one-half hours are to be given to the course each week, and "one-fifth to the teaching of health." Missouri provides

> that a chapter or chapters on dental hygiene be required in all textbooks on physiology used in the public schools of the state of Missouri. That said chapter or chapters shall convey the proper knowledge to the pupil on the care, function, and relation of the teeth to the general health. The aforesaid chapter or chapters in said textbooks shall be edited or approved by a competent committee composed as follows: It shall consist of five members, three of whom shall be selected by the state dental society, one by the state board of health, and one by the state superintendent of schools, and they shall serve without compensation. For the purpose of carrying out the intent of this act, it shall be unlawful to sell in this state for use in the public schools, any textbook on physiology which does not contain the aforesaid chapter or chapters; and the offering for sale of any textbook on physiology in violation of the above sections shall be a misdemeanor.

The following five states have provisions which have not been tabulated under the head of Personal Hygiene. New York and Ohio include "hygiene" among the subjects in which children must be instructed, apart from the physiology and hygiene which is in another section. It may or it may not be intended as an additional requirement. Louisiana had "health" and North Carolina "health education" in connection with the provision for stimulants and narcotics. They have been there tabulated and are accordingly omitted here. Washington includes "laws of health" along with a number of other topics in a section which has been tabulated and will be presented in the discussion of Social and Ethical Outcomes.

COMMUNICABLE DISEASES

One state in 1903 required that instruction be given in the public schools regarding communicable diseases. Such instruction was required in eight states in 1913 and nine in 1923. The following law was in force in Montana in 1913 and also in 1923:

> There shall be taught in every year in every public school of elementary grade in Montana, the principal modes by which each of the dangerous communicable diseases spreads, and the method for the restriction and prevention of each such diseases as smallpox, diphtheria, scarlet fever, measles, tuberculosis, chickenpox and such other diseases as may be named, and attention called to the same by the board of health of this State. School boards shall annually send to the public school superintendents and teachers throughout the state printed data and statements which will enable them to comply with the provisions of this chapter. School boards are hereby required to direct superintendents and teachers to give oral and blackboard instructions, using the data and statements supplied by the state board of health. Neglect or refusal on the part of any superintendent or teacher to comply with the provisions of this chapter shall be considered a sufficient cause for dismissal from the school by the school board. Any member of any school board who shall wilfully neglect or refuse to comply with any provisions of this chapter shall be deemed guilty of a misdemeanor and shall be subject to punishment by a fine not exceeding one hundred dollars.

Michigan had a somewhat similar law which was originally passed in 1895 and amended in 1909 which required that

> such instruction shall be given by the aid of textbooks on physiology supplemented by oral and blackboard instruction;

no textbook on physiology to be adopted unless it gives "at least one-eighth of its space" to the causes and prevention of dangerous communicable diseases. This portion of the textbook must have the approval of the state board of health.

The Indiana law, in force in 1913 and 1923, followed a pattern similar to that of Montana and Michigan. It provided that there should be taught

> in each year in the fifth grade of every public school in Indiana the primary principles of hygiene and sanitary science

and the

> best sanitary methods for the restriction and prevention of each such disease.

The state health commissioner and the state superintendent of public instruction were directed to prepare and furnish printed leaflets to be used by the teachers. Another section of the Indiana law requires instruction to be given regarding "the cause and course of consumption." Missouri in 1913 and 1923 required special instruction to be given regarding "tuberculosis, its nature, causes and prevention." Massachusetts and Pennsylvania in 1913 and 1923 required special reference to "tuberculosis and its prevention." In each of the three last named states the provision is made along with the mandate regarding teaching physiology and hygiene. North Dakota, in connection with the teaching of physiology and hygiene, required instruction in the "nature, treatment and prevention of tuberculosis and other contagious and infectious diseases." The required instruction in hygiene must be given to all pupils above the third year for "not less than four lessons per week for ten weeks of each school year." Utah in 1913 and 1923 required a course of instruction beginning with the eighth grade in "sanitation and the cause and prevention of disease." Wisconsin in 1923 required

> physiology and hygiene with special reference to health, sanitation, the effects of stimulants and narcotics upon the human system, symptoms of disease including the taking of temperature and pulse, and the proper care of the body. Regular class instruction, in the foregoing, equivalent to at least five periods per week for one-half of a school year shall be given in either the sixth, seventh or eighth grade. If the school board or board of education of any district shall refuse or wilfully neglect to comply with the provisions

of this sub-section the district shall forfeit its right to share in the distribution of the common school fund derived from the tax provided for in section 20.25 of the statutes. Provided, that no pupil shall be required to take the instruction herein provided for, if his or her parent or general guardian shall file with the principal or teacher a written objection to the taking of the same.

SANITATION

Instruction in sanitation was required in the two states of Indiana and Utah in 1913 and in five additional states in 1923. The provisions for Utah and Wisconsin have just been quoted in connection with "communicable diseases," and the provision in Indiana has been given in part. Indiana also required instruction regarding

> the dissemination of disease by rats, flies and mosquitoes and the effects thereof and the prevention of disease by the proper selection and consumption of food.

Alabama and Maryland required instruction in "hygiene and sanitation"; Maine, in "community sanitation"; Mississippi, in "home and community sanitation."

ACCIDENT PREVENTION

Three states in 1913 and two additional states in 1923 required instruction regarding accident prevention. The provision in Wisconsin was as follows:

> It shall be the duty of each teacher in a public school in the state of Wisconsin to devote not less than thirty minutes in each month during which such school is in session to instructing the pupils thereof as to ways and means of preventing accidents. The state superintendent of public instruction shall prepare and publish at the expense of the state a book conveniently arranged in chapters or lessons for the purpose of the instruction provided in this section and shall furnish a copy thereof to each teacher required to give such instruction. The members of the boards of education, school directors, trustees, or other bodies or persons having control of the schools of a township, village or city, shall cause a copy of this section to be printed in the manual or handbook prepared for the guidance of teachers, where such manual is in use.

The law in Ohio and New Jersey was similar to that of Wisconsin. In New Jersey the obligation is placed upon teachers in private and parochial as well as public schools and the time devoted shall be "not less than thirty minutes in each two weeks." The manual to be used is to be prepared by

> the State Commissioner of Education acting in conjunction with the Employers' Liability Commission and the Director of the American Museum of Safety."

New Jersey provides also,

> At least once during each school term arrangements shall be made by the principals of all schools for the delivery by a duly authorized representative of the American Museum of Safety of a lecture on accident prevention and industrial, home and school hygiene, the cost of which to be paid by the State.

Pennsylvania in 1923 included among the subjects required to be taught "training in safety first methods." In Virginia,

> each teacher shall devote not less than thirty minutes in each month of the school session in instructing the pupils therein as to ways and means of proper observations in connection with the course of civics and citizenship so as to prevent accidents.

TOBACCO

Specific instruction regarding tobacco, whenever required, is in connection with "stimulants and narcotics" and is isolated here merely as a matter of interest. Tennessee provided for instruction regarding "smoking cigarettes" in 1903, 1913 and 1923. In 1913 and 1923 Indiana required instruction concerning "nicotine," and Alabama and California, concerning "tobacco."

PLACARDS

The use of placards for a specific educational purpose was required in Alabama and Mississippi in 1913 and in Kentucky and Mississippi in 1923. In each case the placards are to deal with stimulants and narcotics, and to these Kentucky adds cigarettes and also uses placards to teach thrift and industry, and Mississippi, the prevention and cure of tuberculosis. The provisions in Alabama regarding the use of placards were given above under "stimulants and narcotics." Mississippi had

> The state board of education shall procure placards, to be hung on the walls of public school-rooms, setting forth the effects of alcohol on the human system and means for the prevention and cure of tuberculosis. It shall be the duty of the county superintendent of education in each county to secure from the state board of education such placards and have them placed on the walls of the public school-rooms in the various counties.

Kentucky provided that

> It shall be the duty of the State Superintendent of Public Instruction to have prepared and furnished to the teachers in the public and high schools, placards printed in large type which shall set forth in attractive style statistics, epigrams, mottoes and up-to-date scientific truths showing the evils of intemperance and especially from the use of alcoholic and intoxicating beverages of all kinds and from cigarettes.

It is also made the duty of the State Superintendent to prepare and furnish similar placards "showing the advantages of thrift and industry." It is made the duty of the teachers to keep these placards posted in a conspicuous place in the schoolroom.

SUMMARY

The results are summarized in Table V. We find a remarkable growth in the legislation which is intended to improve individual and community health conditions; this growth is especially noticeable in the last decade. We find, however, in several instances, a peculiar sensitiveness to the wish of the parent. Lawmakers seem somewhat less willing to assert their authority regarding the body of the child than regarding his mind.

We find greatest stress put upon the teaching of the effects of stimulants and narcotics. Regarding this prescription the law is outspoken and mandatory. It is fortified by numerous provisions to insure its enforcement; the apparent aim being that it should be "taught to and studied by" every pupil in every grade. There has been a slight falling off in the number of states requiring the teaching of this subject; and the particular states where the decrease has taken place have not, as a rule, enacted laws calling for a broader health program.

Still, for the country as a whole the balance shows a decided gain for general hygiene. It would seem probable that, more frequently than formerly, the effects of stimulants and narcotics are considered as a minor topic in a large and important subject rather than as something special and isolated. It would seem probable, also, as a consequence, that the teaching has become more truthful and effective. Moreover, there is no reason to assume that actual instruction regarding stimulants and narcotics is any less effective in those states where it is not now required by law than it was formerly when so required, or than it is in other states where now required.

TABLE V

SUMMARY OF CURRICULAR PRESCRIPTIONS IN HEALTH AND "PROHIBITION" SHOWING INCREASE 1903–1923

Item	Number of States in Which Prescribed			Increase		
	1903	1913	1923	1903 to 1913	1913 to 1923	1903 to 1923
Stimulants and Narcotics	47	45	43	(−2)	(−2)	(−4)
Physiology and Hygiene	46	45	43	(−1)	(−2)	(−3)
Physical Education	5	7	25	2	18	20
Physical Examination	1	13	21	12	8	20
Personal Hygiene	1	2	12	1	10	11
Communicable Diseases	1	8	9	7	1	8
Sanitation	--	2	7	2	5	7
Accident Prevention	--	3	5	3	2	5
Tobacco	1	4	4	3	--	3
Placards	--	2	2	2	--	2
Total Number of Prescriptions	102	131	171	29	40	69

This table is based upon Table IV.
The items are arranged according to the number of states which had the prescription in 1923.

CHAPTER IV

LEGISLATIVE PROVISIONS CONCERNING THE TEACHING OF CONSERVATION OF LIFE AND PROPERTY

The group of subjects which is here called Conservation of Life and Property, including fire drill, fire prevention, and thrift, has grown from one prescription in 1903 to twenty in 1913, and to forty-three in 1923. See Table VI. If Arbor Day and other conservation days had been tabulated with this group, instead of with the Days of Special Observance, the group would have been seventeen in 1903, forty-two in 1913, and seventy in 1923.

FIRE DRILL

Regular fire drills were required in New York in 1903; in fourteen states in 1913, and in twenty-two states in 1923. The laws are of two types: In one type the obligation is placed upon the State Fire Marshal to require the fire drills to be given. In the other type the obligation is placed directly upon some educational authority. Alabama will serve to illustrate the first type.

> It shall be the duty of the State Fire Marshal, his deputies and assistants, to require officials and teachers of public and private schools, and educational institutions to have at least one fire drill each month.

Kansas, Michigan, Pennsylvania, and Tennessee have a similar provision. In Kansas there is an additional provision that a summary dismissal from the building shall be practised each month

> at some time during school hours aside from the regular dismissal at the close of the day's session.

The second type of law may be illustrated by Washington.

> It shall be the duty of the principal or other person in charge

TABLE VI CURRICULAR PRESCRIPTIONS IN CONSERVATION OF LIFE AND
STATES 1903,

Year	Subject or Activity		Alabama	Arizona	Arkansas	California	Colorado	Connecticut	Delaware	Florida	Georgia	Idaho	Illinois	Indiana	Iowa	Kansas	Kentucky	Louisiana	Maine	Maryland
1903	Fire Drill	1																		
	Fire Prevention	2																		
	Thrift	3																		
1913	Fire Drill	1								M				M	M	M				
	Fire Prevention	2													M^T	M^T				
	Thrift	3																		
1923	Fire Drill	1	M		M					M				M	M	M	M			
	Fire Prevention	2				M									M^T	M	M^T			
	Thrift	3				M											M^T			

M=Mandatory. M^T=Mandatory with time specification. (Minimum number of minutes or periods.)

PROPERTY FOR THE PUBLIC ELEMENTARY SCHOOLS IN EACH OF THE FORTY-EIGHT
1913, 1923

	Massachusetts	Michigan	Minnesota	Mississippi	Missouri	Montana	Nebraska	Nevada	New Hampshire	New Jersey	New Mexico	New York	North Carolina	North Dakota	Ohio	Oklahoma	Oregon	Pennsylvania	Rhode Island	South Carolina	South Dakota	Tennessee	Texas	Utah	Vermont	Virginia	Washington	West Virginia	Wisconsin	Wyoming	
1												M																			1
2																															–
3																															–
																															1
1		M	M			M						M			M		M	M	M						M		M				14
2						M^T	M^T								M^T		M^T														6
3																															–
																															20
1		M	M			M		M		M		M		M	M		M	M	M			M			M		M		M		22
2						M^T	M^T			M^T		M^T	M		M^T		M^T	M	M^T	M						M^T		M	M^T		17
3								M							M^T																4
																															43

> of every public or private school or educational institution within the state, to instruct and train the pupils by means of drills, so that they may in a sudden emergency be able to leave the school building in the shortest possible time and without confusion or panic. Such drills or rapid dismissal shall be held at least twice in each month.

A law similar to this is found in a number of states all of which show individual variations. In Rhode Island the law applies to all schools having "more than twenty-five pupils"; in Montana, to schools with "thirty or more children"; in Nevada, "forty or more pupils"; in Ohio and Oregon, fifty or more; in New York, in schools "having more than one hundred pupils or maintained in a building two or more stories high"; in Indiana and North Dakota, in a school having "more than one room"; in Wisconsin it applies to school buildings "exceeding one story in height." In New Jersey it applies to a two-or-more-room school or "a one-room school when located above the first story of a building." Most of the laws require at least one fire drill each month. Nevada, New Jersey, North Dakota, and Washington require at least two fire drills each month. Montana requires one "each week." In New York,

> Such drills or rapid dismissals shall be held at least twelve times in each school year, eight of which required drills shall be held between September first and December first of each such year. At least one-third of all such required drills shall be through use of the fire escapes on buildings where fire escapes are provided, and signals for such drills shall be separate and distinct from signals used for drills through corridors and stairways.

Pennsylvania requires that the scholars and teachers be made thoroughly familiar with the use of fire escapes. Of the states which require fire drills, Florida is the only one which does not definitely indicate a minimum frequency for them.

> The Superintendent of Public Instruction of the State of Florida shall formulate and prescribe tactics of instruction for fire drills for all the public schools of the State of Florida and each teacher teaching in such school shall be provided with a copy of such tactics, and it shall be the duty of each and every (one) of such teachers to instruct the students of their respective schools in such fire drills as prescribed by the State Superintendent of Public Instruction.

North Dakota has an additional prescription regarding one room rural schools "with special reference to prairie fires" which authorizes the county superintendent to require one fire drill each month in such schools. In a few states the law applies only to public schools but usually it applies to all educational institutions.

FIRE PREVENTION

Six states required instruction in fire prevention in 1913; seventeen states in 1923. The six states in 1913 were Iowa, Kansas, Montana, Nebraska, Ohio, Oregon. All of these had laws somewhat similar in type. They all required the preparation of a book or bulletin which was to be used in giving the instruction. Responsibility for the preparation of this required text was placed upon different state officials in the various states. In Iowa, Kansas, and Ohio it was to be prepared by the State Fire Marshal; in Montana, by the Commissioner of Insurance; in Nebraska, by the Chief Deputy Fire Commissioner and the Superintendent of Public Instruction; in Oregon, by the Superintendent of Public Instruction. In Iowa and Kansas the required bulletin dealt with "the causes and dangers of fires" and was to be arranged in not less than four divisions or chapters, and the teachers were required to "instruct their pupils in at least one lesson each quarter of the school year." In Montana, Ohio, and Oregon the book was to deal with "fire dangers" and was to be conveniently arranged in chapters or lessons sufficient in number "to provide a different chapter or lesson for each week of the maximum school year, one of such lessons to be read by the teachers" each week.

In 1923 the law in Iowa, Montana, Nebraska, and Oregon was the same as in 1913. In Kansas the specification as to the divisions of the bulletin and the time requirement were omitted. Ohio in 1923 had a law similar in type to that which was in force in California, New Jersey, New York, Rhode Island, and West Virginia. In these states certain state officials were directed and empowered to provide a course in fire prevention

> dealing with the protection of lives and property against loss and damage as result of preventable fire.

In California the responsibility for prescribing the course is placed upon the local board of education; in New Jersey, upon the Commissioner of Banking and Insurance and the Commissioner of Education; in New York and Rhode Island, upon the Commissioner of Education; in West Virginia, upon the State Superintendent of Schools; and in Ohio upon the State Fire Marshal and the State Superintendent of Public Instruction. In New Jersey and Rhode Island "not less than one hour in each month" shall be devoted to this subject; in New York and Ohio, at least "fifteen minutes in each week"; in California, "a reasonable time in each month." California also specifies,

> The aims and purposes of the courses of fire prevention established under the provisions of this act shall be as follows: (1) To create an understanding of the cause and origin of fires; (2) to emphasize the dangers of carelessness and neglect in homes and public buildings and the necessity of care in the use of fires; (3) to promote an interest in preventing fires and the protection of lives and property.

Virginia and Wisconsin have similar laws which require instruction in

> ways and means of preventing loss and damage to lives and property through preventable fires.

Virginia provides that the teacher "may devote not less than one hour in each month" to this subject and Wisconsin requires "not less than one-half hour in each month." In Pennslyvania, the Department of State Police in consultation with the Superintendent of Public Instruction shall prepare books of instruction with regard to "the dangers of fire and the prevention of fire waste," and

> The curriculum of such schools shall include some regular and continuous study of such subjects during the entire school year.

Kentucky, North Carolina, and South Carolina require that instruction in fire prevention shall be given. In Kentucky it must be given "at least once each week." California, Kansas, North Carolina, Pennsylvania, South Carolina, and West Virginia in 1923 did not specify a time requirement in this subject.

THRIFT

Thrift is a recent addition to the curriculum. The teaching of it was required in four states in 1923. Nevada had this provision:

> It is hereby made the duty of all teachers in the public schools of the State of Nevada to teach in their respective schools lessons on the subject of thrift. These lessons shall emphasize the importance of industry, production, earning, wise spending, regular saving and safe investment; also the importance of thrift in time and material.

It is made the duty of the state board of education to prepare courses of study in the subject of thrift for use in the elementary and high schools. California included "thrift" among the branches in the required course of study. In Ohio,

> as an additional study the subject of thrift shall be taught at least thirty minutes in each week in each grade of the elementary and high schools of the state.

Kentucky required that

> there shall be taught in the public and high schools of the State a course of lessons to inculcate habits of thrift and industry. It shall be the duty of the State superintendent to have prepared and furnished to every teacher in said public and high schools of the State a bulletin covering thrift and industry. Also it shall be the duty of the State Superintendent of Public Instruction to have prepared and furnished to the teachers of public and high schools placards printed in large type, which shall set forth in an attractive style, epigrams and mottoes showing the advantages of thrift and industry. It shall be the duty of every teacher in the State paid entirely or in part by the State, to observe at least one fifteen-minute period each week to the teaching of thrift and industry and to keep placards on thrift and industry posted in the schoolroom.

ARBOR DAY

Special observance of Arbor Day by the public schools was required in sixteen states in 1903, eighteen in 1913, and twenty-one in 1923. It was required in the following fifteen states in all three years:

Arizona	Nevada	Oklahoma
Colorado	New Jersey	Oregon
Connecticut	New Mexico	South Carolina
Idaho	New York	Tennessee
Montana	Ohio	Wyoming

It was required in Georgia in 1903 and 1913; in Indiana and Louisiana in 1913 and 1923; and in California, Maryland, North Carolina, and Rhode Island in 1923. Aside from the slight increase in the number of states making the prescription, there has been very little change during the twenty years; in most of the states the provisions in force in 1903 were still in force in 1923.

The day observed varies in different states; sometimes it is in the spring, sometimes in the fall; sometimes a day is definitely fixed by the law, sometimes it is to be proclaimed by the governor, sometimes it is to be named by an educational authority. The purpose of the observance is variously expressed:

> For the purpose of encouraging the planting of shade and forest trees, shrubs and vines.
> For the benefit and adornment of public and private grounds, places and ways.
> In order to show the value and beauty of forestry.
> To encourage the planting, protection and preservation of trees and shrubs.
> So that a greater understanding of nature may be given to the children and people of this State.

The day must be observed "by planting of trees or other appropriate exercises" or "with appropriate exercises" or "in such manner as the state board of education may direct"; frequently the educational authorities are directed to prepare a program of exercises for the day.

In Ohio,

> The superintendent of public instruction shall issue each year a manual for arbor day exercises. The manual shall contain matters relating to forestry and birds, including a copy of such laws relating to the protection of song and insectivorous birds as he deems proper. He shall transmit copies of the manual to the superintendent of city, village and rural schools and to the clerks of boards of education, who shall cause them to be distributed among the teachers of the schools under their charge. On arbor day, and other days when convenient, the teachers shall cause such laws

> to be read to the scholars of their respective schools and shall encourage them to aid in the protection of such birds.

Also,

> those in charge of the public schools and institutions of learning under state control, or state patronage, for at least two hours must give information to the pupils and students concerning the value and interest of forests, the duty of the public to protect the birds therof, and also for planting forest trees.

In South Carolina,

> The free public schools of this state shall observe the third Friday in November of each year as Arbor Day, and on that day the school officers and teachers shall conduct such exercises and engage in the planting of such shrubs, plants and trees as will impress on the minds of the pupils the proper value and appreciation to be placed on flowers, ornamental shrubbery and shade trees.

In Arizona, Idaho, Montana, New York, Oklahoma, and Oregon the language of the law, in the main, follows a common pattern, that in Arizona being somewhat longer and more comprehensive.

> In order that the children in the public schools shall assist in the work of adorning the school ground with trees, and to stimulate the minds of children towards the benefits of the preservation and perpetuation of the forests, and the growing of timber, it shall be the duty of the authorities in every public school in the State of Arizona to assemble the pupils in their charge on the above day in the school building or elsewhere, as they may deem proper, and to provide for and conduct, under the general supervision of the State Superintendent of Public Instruction, such exercises as shall tend to encourage the planting, protection and preservation of trees and shrubs, and an acquaintance with the best methods to be adopted to accomplish such results; and that the trees may be planted around the school buildings, and that the grounds around such buildings may be improved and beautified; such planting to be attended with appropriate and attractive ceremonies, that the day may be one of pleasure as well as one of instruction for the young; all to be under the supervision and direction of the teacher, who shall see that the trees and shrubs are properly selected and set.
>
> The State Superintendent of Public Instruction shall from year to year prescribe a course of exercises and instructions

in subjects hereinbefore mentioned, which shall be adopted and observed by said public school authorities on Arbor Day.

California in 1923 and Indiana in 1913 and 1923 have laws which introduce a more personal and local coloration.

In California,

> March seventh of each year, being the anniversary of the birthday of Luther Burbank, is hereby set apart and designated conservation, bird and arbor day. All public schools and educational institutions are directed to observe conservation, bird and arbor day, not as a holiday, but by including in the school work of the day suitable exercises having for their object instruction as to the economic value of birds and trees, and the promotion of a spirit of protection towards them, and as to the economic value of natural resources, and the desirability of their conservation.

In Indiana,

> Appropriate exercises shall be introduced in all the schools of the state; and it shall be the duty of the several county and city superintendents to prepare a program of exercises for that day to be observed in all the schools under their respective jurisdictions. The exercises on arbor day shall give due honor to the conservors of forestry, and the founders of the study and conservation of Indiana forestry. And especially to the leading spirit of forestry conservation, Charles Warren Fairbanks.

In Georgia in 1923,

> The County and Local Boards of Education shall see that the following days are observed either by holiday or appropriate exercises and it shall be the duty of the State Superintendent of Schools to arrange programs for the proper observance of these occasions and of the Superintendent and teachers to direct the attention of the pupils to these dates and topics by practical exercises: . . . . Arbor and Bird Day, first Friday in December.[1]

In Maine,

> Arbor day shall not be recognized as a school holiday unless observed by teacher and pupils for the purpose for which it is designated by the governor and council.[2]

[1] Supplement 1923 to Park's Annotated Code, Vol. VIII, p. 358, Sec. 1441*a*.
[2] Revised Statutes 1916, p. 379, Ch. 16, Sec. 109.

BIRD DAY

Louisiana and Utah provided for the observance of bird day in 1913 and 1923; Iowa and Pennsylvania, in 1923. In Louisiana,

> The State and Parish Boards of Public Education are directed to provide for the celebration, by all public schools, of "Bird Day," on May fifth of each year, being the anniversary of the birth of John James Audubon, the distinguished son of Louisiana. On the recurring anniversary days, suitable exercises are to be engaged in, and lessons on the economic and esthetic value of the resident and migratory birds of the State are to be taught by the teachers, to their pupils.

In Utah,

> It shall be the duty of the board of education or school board of every school district within this State to cause to be observed in the schools the last Friday in April of each year as Bird Day, with appropriate lessons and exercises relating to the observation, the study, and the value of birds and other forms of animal life, particularly as aids in the extermination of insects, weeds and other pests.

In Iowa,

> The twenty-first day of March of each year is hereby set apart and designated as Bird Day. It shall be the duty of all public schools to observe said day by devoting a part thereof to a special study of birds, their habits, usefulness and the best means of protection. Should such date fall on other than a school day, such day shall be observed on the next regular school day.

In Pennsylvania,

> The governor of this commonwealth be requested to appoint a day to be designated as "Arbor Day," in Pennsylvania, and to recommend, by proclamation to the people, on the day named, the planting of trees and shrubbery in public school grounds and along public highways throughout the state.

Also,

> From and after the passage of this act, those several days of each year that may be set apart by the Governor as Arbor Days shall also be known as "Bird Day" in Pennsylvania, and it shall be the duty of every teacher in the public schools of this Commonwealth, under penalty of reprimand

> or dismissal, as the case may require, to devote, together with their pupils, at least two hours of such school day to the study of wild birds, and especially to consider the value of the life-work of such birds to the people, and the best methods through which the conservation and increase of useful birds may be secured; and it shall be the duty of all school superintendents within this commonwealth, either county, city or otherwise, to see to it that the requirements of this act are complied with.

In Connecticut, in all three years, bird day was observed in conjunction with arbor day. In California in 1923 the day observed was designated "conservation, bird and arbor day," while in Tennessee it was "Arbor, Bird and Flower Day."

FIRE PREVENTION DAY

In Connecticut in 1923,

> The governor shall, by proclamation, annually designate a day, on or about October ninth, to be known as Fire Prevention Day, which day shall be observed in the schools and in such manner as shall be indicated in such proclamation.

STATE FIRE DAY

In Nebraska in 1913 and 1923,

> For the purpose of creating a public sentiment, and in order that the people of this state shall have called to their attention the great damage caused both to life and property by fire, there is hereby set apart and established the first Friday in November which shall be designated and known as "State Fire Day." This day shall be observed by the public, private and parochial schools of the state with exercises appropriate to the subject and the day.

GOOD ROADS DAY

In Colorado in 1913 and 1923,

> The second Friday in May of each year shall be set apart and known as Good Roads Day, to be observed by the people of this State in the discussion of public highways and in the construction and repair of the same, for the benefit and advacement of good roads in the State of Colorado, and in such further efforts and undertakings as shall be in

harmony with the general character of the day so established. In all public schools of the State, school officers and teachers are required to have scholars in their respective charge observe the day by teaching and educating the children of the schools with respect to the benefit of good roads.

SUMMARY

Table VII gives a summary of this group of subjects. It is perhaps somewhat surprising, in view of the disastrous and fatal school fires which have occurred, to find that Fire Drills are not by law required in all of the states. The increase in such requirements was more marked in the first decade than in the second. They are now required in slightly less than half of the states. Fire Prevention has shown a more rapid increase during the second decade. Time requirements in this subject are very common. It is a frequent practice to place the responsibility for planning the course upon state officials entirely outside of the education department. Sometimes the preparation of a book which is "to be read by the teachers" is also made the duty of those who are not educators.

TABLE VII

Summary of Curricular Prescriptions in Conservation of Life and Property Showing Increase 1903–1923

Item	Number of States in Which Prescribed			Increase		
	1903	1913	1923	1903 to 1913	1913 to 1923	1903 to 1923
Fire Drill	1	14	22	13	8	21
Fire Prevention	--	6	17	6	11	17
Thrift	--	--	4	--	4	4
Total Number of Prescriptions	1	20	43	10	23	42

This table is based upon Table VI.
The items are arranged according to the number of states which had the prescription in 1923.

CHAPTER V

LEGISLATIVE PROVISIONS CONCERNING THE TEACHING OF PRACTICAL AND CULTURAL SUBJECTS

The subjects considered in this chapter are

1. Agriculture	6. Bookkeeping
2. Drawing	7. Exhibitions
3. Music	8. Cotton Grading
4. Household Arts	9. Art
5. Industrial Arts	

They have been called Practical and Cultural because any of them may be taught for either purpose. Agriculture, for example, may be taught in the elementary school as a pre-vocational subject or for general information and apprecation. As will be seen from Table VIII, (pp. 116-17) they show more of an increase during the first decade than during the second. There was a total of twenty-four prescriptions in 1903, forty-four in 1913, and fifty-nine in 1923.

AGRICULTURE

The teaching of agriculture was required in five states in 1903, in seventeen states in 1913, and in nineteen states in 1923. In many instances agriculture is regarded as a regular and ordinary subject of the curriculum. It is included along with the other branches required to be taught, without any elaboration or special comment. Sometimes the subject is referred to as "the elements of agriculture"; sometimes as "elementary agriculture"; again as "the elementary principles of agriculture"; at other times, simply as "agriculture." Alabama in 1903 provided

> In addition to the branches now taught in the public schools instruction shall be given in the elementary principles of agriculture and said subject shall be taught as regularly as other branches are taught in said schools by the use of a textbook in the hands of the pupils and such instruction

> shall be given in all the public schools of the state except in public schools in cities of five hundred inhabitants or over.

In 1913 the same law, without the exception, was found; and in 1923 "agriculture" without further qualification was included in the required courses of study. In Georgia in 1903 the "elementary principles of agriculture" was to be

> included in the branches of study taught in the common or public schools in the State of Georgia and shall be studied and taught as thoroughly and in the same manner as other like required branches are studied and taught in said schools.

The same law was in force in 1913 and essentially the same in 1923, when it is called "the elements and principles of agriculture." In Tennessee in 1903 "the elementary principles of agriculture" was among the subjects to be taught in the "secondary school." At that time the law read:

> the course of study in the primary schools shall consist of five grades and the course of study in the secondary schools shall consist of eight grades, the first five grades in each being identical.

The same law prevailed in 1913 but was not found in 1923. Arkansas in 1913 required the teaching of "elementary agriculture and horticulture," which in 1923 had become "elementary agriculture." In Florida, in 1913 and 1923, the elementary principles of agriculture

> shall be studied and taught as thoroughly and in the same manner as other like required branches are studied and taught.

In Indiana in 1913 and 1923,

> elementary agriculture shall be taught in the grades in all town and township schools,

and the State Board of Education

> shall outline a course of study for each of such grades as they may determine which shall be followed as a minimum requirement.

In Iowa in 1913 and 1923,

> The teaching of elementary agriculture, domestic science and manual training shall be required in the public schools of the state; and the state superintendent of public in-

TABLE VIII CURRICULAR PRESCRIPTIONS IN PRACTICAL AND CULTURAL EIGHT 1903, 1913,

Year	Subject or Activity		Alabama	Arizona	Arkansas	California	Colorado	Connecticut	Delaware	Florida	Georgia	Idaho	Illinois	Indiana	Iowa	Kansas	Kentucky	Louisiana	Maine	Maryland
1903	Agriculture	1	M								M									
	Drawing	2		M		M												M		M
	Music	3				M									M					M
	Household Arts	4																		M
	Industrial Arts	5																		
	Bookkeeping	6		M		M														M
	Exhibitions	7																		
	Cotton Grading	8																		
	Art	9																		
1913	Agriculture	1	M		M					M	M			M	M			M		
	Drawing	2				M												M		M
	Music	3				M									M					M
	Household Arts	4												M	M					M
	Industrial Arts	5												M	M					
	Bookkeeping	6				M														
	Exhibitions	7																		
	Cotton Grading	8																		
	Art	9																		
1923	Agriculture	1	M		M					M	M			M	M		M	M		
	Drawing	2				M												M		
	Music	3				M									M					
	Household Arts	4			M	M								M	M					
	Industrial Arts	5				M								M	M					
	Bookkeeping	6				M														
	Exhibitions	7																		M
	Cotton Grading	8																		
	Art	9																		

M = Mandatory.

SUBJECTS FOR THE PUBLIC ELEMENTARY SCHOOLS IN EACH OF THE FORTY-STATES

1923

	Massachusetts	Michigan	Minnesota	Mississippi	Missouri	Montana	Nebraska	Nevada	New Hampshire	New Jersey	New Mexico	New York	North Carolina	North Dakota	Ohio	Oklahoma	Oregon	Pennsylvania	Rhode Island	South Carolina	South Dakota	Tennessee	Texas	Utah	Vermont	Virginia	Washington	West Virginia	Wisconsin	Wyoming	
1													M							M		M									5
2	M							M					M												M	M					9
3																															3
4																															1
5	M																														1
6																						M						M			5
7																															–
8																															–
9																															–
																															24
1													M	M	M	M				M		M	M					M	M	M	17
2	M							M					M								M				M	M					9
3								M													M										5
4																M															4
5	M							M																							4
6								M														M						M			4
7																															–
8																							M								1
9																															–
																															44
1				M		M	M						M	M	M	M				M			M						M	M	19
2	M						M	M			M		M								M				M	M					10
3								M			M		M					M			M	M									8
4	M										M					M															7
5	M							M			M																				6
6							M	M			M																				4
7							M									M															3
8																							M								1
9																		M													1
																															59

> struction shall prescribe the extent of such instruction in the public schools. Elementary agriculture and domestic science or manual training shall be included among the subjects required in the examination of those applicants for teachers' certificates who are required by the provisions of this section to teach agriculture and domestic science; provided, however, that nothing in this section shall prevent the board of directors from dispensing with the teaching of said subjects in rural schools at its discretion.

In Louisiana, in 1913 and 1923, instruction is required in all the elementary and secondary schools of the state

> in the principles of agriculture or horticulture and in home and farm economy.

In North Dakota, in 1913 and 1923, instruction is required in the "elements of agriculture." In 1923 it is further provided that

> The county commissioners of each county in this state shall provide and purchase one or more standard grain grading and cream testing outfits and any other necessary equipment which is ordinarily used for grading, testing and classifying agricultural products. Said equipment shall at all times be kept in good repair and shall remain the property of the county, to be replaced or added to as circumstances require, and the same shall be placed in the custody of the county superintendent of schools as a part of the educational equipment of that office. It shall be the duty of the county superintendent of schools to arrange a plan so that such equipment shall be in continuous use in the schools of the county which are not consolidated, and to arrange for the instruction of teachers therein in the use of such equipment.

Ohio in 1913 required that agriculture be added to, and made one of the branches of education to be taught in all of the common schools of the state with the exception of those in city school districts. The state was to be divided into four agricultural districts, each to have a district supervisor of agriculture appointed by the Commissioner of Common Schools at a salary of $2000 a year. In 1923 agriculture

> shall hereafter be taught in all the common schools of all the village and rural school districts . . . and may be taught in city school districts at the option of the board of education.

The constitution of Oklahoma in 1913 and 1923 required that

> the legislature shall provide for the teaching of the elements of agriculture, horticulture, stock-raising, and domestic science in the common schools of the state.

The statute law provided

> The elementary principles of agriculture, horticulture, animal husbandry, stock-feeding, forestry, building country roads, and domestic science, including the elements of economics, shall be embraced in all the branches taught in all public schools of this state receiving any part of their support from this state, and these branches shall be as thoroughly studied and taught by observation, practical exercises, and the use of text and reference books, and in the same manner as are other like required branches in said public schools. . . . There is hereby created a chair of agriculture for schools, the occupant of which shall be a member of the faculty of the Agricultural and Mechanical College, whose duty shall be to direct and advise in all matters relating to the teaching of agriculture and allied subjects in the common schools. . . . The State Commissioners of Agricultural and Industrial Education, with the assistance of such experts in agricultural education as may be secured from the State and National Department of Agriculture, shall have the authority, and it shall be their duty to prepare a detailed course of study in the elements of agriculture and allied subjects, domestic science and economics, adapted to the needs of instruction in the elementary and secondary schools of the state. The commission shall prepare a syllabus of the course of study in each subject, in such detail and with such elaboration of the body of knowledge to be considered as may be necessary for the organization and administration of the proper courses of instruction in said branches. The Commission shall with the assistance of members of the faculty of the Agricultural and Mechanical College prepare and have published a textbook on agriculture and allied subjects.

Annual school poultry and egg shows are to be held to promote the study of agriculture. In Texas in 1913 and 1923 elementary agriculture is included in the prescribed course of study but it is provided that it

> shall not be required to be taught in independent school districts having a scholastic population of three hundred or more unless so ordered by the school boards.

In 1923 practical field studies and laboratory experiments were included in the course. In Kentucky in 1923,

> Elementary agriculture shall be taught in the common schools of this state except in cities of the 1st, 2nd, 3rd and 4th classes.

All school officers are required to enforce the teaching of this subject in the same manner as the other branches of the curriculum.

DRAWING

Drawing was included among the subjects in the required course of study in nine states in 1903, nine in 1913 and ten in 1923. California, Louisiana, Massachusetts, North Carolina, Vermont, Virginia, and Nevada required it in all three years. There is some question as to the intent of the law in Nevada. "Industrial drawing" was prescribed in Arizona in 1903; "drawing," in Maryland in 1903 and 1913, South Dakota in 1913 and 1923, and Nebraska and New Mexico in 1923. In Vermont the requirement in all three years was for instruction in "free hand drawing." The law in California in 1903 and 1913 apparently permitted county boards of education in districts having less than one hundred census children to omit instruction in drawing "until they have a practical knowledge of" certain other named subjects. In Nebraska drawing is included in the required course of study for rural schools; it is also included among the subjects from which "the course of study for the first eight grades in common schools shall be composed." Drawing in Nevada is not directly and specifically prescribed, but it is included among the subjects for which a series of textbooks must be adopted. In 1903 the series of textbooks, including drawing, was directly adopted by an act of the legislature to

> be used in all the public schools of the state and no school shall receive its pro rata of public school moneys unless such textbooks are used.

In 1913 and 1923 the language of the law is less explicit. The adopted textbooks are to

> be used in all the public schools of the state to the exclusion of all others,

but the use of supplemental or reference books is permitted.

MUSIC

Music was included among the required subjects in three states in 1903, five in 1913, and eight in 1923. California and Iowa prescribed it in all three years; Maryland in 1903 and 1913; Nevada and South Dakota in 1913 and 1923; North Carolina, Pennsylvania and Tennessee in 1923. In California in 1903 and 1913 it could be omitted in districts having less than one hundred census children. In Nevada the textbooks adopted in music, as in the case of drawing, must be "used in all the public schools of the state to the exclusion of all others." Iowa, in all three years, required that

> The elements of vocal music, including when practical the singing of simple music by note, shall be taught in all of the public schools of Iowa, and all teachers teaching in schools where such instruction is not given by special teachers shall be required to satisfy the county superintendent of their ability to teach the elements of vocal music in a proper manner; provided, however, that no teacher shall be refused a certificate or the grade of his or her certificate lowered on account of lack of ability to sing.

In South Dakota,

> The elements of vocal music including, when practicable, the singing of simple music by note, shall be taught in all the public schools of the state. Music shall be taught in all the state normal schools, and the minimum requirement of graduates from such schools must be at least two hours per week for one school year. In all schools having two or more grades, instruction in music shall be given by an instructor qualified to teach the rudiments of music, who may be a teacher of one of the departments, if qualified to teach this subject. In the country schools conducted by a single teacher, the elements of music notation by vocal and blackboard drill, in connection with simple songs, shall be taught. But no teacher shall be refused a certificate, nor shall the grade of this certificate be lowered on account of his lack of ability to instruct or sing. It shall be the duty of the county superintendent to have taught annually in the normal institutes the elements of vocal music, by some competent person, for at least twenty minutes of each day.

In North Carolina it is the duty of all teachers

> to provide for singing in school and so far as possible to give instruction in public school music.

HOUSEHOLD ARTS

Of the subjects falling under this head there was one in 1903, there were four in 1913, and seven in 1923. Arkansas and California required instruction in "household economics" in 1923. Indiana in 1913 and 1923 required that

> elementary domestic science shall be taught in the grades of all city, town and township schools.

Iowa in 1913 and 1923 required that "domestic science" be taught except in rural schools. Maryland required the teaching of "domestic economy" in 1903 and 1913; no such requirement was found in 1923. Massachusetts in 1923 required that

> Every town of twenty thousand inhabitants shall maintain the teaching of manual training and household arts as part of both its elementary and its high school program of studies.

New Mexico in 1923 included "household economics" among the required branches of learning. In Oklahoma in 1913 and 1923 "domestic science including the elements of economics" was to be taught in all the public schools.

INDUSTRIAL ARTS

The subjects under this head include manual training and other forms of industrial work. One state had such a prescription in 1903, four states in 1913, and six in 1923. California in 1923 required that

> in school districts employing six or more elementary school teachers in any one school, whether housed in one or more buildings, manual training and household economics must be taught.

Indiana in 1913 and 1923 provided that

> elementary industrial work shall be taught in the grades in all city and town schools.

Manual training was required in Iowa in 1913 and 1923. The statutory requirement was quoted above under "agriculture." Massachusetts, in all three years, prescribed the teaching of manual training as part of both its elementary and its high school program of studies in every town of twenty thousand inhabitants.

In Nevada the powers and duties of the state board of education, in 1913 and 1923, included

> to prescribe and cause to be enforced the courses of study for the public schools, such courses to contain in the seventh and eighth grades, among other things, business forms and elementary book-keeping or some features of industrial work; . . . provided that schools of the first class may have modified courses of study subject to the approval of the state board of education.

New Mexico in 1923 included among the prescribed subjects "manual training and other vocational subjects." In Vermont in 1923

> Junior high schools shall have a four-year course, flexible in character, designed for the instruction of pupils who have completed the rural school course or the first six years of the elementary school course, and suitable to the number and needs of local pupils; and the state board of education shall arrange for a course of study, including vocational opportunities, appropriate to the needs of the pupils in the several communities. In a town district where a junior high school is established, said board shall make the necessary readjustment of the course of study in the elementary schools. . . . Junior and senior high schools shall include vocational courses in one or more of the following subjects; agriculture, manual arts, commercial subjects or domestic science, appropriate to the needs and environment of the particular school and for pupils between the ages of twelve and sixteen years.[1]

BOOKKEEPING

Bookkeeping was a required subject in five states in 1903, in four states in 1913, and four in 1923. California is the only state in which it was required in all three years. It is included in Nebraska's course of study for the rural schools in 1923. In Nevada, in 1913 and 1923,

> business forms and elementary bookkeeping or some features of industrial work,

must be offered in the seventh and eighth grades. In Tennessee, in 1903 and 1913, "bookkeeping" was required in the sixth, seventh, or eighth grade. West Virginia required "single entry bookkeeping" in 1903 and "bookkeeping" in 1913.

[1] General Laws 1917, p. 305, Sec. 1294.

EXHIBITIONS

Exhibitions were required in three states in 1923. Maryland and Nebraska required an exhibit of school work; Oklahoma, annual school poultry and egg shows. In Maryland,

> There shall be held in each school, once a year, a public exhibition of school work, of which due notice shall be given, that parents and others interested in education may attend.

In Nebraska,

> There shall hereafter be held at the county seat of each county, under the supervision and direction of the county superintendent, and county board, on or before the first day of May of each year, an exhibition of school work done in each school district of said county during the current school year. The nature and character of said exhibit shall be determined by the county superintendent. Said exhibit shall be open to the public for not less than one nor more than three days. The county superintendent shall annually offer and award premiums intended to stimulate the interest in school affairs. A list of premiums to be awarded shall be published in the various county papers, as other school news, at least sixty days before the date or dates fixed for said exhibit. Each year the county board shall make arrangements to have said county school exhibit taken to the county fair of said county, if there be one, and to the Nebraska state fair at Lincoln. To defray the expenses incident to assembling and carrying on of said annual county school exhibit a sum equal to not less than two and one-half cents nor more than five cents for every pupil of school age shall upon the written request of the teachers of at least one-half of the schools for said county be set aside each year from the general fund of said county by the county board. Said fund shall be known as "——— county school exhibit fund." It shall be the duty of the county board to pay all bills incurred or approved by the county superintendent of said county for the purpose of carrying out the provisions of this act, not exceeding the sum set aside for such purposes. Said board may in its discretion include said item of expense incident to said exhibit in its annual estimate and levy a tax for the payment thereof together with other necessary taxes for the current year.

In Oklahoma,

> For educational purposes, and in furtherance of the study of agriculture, and to encourage industry among the school children of the state, there shall be held annually at each

> school house in the State of Oklahoma, not included within cities of the first class, a poultry show during the week commencing with the last Monday in November of each year and an egg show during the week commencing with the last Monday of January of each year, and the county superintendent of public instruction in each county, and the various officers of each school district, and the teachers at each school house, are hereby directed to co-operate in the holding of said annual school poultry and egg shows, and in aid of such annual school poultry and egg shows, the board of officers of each respective school district are hereby authorized and directed to expend of the fund or funds of each school district not less than five dollars nor more than ten dollars for each of said shows.

Each board of county commissioners is to include in its budget the sum of $250 for holding a county poultry show in December of each year; at least sixty per cent of this money is to be used in connection with the junior department of the county and state shows;

> and the contests in all school house shows shall be limited to specimens of poultry and eggs actually produced and raised by the school children attending each respective school house, and the contests in the junior department of each county show shall be limited to specimens of poultry and eggs actually raised and produced by the school children of such county, and to the work of such children, and the contests in the junior department of the state show shall be limited to specimens of poultry and eggs, actually raised and produced by the school children of the State of Oklahoma, and the work of such children.

The active co-operation of state and county authorities in this field and expert supervision of the children's work are specifically provided for.

COTTON GRADING

The teaching of Cotton Grading was required in Texas in 1913 and 1923.

> *Section 1.* The State Board of Education is authorized and instructed to require the teaching of cotton classification in all the State Normal Schools, Industrial Schools, Summer Normal Schools, teachers' institutes, and in all public schools; *provided,* that the subject of cotton classification

shall not be required to be taught in independent school districts having a scholastic population of three hundred or more, or in districts where the cotton acreage is less than 10 per cent of the total acreage planted to farm products, unless so ordered by the school board or trustees.

Section 2. The grades of cotton taught in all the schools as required in Section 1 of this Act, shall be those established and provided for by the United States Department of Agriculture and known as official types or "standards."

Section 3. It shall be the duty of the State Superintendent of Public Instruction to furnish full information to all schools required to teach the classification of cotton, as to how to obtain the types or "standards" provided for in this Act.

Section 4. The county commissioners' court of all counties coming under the provisions of this Act shall provide for at least one set of the official types or "standards" to be placed in charge of the county superintendent of public instruction, or ex officio county superintendent of public instruction, whose duty it shall be to use them for the purposes of instruction in classification of cotton; to lend them to Summer Normal Schools and Teachers' Institutes held in his county, and to have types of same made for the various schools in his county applying for same; *provided,* that such schools shall pay the cost of making such types.

Section 5. The school board or trustees of every school district required by the provisions of this Act to teach cotton grading, shall furnish the county superintendent of public instruction with samples of the different grades of cotton from which a set of types or "standards" shall be made by comparing them with the official types or "standards" and the county superintendent of public instruction shall certify that the same has been carefully compared with the official types or "standards" in his office, and shall correctly label same, showing the grade thereof; *provided,* that nothing in this section shall prevent school boards or trustees from purchasing the official types or "standards" direct from the United States Department of Agriculture.

Section 6. The State Normal Schools and the State Industrial School shall procure the official types or "standards" from the United States Department of Agriculture and pay for same out of the appropriation made by the Legislature for their support and maintenance.

Section 7. The state schools named in Section 6 of this Act, shall employ a competent instructor to teach the practical art of grading and classing cotton, and the handling of cotton in all of its branches from the field to the factory.

Section 8. Summer normals and county institutes shall make provision for the employment of instructors in cotton classification in the same way that they employ instructors in other required branches.

Section 9. Students of any school in this State where cotton grading or classing is required to be taught shall be entitled to a certificate of proficiency after passing such examination as may be prescribed by the faculty of the school or by the county superintendent of public instruction of the county in which he proposes to teach; *provided,* that the applicant must be able to class 60 per cent or more of the samples presented compared with the types or standards of the Department of Agriculture.

ART

Pennsylvania in 1923 included "art" among the subjects required to be taught.

SUMMARY

The most outstanding gain in this group of subjects was that of agriculture during the first decade when twelve additional

TABLE IX

SUMMARY OF CURRICULAR PRESCRIPTIONS IN PRACTICAL AND CULTURAL SUBJECTS SHOWING INCREASE 1903–1923

Item	Number of States in Which Prescribed			Increase		
	1903	1913	1923	1903 to 1913	1913 to 1923	1903 to 1923
Agriculture	5	17	19	12	2	14
Drawing	9	9	10	--	1	1
Music	3	5	8	2	3	5
Household Arts	1	4	7	3	3	6
Industrial Arts	1	4	6	3	2	5
Bookkeeping	5	4	4	(−1)	--	(−1)
Exhibitions	--	--	3	--	3	3
Cotton Grading	--	1	1	1	--	1
Art	--	--	1	--	1	1
Total Number of Prescriptions	24	44	59	20	15	35

This table is based upon Table VIII.
The items are arranged according to the number of states which had the prescription in 1923.

states prescribed that it be taught; the other subjects show only a slight growth. No time specifications were found for any of these subjects. Frequently there were exceptions or limitations which would make the teaching of a subject necessary in only a part of the schools of the state. Quite obviously there has been less concern regarding the teaching of these subjects than was the case with a number of subjects considered in earlier chapters; such as the observance of special days, the display of the flag, the teaching of fire prevention, of patriotism, and the constitution. A summary of the prescriptions for the three years is shown in Table IX above.

CHAPTER VI

LEGISLATIVE PROVISIONS CONCERNING THE TEACHING OF HUMANENESS

The three subdivisions of Humaneness show, as will be seen from Table X, a total of twelve prescriptions in 1903, twenty-eight in 1913, and thirty-six in 1923. In the majority of instances the three items, here isolated as a matter of interest, are to be found embodied in the same law. The three subjects are:

1. Humane Treatment and Protection of Animals and Birds
2. Importance of Animals and Birds
3. Animal Experimentation

HUMANE TREATMENT AND PROTECTION OF ANIMALS AND BIRDS

The teaching of the humane treatment and protection of animals and birds was required in eight states in 1903, fifteen in 1913, and seventeen in 1923.

1903	1913	1923
		Alabama
California	California	California
Colorado	Colorado	
	Delaware	
		Florida
	Illinois	Illinois
		Kentucky
Maine	Maine	Maine
	Michigan	Michigan
Montana		
	New Hampshire	
		New York
	North Dakota	North Dakota
	Oklahoma	Oklahoma
		Oregon
	Pennsylvania	Pennsylvania
South Dakota	South Dakota	South Dakota
Texas	Texas	Texas
Washington	Washington	Washington
	Wisconsin	Wisconsin
Wyoming	Wyoming	Wyoming

TABLE X CURRICULAR PRESCRIPTIONS IN HUMANENESS FOR THE PUBLIC

Year	Subject or Activity		Alabama	Arizona	Arkansas	California	Colorado	Connecticut	Delaware	Florida	Georgia	Idaho	Illinois	Indiana	Iowa	Kansas	Kentucky	Louisiana	Maine	Maryland
1903	Humane Treatment&Protection	1				M	M^T												M^T	
	Importance of Animals & Birds	2																		
	Animal Experimentation......	3																		
1913	Humane Treatment&Protection	1				M	M^T		M^T				M^T						M^T	
	Importance of Animals & Birds	2							M^T				M^T							
	Animal Experimentation......	3							F				F							
1923	Humane Treatment&Protection	1	M^T			M				M^T			M^T				M^T		M^T	
	Importance of Animals & Birds	2	M^T							M^T		M	M^T				M^T			
	Animal Experimentation......	3	F										F						F	

M = Mandatory. F = Forbidden. M^T = Mandatory with a time specification. (Minimum number of minutes or periods.)

ELEMENTARY SCHOOLS IN EACH OF THE FORTY-EIGHT STATES, 1903, 1913, 1923

	Massachusetts	Michigan	Minnesota	Mississippi	Missouri	Montana	Nebraska	Nevada	New Hampshire	New Jersey	New Mexico	New York	North Carolina	North Dakota	Ohio	Oklahoma	Oregon	Pennsylvania	Rhode Island	South Carolina	South Dakota	Tennessee	Texas	Utah	Vermont	Virginia	Washington	West Virginia	Wisconsin	Wyoming	
1						M^T															M^T		M^T				M^T			M^T	**8**
2								M^T																							**1**
3	**F**																				**F**						**F**				**3**
																															12
1		M							M					M^T		M^T		M			M^T		M^T				M^T		M	M^T	**15**
2		M						M^T								M^T													M		**6**
3	**F**															F		F			F						F				**7**
																															28
1		M										M		M^T		M^T	M^T	M			M^T		M^T				M^T		M^T	M^T	**17**
2		M						M^T				M				M^T	M^T												M^T		**11**
3	**F**															F		F			F						F				**8**
																															36

California, Maine, South Dakota, Texas, Washington, and Wyoming required instruction in each of the three years, the legal provisions remaining practically unchanged. California required instruction in "humane education"; South Dakota and Wyoming prescribed "a system of humane treatment of animals." Texas provided that

> suitable instruction shall be given in the primary grades once each week regarding kindness to animals of the brute creation and the protection of birds and their nests and eggs.

Washington required that

> not less than ten minutes each week must be devoted to the systematic teaching of kindness to not only our domestic animals but to all living creatures.

Maine, in 1903 and 1913, required instruction in "the principles of kindness to birds and animals"; in 1923 instruction is to be given

> in correlation with other studies of the school curriculum the great principles of humanity as illustrated by kindness to birds and animals and regard for all factors which contribute to the well being of man.

In Colorado in 1903 and 1913,

> The school boards . . . shall cause to be given in each school week two lessons of not less than ten minutes duration each on the subject of humane treatment to animals.

Montana in 1903 required that

> Instruction shall be given in . . . a system of humane treatment of animals as embodied in the laws of Montana. Such instruction to consist of, at least, two (2) lessons of not less than ten minutes each per week. The principal or teacher in every school shall certify in each of his or her reports that such instruction has been given in the school under his or her control.

South Dakota and Wyoming likewise required that the instruction give special emphasis to the laws of the state pertaining to humaneness. Provision for the teaching of

> kindness and justice to and humane treatment and protection of animals and birds and the important part they fulfil in the economy of nature,

was found in Michigan in 1913 and 1923 and in Florida and Kentucky in 1923. Essentially the same provision was found in Delaware, Illinois, Oklahoma, and Wisconsin in 1913 and 1923, and in Alabama, New York, and Oregon in 1923. In addition to the provisions just indicated, Michigan, Kentucky, and Florida have the following:

> For the purpose of lessening crime and raising the standard of good citizenship, and inculcating the spirit of humanity, such humane education shall be given in the public schools as shall include the kind and just treatment of horses, dogs, cats, birds and all other animals.

In Oregon birds are not specifically mentioned but there is this added provision:

> They shall be taught the true relation of the human to the animal life, the value of life, and the cowardice of needless killing or any act of cruelty to man or beast, inculcating a love for truth, justice, and that beautiful generosity that makes the strong supporters, instead of oppressors, of the weak.

North Dakota in 1913 and 1923 prescribed

> instruction in the humane treatment of animals; such instruction shall be oral and shall consist of not less than two lessons of ten minutes each per week.

The Pennsylvania law in 1913 and 1923 read,

> Instruction in humane education shall be given to all pupils up to and including the fourth grade and need not exceed half an hour each week during the whole school term. No cruel experiment on any living creature shall be permitted in any public school of this commonwealth.

In another section of the law we find, for 1913, required instruction in

> a system of humane education which shall include kind treatment of horses, birds and other animals.

In 1923 the required instruction is in "the humane treatment of birds and animals." In New Hampshire in 1913 the local school board

> shall see that a well prescribed reading course dealing with the principles of the humane treatment of the lower animals

> shall be included in the ordinary instruction in reading or otherwise.

In New Hampshire a law approved April 8, 1921, prescribed a reading course on "the humane treatment of live animals" which was, apparently, rendered void by a law approved April 14, 1921.[1]

Time specifications are to be found in most of the states which require the teaching of this subject.

In Delaware 1913, Illinois and Oklahoma 1913 and 1923, Florida, Kentucky, and Maine 1923 it was

> not less than one-half hour of each week,

it being optional with the teacher, in Florida, Kentucky, and Illinois, whether the instruction be given in a consecutive half-hour or in shorter periods through the week; in Alabama 1923,

> twenty minutes or more each week;

in Montana 1903, Colorado 1903 and 1913, North Dakota 1913 and 1923, and Wyoming 1903, 1913, and 1923,

> not less than two lessons of ten minutes each per week;

in Oregon in 1923,

> not less than one-quarter hour each week,

and

> it shall be optional with each teacher whether it shall be a consecutive half-hour [*sic*] or shorter periods daily;

in Maine 1903 and 1913, South Dakota and Washington 1903, 1913, and 1923,

> not less than ten minutes each week.

In Wisconsin, 1923, it was

> not less than thirty minutes in each month.

In Texas 1903, 1913, and 1923, it was

> at least once each week.

Pennsylvania in 1923 stipulated that the instruction

> need not exceed half an hour each week.

[1] Laws 1921, p. 114, Ch. 85, Part I, Sec 5, Subsec. 3. Laws 1921, p. 230, Ch. 125, Sec. 2.

In New York,

> Such instruction shall be for such period of time during each school year as the Board of Regents may prescribe and may be joined with work in literature, reading, language, nature study or ethnology. Such weekly instruction may be divided into two or more periods. A school district shall not be entitled to participate in the public school money on account of any school subject to the provisions of this section if the instruction required hereby is not given therein.

Florida, Kentucky and Michigan make it optional with the teacher whether such teaching shall be through humane reading, stories, narratives of daily incidents or illustrations taken from personal experience. Illinois had essentially the same provision; and Delaware in 1913 provided,

> It shall be optional with each teacher whether it shall be a consecutive half-hour or a few minutes daily, or whether such teaching shall be through humane reading, daily incidents, stories, personal example or in connection with nature-study or recitations or quotations bearing upon these virtues memorized by the pupil. The memorizing and reciting by each pupil to the teacher of quotations or a declamation of not less than fifty words, and upon these subjects, shall be equivalent to and take the place of four weeks' requirements named in this Section.

In a number of states, including Alabama, Florida, Illinois, Kentucky, Michigan, Montana, and Wyoming, the principal or teacher is required to certify in his report that this instruction has been given.

IMPORTANCE OF ANIMALS AND BIRDS

The teaching of the importance and usefulness of animals and birds was prescribed in one state in 1903, in six in 1913, and in eleven in 1923.

1903	1913	1923
		Alabama
	Delaware	
		Florida
		Idaho
	Illinois	Illinois
Nevada		Kentucky
	Michigan	Michigan
	Nevada	Nevada

	New York
Oklahoma	Oklahoma
	Oregon
Wisconsin	Wisconsin

Wherever required it is, except in two states, included in the same provision as humane treatment and protection. Idaho and Nevada are the two exceptions. Idaho in 1923 required instruction to be given to all school children concerning

> the usefulness of insectivorous, song and innocent birds in the destruction of insects and pests that destroy plant life. It shall be their duty to inform school children of the destructiveness of the common house cat to bird life, and of the necessity of protecting the same against the destructiveness of the said common house cat.

In Nevada in 1903,

> It is hereby made the duty of each and every teacher in the public schools of this State to give oral instruction, at least once a month to all children attending such schools relative to the preservation of song-birds, fish and game; and to read or cause to be read to such children at least twice during each school year the Fish and Game Laws of the State of Nevada. No teacher shall be entitled to receive any portion of the public school moneys as compensation for services unless such teacher shall have complied with the provisions of this Act.

In 1913 and 1923, instead of reading the law, it was to be explained; and in 1923 the penalty clause was omitted. Illinois and Michigan in 1913 and 1923, and Alabama, Florida, Kentucky, and Oregon in 1923, prescribed instruction regarding

> the important part they fulfil in the economy of nature;

Oklahoma and Wisconsin in 1913 and 1923,

> their lives, habits and usefulness and the important part they are intended to fulfil in the economy of nature;

Delaware in 1913,

> their important part in the economy of nature;

and New York in 1923,

> the importance of the part they play in the economy of nature.

ANIMAL EXPERIMENTATION

Vivisection and animal experimentation were forbidden in three states in 1903, seven in 1913, and eight in 1923.

1903	1913	1923
		Alabama
	Delaware	
	Illinois	Illinois
		Maine
Massachusetts	Massachusetts	Massachusetts
	Oklahoma	Oklahoma
	Pennsylvania	Pennsylvania
South Dakota	South Dakota	South Dakota
Washington	Washington	Washington

No experiments were permitted upon "any living creature" in Alabama and Oklahoma; "upon live animals to demonstrate facts in physiology," in South Dakota; "upon any living creature for the purpose of demonstration in any study," in Delaware and Illinois. "No cruel experiment on any living creature" was allowed in Pennsylvania.

The law in Massachusetts reads,

> No person shall, in the presence of a pupil in any public school, practice vivisection, or exhibit a vivisected animal. Dissection of dead animals or any portions thereof in such schools shall be confined to the class room and to the presence of pupils engaged in the study to be promoted thereby, and shall in no case be for the purpose of exhibition. Violation of this section shall be punished by a fine of not less than ten nor more than fifty dollars.

Provisions somewhat similar to those in Massachusetts are to be found in Washington and Illinois. In Maine,

> No person in any of the schools of the state supported wholly or in part by public money, shall practice vivisection or perform any experiment upon a living animal, or exhibit to any pupil in such school an animal which has been vivisected or experimented upon. Whoever wilfully violates the provisions of this act shall be punished by a fine of not less than ten nor more than twenty-five dollars, and if the person found guilty of such violation is a teacher in any of the said schools, the state superintendent of schools shall revoke the certificate of said teacher.

In Washington,

> No teacher or other person employed in any school in the state of Washington, except a medical or dental school, shall practice vivisection upon any vertebrate animal in the presence of any pupil in said school, or any child or minor there present; nor in such presence shall exhibit any vertebrate animal upon which vivisection has been practiced.

In Illinois,

> No animal provided by, nor killed in the presence of any pupil of a public school, shall be used for dissection in such school, and in no case shall dogs or cats be killed for such purpose.

SUMMARY

The three items under humaneness show an increase of twenty-four prescriptions in twenty years; from twelve to thirty-six. If these three subdivisions had been combined there would have been ten in 1903, seventeen in 1913, and twenty in 1923, an increase for the twenty years of ten prescriptions; which is, doubtless, more nearly in accord with the change which has actually taken place. The results as here classified are summarized in Table XI.

TABLE XI

SUMMARY OF CURRICULAR PRESCRIPTIONS IN HUMANENESS SHOWING INCREASE 1903–1923

Item	Number of States in Which Prescribed			Increase		
	1903	1913	1923	1903 to 1913	1913 to 1923	1903 to 1923
Humane Treatment and Protection of Animals and Birds....	8	15	17	7	2	9
Importance of Animals and Birds	1	6	11	5	5	10
Animal Experimentation.......	3	7	8	4	1	5
Total Number of Prescriptions..	12	28	36	16	8	24

This table is based upon Table X.
The items are arranged according to the number of states which had the prescription in 1923.
Animal Experimentation.—The "prescriptions" were all prohibitive.

CHAPTER VII

LEGISLATIVE PROVISIONS CONCERNING THE TEACHING OF "FUNDAMENTAL" SUBJECTS

The "fundamentals" or "fundamental subjects" will be understood to include

1. Arithmetic	4. Penmanship
2. English	5. Reading
3. Geography	6. Spelling

Arithmetic includes also "oral arithmetic," "written arithmetic," "mental arithmetic," and "numbers." *English* includes "grammar" or "English grammar," "language" or "English language," "composition" or "English composition," "language lessons" or "English language lessons," "oral and written English," "primary language," and "elementary English." *Geography* includes "elementary geography," "modern geography," and geography of the state. *Penmanship* is occasionally "handwriting" and more frequently "writing." *Reading,* in two or three states, is referred to as "reading in English." *Spelling* is almost as frequently called "orthography."

In view of the persistent adverse criticism of "fads and frills" in the school program it is, perhaps, a little surprising to learn that the fundamental subjects are not the ones about which the people's representatives have exhibited most concern. These subjects are directly and specifically required to be taught in only three-fourths of the states; and even this number is obtained only by a liberal interpretation of the law.

Table XII shows that there are nine states which have not prescribed any of the fundamental subjects in any of the years covered by this study:

Delaware	Minnesota	Oregon
Maine	Missouri	Rhode Island
Michigan	New Hampshire	Utah

There has been a slight increase in the number of prescriptions

TABLE XII CURRICULAR PRESCRIPTIONS IN "FUNDAMENTAL" SUBJECTS FOR 1903, 1913,

Year	Subject or Activity		Alabama	Arizona	Arkansas	California	Colorado	Connecticut	Delaware	Florida	Georgia	Idaho	Illinois	Indiana	Iowa	Kansas	Kentucky	Louisiana	Maine	Maryland
1903	Arithmetic	1	M	M		M	M	M		M			M	M	M	M	M	M		M
	English	2	M	M		M	M	M		M			M	M	M	M	M	M		M
	Geography	3	M	M		M	M	M		M			M	M	M	M	M	M		M
	Penmanship	4	M	M		M	M	M		M			M	M	M	M	M	M		M
	Reading	5	M	M		M	M	M		M			M	M	M	M	M	M		M
	Spelling	6	M	M		M	M	M		M			M	M	M	M	M	M		M
1913	Arithmetic	1	M			M	M	M		M	M	M	M	M	M	M	M	M		M
	English	2	M			M	M	M		M	M	M	M	M	M	M	M	M		M
	Geography	3	M			M	M	M		M	M	M	M	M	M	M	M	M		M
	Penmanship	4	M			M	M	M		M	M	M	M	M	M	M	M	M		M
	Reading	5	M			M	M	M		M	M	M	M	M	M	M	M	M		M
	Spelling	6	M			M	M	M		M	M	M	M	M	M	M	M	M		M
1923	Arithmetic	1	M		M	M	M	M		M	M	M		M	M	M	M	M		M
	English	2	M		M	M	M	M		M	M	M		M	M	M	M	M		M
	Geography	3	M		M	M	M	M		M	M	M		M	M	M	M	M		M
	Penmanship	4	M		M	M	M	M		M	M	M		M	M	M	M	M		M
	Reading	5	M		M	M	M	M		M	M	M		M	M	M	M	M		M
	Spelling	6	M		M	M	M	M		M	M	M		M	M	M	M	M		M

M = Mandatory. M^T = Mandatory with a time specification. (Minimum number of

THE PUBLIC ELEMENTARY SCHOOLS IN EACH OF THE FORTY-EIGHT STATES 1923

	Massachusetts	Michigan	Minnesota	Mississippi	Missouri	Montana	Nebraska	Nevada	New Hampshire	New Jersey	New Mexico	New York	North Carolina	North Dakota	Ohio	Oklahoma	Oregon	Pennsylvania	Rhode Island	South Carolina	South Dakota	Tennessee	Texas	Utah	Vermont	Virginia	Washington	West Virginia	Wisconsin	Wyoming	
1	M			M		M		M			M	M	M	M	M	M		M		M	M	M	M		M	M	M	M	M		33
2	M			M		M		M			M	M	M	M	M	M		M		M	M	M	M		M	M	M	M	M		33
3	M			M		M		M			M	M	M	M	M	M		M		M	M	M	M		M	M	M	M	M		33
4	M					M		M			M	M	M	M	M	M		M		M	M	M	M		M	M	M	M	M		32
5	M			M		M		M			M	M	M	M	M	M		M		M	M	M	M		M	M	M	M	M		33
6	M			M		M		M			M	M	M	M	M	M		M		M	M	M	M		M	M	M	M	M		33
																															197
1	M			M		M		M		M	M	M	M	M	M	M		M		M	M	M	M		M	M	M	M	M	M	36
2	M			M		M		M		M	M	M	M	M	M	M		M		M	M	M	M		M	M	M	M	M	M	36
3	M			M		M		M		M	M	M	M	M	M	M		M		M	M	M	M		M	M	M	M	M	M	36
4	M			M		M		M		M	M	M	M	M[T]	M	M		M		M	M	M	M		M	M	M	M	M	M	36
5	M			M		M		M		M	M	M	M	M	M	M		M		M	M	M	M		M	M	M	M	M	M	36
6	M			M		M		M		M	M	M	M	M	M	M		M		M	M	M	M		M	M	M	M	M	M	36
																															216
1	M			M		M	M	M		M	M	M	M	M	M	M		M		M	M	M	M		M	M	M		M	M	36
2	M			M		M	M	M		M	M	M	M	M	M	M		M		M	M	M	M		M	M	M		M	M	36
3	M			M		M	M	M		M	M	M	M	M	M	M		M		M	M	M	M		M	M	M		M	M	36
4	M			M		M	M	M		M	M	M	M	M[T]	M	M		M		M	M	M	M		M	M	M		M	M	36
5	M			M		M	M	M		M	M	M	M	M	M	M		M		M	M	M	M		M	M	M		M	M	36
6	M			M		M	M	M		M	M	M	M	M	M	M		M		M	M	M	M		M	M	M		M	M	36
																															216

minutes or periods.)

in this group of subjects during the twenty years but it is not marked and there have been few important changes. Arkansas, Georgia, Idaho, Nebraska, New Jersey, and Wyoming, for which no prescriptions were found in 1903, all had such prescriptions in 1923. On the other hand, Arizona, Illinois, and West Virginia which required these subjects in 1903 did not do so in 1923. Arizona has placed full responsibility upon the State Board of Education

> to prescribe and enforce a course of study in the common schools of the state.

In West Virginia

> the state board of education shall prescribe minimum standards of the courses of study to be offered in the elementary schools, high schools. . . .

Other states have increased the authority of their state educational board of control regarding the course of study without eliminating the legal mandate that these subjects be taught.

No single formula has been followed in the different states in creating the obligation to teach the fundamentals. Sometimes the responsibility to see that it is done is placed upon the state board of education, sometimes upon the county board, sometimes upon the local board, sometimes upon the teacher. Sometimes the mandate reads that these subjects "shall be taught" in every school district; sometimes the "instruction must be given"; sometimes "the courses of study in the elementary school shall embrace"; sometimes the law applies to private as well as public schools. New York in 1903, Colorado in 1923, Idaho and New Jersey in 1913 and 1923, and Iowa in all three years placed the obligation upon the parent or other person having the care of children to see that they receive instruction in these subjects. For example, the provision in New Jersey is

> Every parent, guardian, or other person having custody and control of a child between the ages of seven and sixteen years, shall cause such child regularly to attend a day school in which at least reading, writing, spelling, English grammar, arithmetic and geography are taught in the English language by a competent teacher, or to receive equivalent instruction elsewhere than at school.

It may be contended that this is not a legal obligation resting upon the public schools; and yet it is hard to imagine responsible public school administrators refusing to furnish instruction which children are required to have. In this study such provisions have been considered mandatory. There are several instances where the obligation is established only through adopted textbooks which are required to be used. This was the situation in Alabama in 1903 and 1913; in Georgia in 1913 and 1923, and in Nevada in 1903, 1913, and 1923. It was also the case with respect to reading in North Carolina in 1903 and penmanship in Mississippi in 1913 and 1923. Adopted textbooks are, of course, required to be used in many other states. We are not here following the textbook requirements except to the extent necessary to get the complete record regarding the prescription of subjects. If there is a definite and specific mandate that a subject must be taught it has not been considered necessary to consult the law regarding textbooks. When there is no such direct mandate, however, the obligation to teach the subject may still be effectively created through provisions regarding the use of textbooks. The legislature of Nevada in 1901 adopted a series of textbooks for the fundamental subjects.

> Said series of text-books shall be used in all the public schools of this state and no school shall receive its pro rata of public school moneys unless such text-books are used. No change shall be made in said series except by an act of the Legislature; provided no such change in books shall be made more often than once in four years.

Georgia passed a law in 1903 creating a school-book commission to adopt a uniform series which was to be in use in all the common schools of the state within sixty days after January 1st, 1904. This law was in force in 1913. It provided that the uniform series of books

> shall include the following elementary branches of an English education only, to wit: Orthography, reading, writing, arithmetic, geography, English language lessons, English grammar . . . . The books adopted under the provisions of the act shall be used to the exclusion of all others on the same subject in all the public common schools of the State; provided that supplementary readers may be used in any of the common schools of the State, but even supplementary readers shall not be used until after the regular readers prescribed have been completed.

These provisions, reinforced by amendment, were also found in 1923. In Mississippi in 1903

> The branches of study upon which teachers are required to be examined constitute the curriculum of the free public schools.

Penmanship is not mentioned among the subjects required for the teachers' examination nor is a "textbook" in it prescribed for use. In 1913 and 1923 "writing" is included among the branches for which a textbook must be provided for use in the public schools of the state. The intent of the law in Nebraska is somewhat vague. The county board may establish a course of study with the advice and consent of the state superintendent. "This course of study shall apply only to rural schools and shall include" among other subjects the fundamentals. But in another article, dealing with free public high schools, the following provision is found:

> The course of study for the first eight grades in common schools shall be composed of the following subjects: Agriculture, bookkeeping, civics, drawing, arithmetic, English composition, geography, grammar, history, mental arithmetic, orthography, penmanship, physiology, reading. The state superintendent with these subjects for a foundation shall lay out a feasible course of study adapted to rural school conditions keeping in view the good of a thorough education for the child in these branches rather than to the completion of the course in a given number of years.

The fundamental subjects must be taught at least in the rural schools. New Hampshire nowhere definitely prescribes the teaching of the fundamental subjects but they are enumerated three separate times with an apparent implication that they are to be taught. The three provisions are as follows:

> (1) In the instruction of children in all schools, including private schools, in reading, writing, spelling, arithmetic, grammar, geography, physiology, history, civil government, music and drawing, the English language shall be used exclusively, both for the purpose of instruction thereon and for purposes of general administration.[1]
>
> (2) A foreign language may be taught in elementary schools provided the course of study (or its equivalent) outlined by the state board of education in the common

[1] Laws of 1921, p. 125, Ch. 85, part II, Sec. 10, Subsec. 1.

English branches, that is, in reading, writing, spelling, arithmetic, grammar, geography, physiology, history, civil government, music and drawing, be not abridged but be taught in compliance with the law of the state.[2]

(3) The selectmen in each town shall assess an annual tax of three dollars and fifty cents on each thousand dollars of the value of the ratable estate taxable therein for the support of the public schools.

The sum so raised shall be appropriated to the sole purpose of maintaining public schools within the district for teaching reading, writing, English grammar, arithmetic, geography, and such other branches as are adapted to the advancement of the schools, including the purchase of fuel and other supplies, the making of occasional repairs upon schoolhouses, appurtenances, and furniture, and the conveyance of pupils to and from school as provided by law.[3]

From the foregoing it seems reasonable to assume that the lawmakers fully expected these subjects to be taught; nevertheless New Hampshire was not included in the tabulation. In North Dakota in 1913 and 1923,

> Each pupil in the common schools as they shall become sufficiently advanced to pursue the same, shall be required to devote at least fifteen minutes practice in writing each day during the school year.

This is the only instance of a specific time requirement applying exclusively to any of the fundamental subjects. California had in 1923 a blanket provision regarding time allotment which applies to the fundamental subjects and several others.

> Instructions must be given in the following branches in the several grades in which they may be required, viz: reading, writing, spelling, arithmetic, geography, language and grammar, with special reference to composition, history of the State of California, history of the United States with special reference to the history of the constitution of the United States; and the history of the reasons for the adoption of each of its provisions, the duties of citizenship, together with instruction in local civil government; elements of physiology and hygiene, with special reference to the injurious effects of tobacco, alcohol and narcotics on the human system; morals and manners. In the first six grades of the elementary schools, at least two-thirds of the pupil's time

[2] Laws of 1921, p. 125, Ch. 85, part II, Sec. 10, Subsec. 3.

[3] Laws of 1921, p. 146, Ch. 85, part VI, Secs. 1, 2.

> during each week shall be devoted to study and recitation of the subjects hereinbefore enumerated, and in the seventh and eighth grades at least twelve and one-half hours of the pupil's time each week shall be devoted to the study and recitation of such subjects.

In the time remaining physical training, nature study, music, drawing, elementary bookkeeping, humane education, and thrift must be taught. The next section contains the following unusual provision:

> Other studies may be authorized by the board of education of any county, city, or city and county, but such studies, if so authorized shall be in lieu of a corresponding number of such enumerated studies specified in the preceding section, and not in addition thereto.

In California in 1903 and 1913 the following provision was in force:

> County board of education may in districts having less than 100 census children confine the pupils to reading, writing, orthography, arithmetic, language and grammar, geography, history of United States and civil government, elements of physiology and hygiene and elementary bookkeeping until they have a practical knowledge of these subjects . . . and no pupils under the age of 15 years in any elementary school shall be required to do any home study.

The law in Tennessee in 1903 and 1913 was unique; it prescribed that certain subjects must be taught, it permitted certain others to be taught and then prohibited the teaching of any other subjects.

> There shall be two classes of district public schools, designated respectively Primary Schools and Secondary Schools. The course of study in the primary schools shall consist of five grades and the course of study in the secondary schools shall consist of eight grades—the first five grades in each being identical.
>
> In every primary school shall be taught orthography, reading, writing, arithmetic, grammar, geography, History of Tennessee, the constitution of Tennessee, History of the United States containing the Constitution of the United States, physiology and hygiene; vocal music and elocution, or the art of public speaking, may be taught therein, and no other branches shall be introduced. The directors of each school district, whenever the interests of the district shall require it, may establish and maintain therein one or

> more secondary schools. . . . In every secondary school shall be taught the following branches: Orthography, reading, writing, arithmetic, grammar, geography, History of Tennessee, the constitution of Tennessee, History of the United States, containing the Constitution of the United States, elementary geology of Tennessee, elementary principles of agriculture, elements of algebra, elements of plane geometry, elements of natural philosophy, bookkeeping, elementary physiology and hygiene, elements of civil government, and rhetoric or higher English. Practice shall be given in elocution or the art of public speaking. Vocal music may be taught, and no other branches shall be introduced.

In 1923 we find

> The elementary schools shall consist of the first eight grades of the public system. . . . The course of study in the elementary schools shall embrace the following subjects: Orthography, reading, writing, arithmetic, grammar, geography, history of Tennessee, containing the Constitution of Tennessee, history of the United States, elementary physiology and hygiene, and vocal music, drawing may be taught, and such kindred supplemental work as the County Board of Education may determine from time to time, and approved by the State Board of Education.

Vermont in its nine-year elementary course includes

> special instruction in the geography, history, constitution and principles of government of Vermont.

In New Jersey,

> For the elementary grades, a course in the geography, history and civics of New Jersey shall be provided, which course shall be prescribed by the Commissioner of Education, with the approval of the State Board of Education; and the course thus prescribed shall be required in all public elementary schools and shall be taken by all pupils in the grade in which it is given.

North Carolina, also, in addition to the general geography, requires instruction in the geography of the state.

In Nevada,

> The publishers, contracting and agreeing to furnish books for use in the State of Nevada under the provisions of this act, shall cause to be prepared a special map and a special supplement descriptive of Nevada for the geography adopted by said commission. The map and descriptive geography

of Nevada shall be revised every four years by the publishers.[4]

In 1903 "defining" was included among the required branches of the course of study in North Carolina, while Wisconsin required "orthoepy" in 1903 and 1913.

SUMMARY

The six subjects classified as fundamental are invariably included in the same section of the law. Prescriptions regarding them have undergone very little change. Time specifications and other special provisions to make sure that they receive proper attention are almost never resorted to. It is apparently assumed that they are adequately provided for. The results are summarized in Table XIII.

TABLE XIII

SUMMARY OF CURRICULAR PRESCRIPTIONS IN "FUNDAMENTAL" SUBJECTS SHOWING INCREASE 1903–1923

Item	Number of States in Which Prescribed			Increase		
	1903	1913	1923	1903 to 1913	1913 to 1923	1903 to 1923
Arithmetic	33	36	36	3	--	3
English	33	36	36	3	--	3
Geography	33	36	36	3	--	3
Penmanship	32	36	36	4	--	4
Reading	33	36	36	3	--	3
Spelling	33	36	36	3	--	3
Total Number of Prescriptions	197	216	216	19	--	19

This table is based upon Table XII.

[4] Revised Laws 1912, Vol. I, p. 982, Sec. 3402.

CHAPTER VIII

LEGISLATIVE PROVISIONS CONCERNING THE TEACHING OF RELIGIOUS AND ETHICAL SUBJECTS

The subjects classified as Religious and Ethical are

1. Sectarian Doctrine
2. Bible Reading
3. Social and Ethical Outcomes
4. Manners
5. Morals

The prescriptions for each of the three years are shown in Table XIV.

SECTARIAN DOCTRINE

The provisions listed under this heading include not only direct prohibitions against sectarian instruction and against the use of textbooks which are sectarian in character, but also prohibitions against sectarian control of public school money and against public support of sectarian schools. Some such prescription is to be found in all three years in thirty-eight states, with North Carolina in addition in 1903 and 1913. No provision was found in any of the three years in Connecticut, Iowa, Rhode Island, Vermont, Virginia, or West Virginia. New Jersey and Oregon had special limited provisions which will be given below but which were not included in the tabulation. There has been no significant development during the twenty-year period. Apparently the intention to keep public education non-sectarian has been, throughout, widespread and generally accepted. There is little uniformity in the wording of the law. Sometimes the provision is in the constitution where the expression that occurs most frequently is to the effect that the public school funds shall be kept "free from sectarian control"; sometimes the provision is in the statutes where the most common expression occurs in connection with the adoption of textbooks; "none of said textbooks shall contain anything of a partisan or sectarian character." Not infrequently provisions are to be found in both the constitution

ABLE XIV CURRICULAR PRESCRIPTIONS IN RELIGIOUS AND ETHICAL
EIGHT
1903, 1913,

Year	Subject or Activity		Alabama	Arizona	Arkansas	California	Colorado	Connecticut	Delaware	Florida	Georgia	Idaho	Illinois	Indiana	Iowa	Kansas	Kentucky	Louisiana	Maine	Maryland
1903	Sectarian Doctrine	1	F	F	F	F	F		F	F	F	F	F	F		F	F	F		F
	Social and Ethical Outcomes	2		M		M				M		M							M	
	Bible Reading	3									P			P	P	P				
	Manners	4		M		M								M						M
	Morals	5		M		M														
1913	Sectarian Doctrine	1	F	F	F	F	F		F	F	F	F	F	F		F	F	F		F
	Social and Ethical Outcomes	2				M			M	M		M	M						M	
	Bible Reading	3												P	P	P				
	Manners	4				M								M						M
	Morals	5				M														
1923	Sectarian Doctrine	1	F	F	F	F	F		F	F	F	F	F	F		F	F	F		F
	Social and Ethical Outcomes	2			M	M				M		M	M						M	
	Bible Reading	3	M						M		M			P	P	P			M	
	Manners	4				M								M						M
	Morals	5				M														

M=Mandatory. P=Permissive. F=Forbidden.

Subjects for the Public Elementary Schools in Each of the Forty-States

1923

	Massachusetts	Michigan	Minnesota	Mississippi	Missouri	Montana	Nebraska	Nevada	New Hampshire	New Jersey	New Mexico	New York	North Carolina	North Dakota	Ohio	Oklahoma	Oregon	Pennsylvania	Rhode Island	South Carolina	South Dakota	Tennessee	Texas	Utah	Vermont	Virginia	Washington	West Virginia	Wisconsin	Wyoming	
1	F	F	F	F	F	F	F	F	F		F	F	F	F	F	F		F		F	F	F	F	F			F		F	F	39
2	M					M							M	M			M				M			M			M	M			14
3	M			P						P				P		P					P										10
4	M																			M					M						7
5																			M	M											4
																															74
1	F	F	F	F	F	F	F	F	F		F	F	F	F	F	F		F		F	F	F	F	F			F		F	F	39
2	M					M							M	M		M	M				M			M			M		M		16
3	M			P						P				P		P		M			P										10
4	M																			M					M						6
5			M																M	M						M					5
																															76
1	F	F	F	F	F	F	F	F	F		F	F		F	F	F		F		F	F	F	F	F			F		F	F	38
2	M					M					M		M	M		M	M				M						M		M		16
3	M			P						M				P		P		M			P	M									15
4	M			M							M									M					M						8
5			M	M							M								M	M						M					7
																															84

and the statutes. Some of the provisions in force in 1923 will be given; in most cases these provisions were practically the same in 1903; there has been very little change in any given state.

Arizona, California, Colorado, Idaho, Montana, Nebraska, Nevada, South Dakota, Wisconsin, and Wyoming have constitutional provisions which prohibit the teaching of sectarian tenets or doctrines in such parts of the educational system as would always include the elementary schools. For example, in Arizona

> No sectarian instruction shall be imparted in any school or state educational institution that may be established under this constitution.

In Idaho,

> No sectarian or religious tenets or doctrines shall ever be taught in the public schools.

In California,

> Nor shall any sectarian or denominational doctrine be taught or instruction thereon be permitted, directly or indirectly, in any of the common schools of this state.

Similar provisions, by statutory enactment, are to be found in Mississippi, New Mexico, Oklahoma, South Carolina, Kentucky, and Utah. Kentucky has

> No books or other publications of a sectarian, infidel or immoral character, shall be used or distributed in any common school, nor shall any sectarian doctrines be taught therein;

and Utah,

> It shall be unlawful to teach in any of the district schools of this State, while in session, any atheistic, infidel, sectarian, religious, or denominational doctrine and all such schools shall be free from sectarian control.

Kansas has a statute forbidding the teaching of sectarian or religious doctrine in cities of the first and second class, and also the constitutional prohibition,

> No religious sect or sects shall ever control any part of the common school or university funds of the state.

Massachusetts, Minnesota, and New York in their constitutions forbid support by public money of educational institutions in which denominational tenets are taught. It is common to find in the law dealing with the adoption of textbooks this clause:

> none of said textbooks shall contain anything of a partisan or sectarian character.

This was the case in Indiana, Tennessee, and Texas; it was substantially the case in Alabama, Georgia, and Maryland. In Arkansas,

> No teacher employed in any of the common schools shall permit sectarian books to be used as a reading or textbook in the school under his care.

In New Hampshire,

> No books shall be introduced into the public schools calculated to favor any particular religious sect or political party.

In Washington the board of directors shall have the power and duty

> to exclude from schools and school libraries all books, tracts, papers and other publications of an immoral or pernicious tendency.[1]

Washington also has the constitutional provision,

> All schools maintained or supported wholly or in part by the public funds shall be forever free from sectarian control or influence.

Delaware, Florida, Illinois, Louisiana, Missouri, North Dakota, Pennsylvania, and Ohio have constitutional provisions which forbid the use of public school moneys for the support of sectarian schools. For example, in Louisiana,

> No public funds shall be used for the support of any private or sectarian school.

In Pennsylvania,

> No money raised for the support of the common schools of the Commonwealth shall be appropriated to or used for the support of any sectarian school.

In Ohio,

> No religious or other sect or sects shall ever have any exclusive right to, or control of any part of the school funds of this state.

[1] Remington's Compiled Statutes 1922, Vol. II, p. 726, Sec. 4776, ninth.

Michigan has a statutory provision of similar import:

> No school district shall apply any of the moneys received by it from the primary school interest fund or from any and all other sources for the support and maintenance of any school of a sectarian character, whether the same be under the control of any religious society or made sectarian by the school district board.

The foregoing will serve to give a fair idea of the situation in this field, not only as it is now but as it has been during the past two decades. Several of the states have other provisions besides those already indicated which it has not seemed necessary to present. A few additional provisions should be noted. North Carolina in 1903 and 1913 had the prohibition regarding partisan or sectarian subject matter in textbooks but nothing of the sort was found in 1923. In Massachusetts in 1903 and 1913 the constitution provided, regarding public school moneys, that

> such moneys shall never be appropriated to any religious sect for the maintenance exclusively of its own schools.

There was a statutory provision in all three years which prohibited the school committee from purchasing or using school books calculated to favor

> the tenets of any particular religious sect.

The following statute was in force in Louisiana in 1923 and a similar provision in 1903 and 1913:

> The school boards of the several parishes of this State are prohibited from entering into any contract, agreement, understanding or combination, tacitly or expressly, directly or indirectly, with any church, monastic or other order or association of any religious sect or denomination whatsoever, with the representatives thereof or with any person or corporation conducting a school which solicits patronage from those of any particular religious faith, affiliation or persuasion, for the purpose of running any public school or schools of this State together, in connection, or in combination with any private or parochial school, or other institution of learning which may be under the control or management of any church, monastic or other religious order or association of any religious sect or denomination whatsoever, or under the control of any person or corporation conducting a school

> which solicits patronage especially from those of any particular religious faith, affiliation or persuasion. [2]

Arizonia, New Mexico, and Oklahoma were territories in 1903. Arizona and Oklahoma prohibited by statute the teaching of sectarian doctrine, and New Mexico did the same "in any of the public schools of the city or town." When they became states each of the three included some sort of prescription in the constitution. Maine, in the law dealing with Bible reading, provided in 1923 that

> there shall be no denominational or sectarian comment or teaching;

no provision was found in the earlier years. New Jersey had the following provision in all three years:

> No religious service or exercise, except the reading of the Bible and the repeating of the Lord's Prayer, shall be held in any school receiving any portion of the moneys appropriated for the support of public schools. [3]

Oregon in 1923 enacted the following:

> After the passage of this act it shall be unlawful for any teacher in any public school in the state of Oregon to wear in said school, and while engaged in the performance of his or her duty, any dress or garb of any religious order, sect or denomination. [4]

BIBLE READING

There were ten states in 1903 with prescriptions regarding the reading of the Bible in the public school, ten in 1913, and fifteen in 1923. Of these prescriptions one in 1903 was mandatory, two in 1913, and eight in 1923. The development is striking because it is entirely in the direction of mandatory legislation. There has been no increase in the number of permissive laws. The seven states, Indiana, Iowa, Kansas, Mississippi, North Dakota, Oklahoma, and South Dakota, which had permissive laws in 1923 had the same laws in 1903 and 1913. Georgia had a permissive law in 1903, no law in 1913, and a mandatory law in 1923. New Jersey had a permissive law in 1903 and 1913 and a mandatory law in

[2] Wolff's Revised Laws of 1904, Vol. I, p. 610 (Acts of 1902, p. 410, No. 214, Sec. 14).

[3] Acts of 1903 (Second Special Session), p. 45, Ch. 1, Sec. 114.

[4] Laws of 1923, p. 19, Ch. 11.

1923. Massachusetts had the same mandatory law in all three years. Pennsylvania had a mandatory law in 1913 and 1923. Alabama, Delaware, Maine, and Tennessee each had a mandatory law in 1923.

The permissive laws are brief and provide that the Bible shall not be excluded from the public schools or that the reading of the Holy Scriptures shall not be prohibited or that the Bible may be read without comment. In Kansas, Oklahoma, and South Dakota the provision is found in connection with the prohibition regarding sectarian doctrine. In Mississippi it is a constitutional provision. In Iowa,

> The Bible shall not be excluded from any public school or institution in the state, nor shall any child be required to read it contrary to the wishes of his parent or guardian.

In North Dakota,

> The Bible shall not be deemed a sectarian book. It shall not be excluded from any public school. It may at the option of the teacher be read in school without sectarian comment, not to exceed ten minutes daily. No pupil shall be required to read it or to be present in the school room during the reading thereof, contrary to the wishes of his parents or guardians or other person having him in charge.

In New Jersey the following provision, in force in all three years, was supplemented by a mandatory law in 1923.

> No religious service or exercise, except the reading of the Bible and the repeating of the Lord's Prayer, shall be held in any school receiving any portion of the moneys appropriated for the support of public schools.

The mandatory laws, with the possible exception of that of Maine, require that the Bible be read every school day. Five states specify the minimum amount; five verses in Delaware and New Jersey, ten verses in Pennsylvania and Tennessee, one chapter in Georgia. In four states, Delaware, New Jersey, Pennsylvania, and Tennessee, the reading must be done at the opening of the school day. In Massachusetts, in all three years,

> A portion of the Bible shall be read daily in the public schools, without written note or oral comment, but a pupil whose parent or guardian informs the teacher in writing that he has conscientious scruples against it, shall not be

> required to read from any particular version, or to take any personal part in the reading.

Pennsylvania in 1913 and 1923 required that

> At least ten verses from the Holy Bible shall be read or caused to be read, without comment, at the opening of each and every public school, upon each and every school day by the teacher in charge: Provided, That where any teacher has other teachers under and subject to direction, then the teacher exercising this authority shall read the Holy Bible, or cause it to be read, as herein directed. If any school teacher, whose duty it shall be to read the Holy Bible, or cause it to be read, as directed in this act, shall fail or omit so to do, said school teacher shall, upon charges preferred for such failure or omission, and proof of the same, before the governing board of the school district, be discharged.

Tennessee in 1923 had this same law, practically verbatim, with the added provision that

> the teacher does not read the same chapter more than twice during the same session.

Georgia permits an individual pupil to be excused from hearing the Bible read upon written request of parent or guardian, one such request being sufficient to cover a school year, and provides that

> the Bible, including the Old and the New Testament, shall be read in all the schools of this State receiving State funds, and that not less than one Chapter shall be read at some appropriate time during each school day.

In New Jersey the reading is to be "from that portion of the Holy Bible known as the Old Testament." The law in Maine reads,

> To insure greater security in the faith of our fathers, to inculcate into the lives of the rising generation the spiritual values necessary to the well being of our and future civilizations, to develop those high moral and religious principles essential to human happiness, to make available to the youth of our land the book which has been the inspiration of the greatest masterpieces of literature, art and music and which have been the strength of the great men and women of the Christian era, there shall be, in all the public schools of the state, daily or at suitable intervals, readings from the scriptures with special emphasis upon the Ten Commandments,

> the Psalms of David, the Proverbs of Solomon, the Sermon on the Mount and the Lord's Prayer. It is provided further, that there shall be no denominational or sectarian comment or teaching and each student shall give respectful attention but shall be free in his own forms of worship.

In Alabama,

> All schools in this State that are supported in whole or in part by public funds are hereby required to have once every school day, readings from the Holy Bible. Teachers in making monthly reports shall show on the same that they have complied with this act, and superintendents of city schools in drawing public funds shall certify that each teacher under his supervision has complied with this act. Schools in the State subject to the provisions of this act shall not be allowed to draw public funds unless the provisions of this act are complied with, and the State Superintendent of Education is charged with the enforcement of the provisions hereof.

SOCIAL AND ETHICAL OUTCOMES

The term Social and Ethical Outcomes is here used to denote various virtues, attributes, and qualities the "teaching" of which was required in fourteen states in 1903, sixteen in 1913, and sixteen in 1923. A composite list of the qualities and habits desired would include the following:

Benevolence	Morality
Chastity	Morals
Cleanliness	Neatness
Economy	Obedience to parents
Frugality	Order
Gentility	Patriotism
Good behavior	Piety
Honesty	Politeness
Honor	Promptness
Humanity	Public spirit
Industry	Purity
Integrity	Refinement
Justice	Regard for others
Kindness	Respect for labor
Love of country	Sobriety
Manners	Temperance
Moderation	Truth
Moral courage	Truthfulness

A corresponding list to be avoided would include Falsehood, Idleness, Intemperance, Profanity, Vulgarity. Certain other objectives and outcomes are enumerated, such as "the true comprehension of the rights, duties and dignity of American citizenship," "their own responsibilities and duties as citizens," "the principles of free government" and "international peace." The legislation regarding this group of social and ethical outcomes has undergone comparatively little change. California, Florida, Idaho, Maine, Massachusetts, Montana, North Carolina, North Dakota, Oregon, South Dakota, and Washington have had laws throughout the period of this study which have remained practically the same. Arizona and West Virginia had laws in 1903 which had disappeared before 1913. The law in Utah which was mandatory in 1903 and 1913 had become permissive in 1923. Delaware had a law only in 1913; Illinois, Oklahoma and Wisconsin, in 1913 and 1923; Arkansas, and New Mexico, in 1923 only. The laws of Maine and Massachusetts are almost identical and reveal an early origin. In Maine,

> The president, professors and tutors of colleges, the preceptors and teachers of academies, and all other instructors of youth, in public or private institutions, shall use their best endeavors to impress on the minds of the children and youth committed to their care and instruction, the principles of morality and justice, and a sacred regard for truth; love of country, humanity and a universal benevolence; sobriety, industry and frugality; chastity, moderation and temperance; and all other virtues which ornament human society; and to lead those under their care, as their ages and capacities admit, into a particular understanding of the tendency of such virtues to preserve and perfect a republican constitution, secure the blessings of liberty, and to promote their future happiness; and the tendency of the opposite vices, to slavery, degradation and ruin.

Massachusetts places the obligation upon

> The president, professors and tutors of the university at Cambridge and of the several colleges, all preceptors and teachers of academies and all other instructors of youth.

In Washington,

> Attention must be given during the entire course to the cultivation of manners, and the fundamental principles of honesty, honor, industry and economy, to the laws of health,

> physical exercise, ventilation and temperature of the school room;

and also,

> It shall be the duty of all teachers to endeavor to impress on the minds of their pupils the principles of morality, truth, justice, temperance, humanity and patriotism; to teach them to avoid idleness, profanity and falsehood; to instruct them in the principles of free government, and to train them up to the true comprehension of the rights, duties and dignity of American citizenship.

California and Montana in all three years and Arizona in 1903 had laws essentially like the second provision just given for Washington, but did not include temperance and humanity. Washington did not include humanity in 1903. Oklahoma had the following law in 1913 and 1923, which is practically the same as Wisconsin's law in 1913 and 1923:

> In each and every public school, it shall be the duty of each and every teacher to teach morality, in the broadest meaning of the word, for the purpose of elevating and refining the character of school children up to the highest plane of life; that they may know how to conduct themselves as social beings in relation to each other, as respects right and wrong, and rectitude of life, and thereby lessen wrong-doing and crime.

North and South Dakota had identical laws in 1903. In South Dakota the law has not been changed. In North Dakota it was amended in 1911 by adding "international peace," a change worthy of note because of its exceptional character; we have here an apparent recognition by lawmakers, when dealing with instruction in the public schools, of a world which extends beyond the boundary of the United States.

> Moral instruction tending to impress upon the minds of pupils the importance of truthfulness, temperance, purity, public spirit, patriotism, international peace, respect for honest labor, obedience to parents and due deference for old age, shall be given by each teacher in the public schools.

North Dakota also has the following constitutional provision:

> In all schools instruction shall be given as far as practicable in those branches of knowledge that tend to impress upon the mind the vital importance of truthfulness, temperance,

purity, public spirit, and respect for honest labor of every kind.

In Florida,

> Every teacher is directed . . . to embrace every opportunity to inculcate, by precept and example, the principles of truth, honesty and patriotism and the practice of every christian virtue. To require the pupils to observe personal cleanliness, neatness, order, promptness and gentility of manners, to avoid vulgarity and profanity, and to cultivate in them habits of industry and economy, a regard for the rights and feelings of others, and their own responsibilities and duties as citizens.

In Idaho, every teacher

> shall keep himself or herself without reproach, and endeavor to impress upon the minds of the pupils the principles of truth, justice, morality, patriotism, and refinement, and to avoid idleness, falsehood, profanity, vulgarity and intemperance, give attention during every school term to the cultivation of manners.

In Oregon,

> A teacher's duty, while in charge of a school, shall be as follows . . . to create in their minds a desire for knowledge, principle, morality, politeness, cleanliness, and the preservation of physical health.

In Illinois in 1913 and 1923 and in Delaware in 1913 the provision was part of the law regarding humaneness and was substantially the same in the two states. In Illinois,

> It shall be the duty of every teacher of a public school in this State to teach to all the pupils thereof honesty, kindness, justice and moral courage for the purpose of lessening crime and raising the standard of good citizenship.

In West Virginia in 1903,

> All teachers, boards of education and other school officers are hereby charged with the duty of providing that moral training for the youth of this state which will contribute to securing good behavior and manners and furnish the state with exemplary citizens.

New Mexico in 1923 included among the branches to be taught

> the fundamental principles of common honesty, honor, industry and economy.

In Utah in 1903 and 1913 the following was in force:

> No atheistic, infidel, sectarian, religious or denominational doctrine shall be taught in any of the district schools of this state. Moral instruction tending to impress upon the minds of the pupils the importance of good manners, truthfulness, temperance, purity, patriotism and industry, shall be given in every district school, and all such schools shall be free from sectarian control.

This was amended in 1921 to read as follows:

> It shall be unlawful to teach in any of the district schools of this State, while in session, any atheistic, infidel, sectarian, religious or denominational doctrine and all such schools shall be free from sectarian control. Nothing in this Act shall be deemed to prohibit the giving of any moral instruction tending to impress upon the minds of the pupils the importance and necessity of good manners, truthfulness, temperance, purity, patriotism, and industry but such instruction shall be given in connection with the regular school work.[5]

The following was adopted in Arkansas in 1923:

> *Whereas,* training in morals and patriotism is important to child life and education, and to the welfare of the State, and
> *Whereas,* the prevalence and persistence of crime and immorality indicates a lack of such training in our present day citizenship, and
> *Whereas,* the present course of study for our State public schools does not provide especially for such training; therefore
> Be It Enacted by the General Assembly of the State of Arkansas:
> Section 1. That a course in morals, manners, patriotism, and business and professional integrity be, and is hereby, included in the course of study for the State public schools.
> Section 2. That the State Textbook Commission is hereby authorized to adopt suitable textbooks on such subjects, for use in the public schools.

MANNERS

No clear-cut line can be drawn between the manners and morals listed separately and the same terms included in social and ethical outcomes. At the extreme in one case we have them enumerated along with required branches of study such as read-

[5] Laws of 1921, p. 284, Ch. 95.

ing or arithmetic, as if they were to be taught as separate subjects; at the other, they are enumerated along with qualities such as truth and purity which are to be inculcated. Whether or not this betokens a distinction in the intent of the lawmakers is not evident and probably is not important. The law as framed in a few of the states can be classified only arbitrarily. Manners or good behavior was required in seven states in 1903, six in 1913, and eight in 1923. Indiana, Maryland, Massachusetts, South Carolina, and Vermont included "good behavior" in the prescribed course of study in all three years. California in 1913 and 1923 and New Mexico in 1923 included "morals and manners" in the course of study. California in all three years also had

> Instruction must be given in all grades of school and in all classes during the entire school course, in manners and morals.

Arizona in 1903 had

> Instruction must be given during the entire course in manners and morals.

Mississippi required "good manners" in 1923 in connection with a course in morality.

MORALS

Morals or morality was required to be taught in four states in 1903, three in 1913, and five in 1923. South Carolina included "morals" in the course of study in all three years along with good behavior. California provided for "morals" along with manners in all three years. New Mexico did the same in 1923. Arizona provided for "manners and morals" in 1903. In Rhode Island in all three years,

> Every teacher shall aim to implant and cultivate in the minds of all children committed to his care the principles of morality and virtue.

In Minnesota in 1913 and 1923,

> The teachers in all public schools shall give instruction in morals.
>
> Provision shall further be made for moral education in the public schools to be extended throughout the entire course.

In Virginia in 1913 and 1923,

> Such instruction shall be imparted by reading books and textbooks inculcating the virtues of a pure and noble life. The textbooks shall be selected as are other textbooks by the State Board of Education.

In Mississippi in 1923,

> The board of education is hereby directed to prepare or cause to be prepared a suitable course of instruction in the principles of morality and good manners to be used in all of the public schools of the state. Such course shall include what is known as the Mosaic Ten Commandments and may be graded and may be formulated with the idea that a certain amount of time will be devoted to it.
> Provided, that no doctrinal nor sectarian teaching shall be permitted in any public school in this state, and provided that no pupil shall be required to attend the course provided for herein when the parent or parents or guardian of said pupil shall so request in writing filed with the superintendent or teacher. When so prepared and published such a course shall be used in all the public schools of the state. It shall be the duty of the several county and city superintendents of schools to see that the provisions of this act are carried out. There are not to be any extra employees under this act, either state or county.

If "Social and Ethical Outcomes," "Manners," and "Morals" had been grouped under a single caption there would have been nineteen states with prescriptions in 1903, twenty-three in 1913, and twenty-three in 1923.

SUMMARY

Table XV shows that there has been very little increase in the number of prescriptions in this group during the twenty years. The gain was somewhat larger in the second decade. The most significant change is the increase in mandatory legislation regarding the reading of the Bible. Whether this growth has been due to a popular demand or to an aggressive campaign by a small zealous group is, of course, not evident from the law. The legal provisions found in connection with the subjects presented in this chapter illustrate with especial clearness a characteristic which is common to much of the legislation affecting the curriculum; namely, a tacit disregard of the laws of learning and an implicit faith in the efficacy, for character formation, of mere exposure to ideas. Those who promote the sort of legislation that is found, for example, in connection with Morals and with Social and Ethical Outcomes appear to be actuated by the assumption that desirable habits, attitudes, and ideals can, with certainty, be imparted by the written or spoken word.

TABLE XV

SUMMARY OF CURRICULAR PRESCRIPTIONS IN RELIGIOUS AND ETHICAL SUBJECTS SHOWING INCREASE 1903–1923

Item	Number of States in Which Prescribed			Increase		
	1903	1913	1923	1903 to 1913	1913 to 1923	1903 to 1923
Sectarian Doctrine	39	39	38	--	(−1)	(−1)
Social and Ethical Outcomes	14	16	16	2	--	2
Bible Reading	10	10	15	--	5	5
Manners	7	6	8	(−1)	2	1
Morals	4	5	7	1	2	3
Total Number of Prescriptions	74	76	84	2	8	10

This table is based upon Table XIV.
The items are arranged according to the number of states which had the prescription in 1923.
Sectarian Doctrine.—The "prescriptions" were all prohibitive.
Bible Reading.—Of the "prescriptions" in 1903, one was mandatory and nine were permissive; in 1913 two were mandatory and eight were permissive; in 1923 eight were mandatory and seven were permissive.

CHAPTER IX

LEGISLATIVE PROVISIONS CONCERNING THE TEACHING OF MISCELLANEOUS SUBJECTS

In this chapter seven miscellaneous subjects are considered:

1. Elementary Science
2. Algebra
3. Metric System
4. Forestry and Plant Life
5. Dictionary
6. Darwinism
7. Land Designation

Prescriptions of these subjects are not numerous, as may be seen from Table XVI. They show very little increase during the last twenty years. In addition to the seven items tabulated, mention should be made of a few which have been omitted. North Carolina in 1903 included "theory and practice of teaching" among the branches to be taught in the public schools. Colorado in 1903 and 1913 directed school boards to provide to have taught in the public schools the branches included in the examination for a teacher's certificate among which were "theory and practice of teaching and the school law of the state." In West Virginia in 1903,

> In the primary schools there shall be taught . . . general United States and state history . . . and in addition thereto the theory and art of teaching.

General history was also included among the required branches of study in 1913.

ELEMENTARY SCIENCE

Elementary science or nature study was prescribed in two states in 1903, four in 1913, and six in 1923. California in 1903 included "nature study" among the branches of study in which instruction must be given in the several grades as required but provided that the instruction might be "oral," no textbook being required to be purchased by the pupil; also, apparently the subject could be omitted in school districts of less than one hundred census children. In 1913 instruction in

> nature study with special reference to agriculture

was required under similar conditions. In 1923,

> instruction must be given in nature study with special reference to agriculture and animal and bird life.

Florida prescribed, in all three years, in the primary grades (first and second) such lessons in "nature study" as were provided in the county course of study; in the intermediate grades (third, fourth, fifth and sixth) "elementary science" and such lessons in "nature study" as were provided in the county course of study; and in the grammar grades (seventh and eighth) "science." North Dakota in 1913 and 1923 included "lessons in nature study" among the branches in which

> each teacher in the common schools shall teach pupils as they are sufficiently advanced to pursue the same.

Wyoming in 1913 and 1923 included "nature study" in the required course of study for the elementary schools. Alabama in 1923 required that "elementary science" be taught in every elementary school in the state. Mississippi in 1923 included "general science" in the curriculum of the free public schools where there were three or more teachers.

ALGEBRA

Maryland in 1903 prescribed that "algebra, bookkeeping and natural philosophy," in addition to a number of obviously elementary subjects, should be taught in every district school. South Carolina in all three years had algebra among the subjects which must be taught "as far as practicable" in every public school. Tennessee in 1903 and 1913 had two classes of district public schools, primary and secondary. The primary schools had five grades and the secondary schools eight; the first five grades being identical. The prescribed course of study for the secondary schools included the following branches in addition to those prescribed for the primary schools:

> elementary geology of Tennessee, elementary principles of agriculture, elements of algebra, elements of plane geometry, elements of natural philosophy, bookkeeping, . . . elements of civil government and rhetoric or higher English,[1]

[1] Shannon's Code of 1896, p. 420, Sec. 1454.

TABLE XVI CURRICULAR PRESCRIPTIONS IN MISCELLANEOUS SUBJECTS 1903, 1913,

Year	Subject or Activity		Alabama	Arizona	Arkansas	California	Colorado	Connecticut	Delaware	Florida	Georgia	Idaho	Illinois	Indiana	Iowa	Kansas	Kentucky	Louisiana	Maine	Maryland
1903	Elementary Science	1				M				M										
	Algebra	2																		M
	Metric System	3																		
	Forestry and Plant Life	4																		
	Dictionary	5																		
	Darwinism	6																		
	Land Designation	7			M															
1913	Elementary Science	1				M				M										
	Algebra	2																		
	Metric System	3																		
	Forestry and Plant Life	4																M		
	Dictionary	5																		
	Darwinism	6																		
	Land Designation	7			M															
1923	Elementary Science	1	M			M				M										
	Algebra	2			M															
	Metric System	3																		
	Forestry and Plant Life	4																		
	Dictionary	5			M															
	Darwinism	6																		
	Land Designation	7																		

M = Mandatory. F = Forbidden.

FOR PUBLIC ELEMENTARY SCHOOLS IN EACH OF THE FORTY-EIGHT STATES
1923

	Massachusetts	Michigan	Minnesota	Mississippi	Missouri	Montana	Nebraska	Nevada	New Hampshire	New Jersey	New Mexico	New York	North Carolina	North Dakota	Ohio	Oklahoma	Oregon	Pennsylvania	Rhode Island	South Carolina	South Dakota	Tennessee	Texas	Utah	Vermont	Virginia	Washington	West Virginia	Wisconsin	Wyoming	
1																															2
2																				M		M									3
3																								M							1
4																															-
5																															-
6																															-
7																															1
																															7
1														M																M	4
2																				M		M									2
3																								M							1
4																															1
5																															-
6																															-
7																															1
																															9
1				M										M																M	6
2				M																M											3
3																								M							1
4																						M									1
5																															1
6																F															1
7																															-
																															13

and also "elocution or the art of public speaking" which had been merely permissive in the primary school. Mississippi in 1923 provided that "elementary algebra" should be included in the curriculum of the free public schools where there were three or more teachers. Arkansas in 1923 included "elementary algebra" among the branches embraced in the regular work of the first eight grades of the public schools.

METRIC SYSTEM

Utah in all three years had a constitutional provision:

> The metric system shall be taught in the public schools of the State.

FORESTRY AND PLANT LIFE

In Louisiana in 1913,

> The State and parish boards of public education are directed to provide for proper courses of instruction by textbooks or lectures on the general subject of forestry in all the public schools of this State.

In Tennessee in 1923,

> The curriculum of every public school in this State shall include a study of forestry and plant life, which shall be taught therein, and which study shall include the names and varieties of trees grown in the State, their age of maturity, their value to the soil, to animals and birds, and when possible or practical, the children of such schools be given an object lesson in study of Forestry by one or more visits during each semi-annual session, to some conveniently located forests, and there instructed and taught by their respective teachers or some competent person selected for such purposes. Every pupil, unless excused by his or her teacher, shall be required to write at least one short essay or story during the session on forestry along such lines as the teacher may direct.
>
> It shall be the duty of the State Commissioner of Education, County Superintendent and City School Superintendent to see that this statute is enforced in the public schools of the State and its requirements are complied with and that this Act take effect from and after its passage, the public welfare requiring it. The correlation of the study of Forestry in connection with other studies in the public schools is ex-

plained as follows: An art lesson may be taught in the drawing of trees and plants, a composition lesson be taught in writing of trees and plants. A language and memory lesson be taught in knowledge gained by the observation and reading of books on trees and plants, so that the child may grow up with the knowledge of the value of Forestry.

DICTIONARY

Arkansas in 1923 included "dictionaries" among the subjects for which a uniform series of books must be adopted and which must be embraced in the regular work of the first eight grades.

DARWINISM

Oklahoma in 1923 had the provision that

> no copy-right shall be purchased nor textbook adopted that teaches the "Materialistic Conception of History" (i.e) the Darwin Theory of Creation *vs.* the Bible Account of Creation.

Florida in 1923 passed the following resolution:

> *Whereas,* the Constitution of the State of Florida expressly states in section 6 of the Declaration of Rights that, "No preference shall be given by law to any church, sect or mode of worship, and no money shall ever be taken from the public treasury directly or indirectly in aid of any church, sect or religious denomination, or in aid of any sectarian institution." And
> *Whereas,* The public schools and colleges of this State, supported in whole or in part by public funds, should be kept free from any teachings designed to set up and promulgate sectarian views, and should also be equally free from teachings designed to attack the religious beliefs of the public. Therefore, Be It Resolved by the House of Representatives, the Senate concurring: That it is the sense of the Legislature of the State of Florida that it is improper and subversive of the best interests of the people of this State for any professor, teacher or instructor in the public schools and colleges of this State, supported in whole or in part by public taxation, to teach or permit to be taught atheism, or agnosticism, or to teach as true Darwinism, or any other hypothesis that links man in blood relationship to any other form of life.[2]

[2] Acts and Resolutions, 1923, p. 506, House Concurrent Resolution No. 7.

LAND DESIGNATION

In Arkansas in 1903 and 1913,

> In addition to the branches now prescribed by law to be taught in the common schools of the state, it is hereby made the duty of the county examiner of the several counties of this state to examine all persons applying for examination and license to teach in such schools as to their knowledge and proficiency in the methods of designating and reading the survey of the lands of this State by ranges, townships, and sections and parts of sections and surveyed, platted and designated by the government of the United States, and no such applicant shall be authorized or licensed to teach in any of such schools unless found upon such examination proficient in the method of designating and reading land surveys, as in this act provided. It is hereby made the duty and specially imposed upon all persons teaching in the public schools of this State, to teach and impart the instructions here provided for whenever practicable to do so, and a willful neglect or failure to discharge the duties by this act imposed shall be deemed sufficient cause for the revocation of license to teach.

SUMMARY

Table XVII indicates that this group of subjects has not been regarded by our lawmakers as very important. Elementary Sci-

TABLE XVII

SUMMARY OF CURRICULAR PRESCRIPTIONS IN MISCELLANEOUS SUBJECTS SHOWING INCREASE 1903–1923

Item	Number of States in Which Prescribed			Increase		
	1903	1913	1923	1903 to 1913	1913 to 1923	1903 to 1923
Elementary Science	2	4	6	2	2	4
Algebra	3	2	3	(−1)	1	--
Metric System	1	1	1	--	--	--
Forestry and Plant Life	--	1	1	1	--	1
Dictionary	--	--	1	--	1	1
Darwinism	--	--	1	--	1	1
Land Designation	1	1	--	--	(−1)	(−1)
Total Number of Prescriptions	7	9	13	2	4	6

This table is based upon Table XVI.
Darwinism.—The "prescription" is a prohibition relating to textbook adoption.

ence shows the most growth. Doubtless the provisio[illegible] ing Darwinism are of greatest interest. Not as much was found as the writer had been led to expect from t[illegible] which has been given to various bills which have [illegible] legislatures in recent years. The provision in Florida [illegible] tion. That in Oklahoma would, apparently, not [illegible] teaching of Darwinism or the use of supplement [illegible] reference.

CHAPTER X

GENERAL SUMMARY OF THE FINDINGS

In the preceding eight chapters there have been presented the conditions which have been found to exist at each of three periods as regards legislative enactments directly affecting the curriculum of the public elementary school. The provisions have been presented with considerable detail but by no means exhaustively. The aim has been to portray fairly accurately the variety and scope of the provisions. This has been done through selected quotations, descriptions, and two series of tables. The first series of tables has shown for each of the three years, 1903, 1913, and 1923, the states which have prescribed each of the sixty items. The second series has been based upon the first and has shown a summary for each item, and the amount of increase by decades and also for the twenty-year period. Totals from the tables of this second series have been brought together under eight headings and are shown in Table XVIII. The topics in this table are arranged in accordance with the amount of increase during the twenty-year interval, which is also the order of their consideration in the foregoing chapters.

INCREASE IN PRESCRIPTIONS

It will be observed that the total number of prescriptions was 564 in 1903, 720 in 1913, and 926 in 1923. There was an increase of 156 prescriptions during the first decade and of 206 during the second; this is an increase of 362 during the twenty-year interval or of about 65 per cent. Four of the eight topics have more than doubled in number of prescriptions in the twenty years: Conservation of Life and Property, Humaneness, Practical and Cultural Subjects, and Nationalism. Conservation of Life and Property, on a percentage basis, shows the largest increase, since only one prescription in this group was found in 1903. Nationalism has

TABLE XVIII

General Summary of Curricular Prescriptions for the Public Elementary Schools of the United States 1903, 1913, 1923

Topic	Number of Prescriptions			Increase		
	1903	1913	1923	1903 to 1913	1913 to 1923	1903 to 1923
Nationalism	147	196	304	49	108	157
Health and "Prohibition"	102	131	171	29	40	69
Conservation of Life and Property	1	20	43	19	23	42
Practical and Cultural Subjects	24	44	59	20	15	35
Humaneness	12	28	36	16	8	24
Fundamental Subjects	197	216	216	19	--	19
Religious and Ethical Subjects	74	76	84	2	8	10
Miscellaneous Subjects	7	9	13	2	4	6
Total	564	720	926	156	206	362

This table is based upon Tables III, V, VII, IX, XI, XIII, XV and XVII.
The topics are arranged according to the amount of increase 1903–1923.

made the greatest numerical gain. There are more items classified under this topic than under any other, and together they account for more than two-fifths of the total increase found. On the whole, there was more of an increase during the second period than during the first.

Among the individual subjects an increase in number of prescriptions is the rule. Very few of the items show a net loss. Individual states have occasionally amended the law so as to eliminate the requirement of a particular subject but this has, usually, been more than offset by new prescriptions in other states. In the main, a subject once required continues to be required and to spread to other states.

SUBJECTS SHOWING LARGEST GAIN

Below are given the twelve subjects which were found to have made the largest increase during the twenty years; following each item is the net number of additional states in which it was required in 1923 as compared with 1903. The list includes those items which made a gain of twelve states or more; that is, a gain equal to or exceeding one-fourth of all the states.

1. Flag Display 22
2. Days of Special Observance 22
3. Fire Drill 21
4. Physical Examination 20
5. All Instruction in English 20
6. Physical Education 20
7. Fire Prevention 17
8. Agriculture 14
9. Constitution of the United States 14
10. Citizenship 13
11. History of the State 12
12. Patriotism 12

NEW SUBJECTS ADDED

Fourteen items were added to the list of prescribed subjects during the twenty years; of these six were introduced during the last decade. A list of the fourteen additional subjects together with the number of states in which they were required in 1923 follows:

1. Fire Prevention 17
2. Patriotism 12
3. Sanitation 7
4. Accident Prevention 5
5. Thrift 4
6. Exhibitions 3
7. Patriotic Songs 3
8. Declaration of Independence 2
9. Placards 2
10. Art 1
11. Cotton Grading 1
12. Darwinism 1
13. Dictionary 1
14. Forestry and Plant Life 1

Thrift, Exhibitions, Declaration of Independence, Art, Darwinism, and Dictionary were added during the last ten years.

PROVISIONS TO SECURE ENFORCEMENT

Many of the recent laws contain provisions intended to insure the carrying out of the legislative prescription. A direct obligation to teach a given subject is often placed upon the teacher. The local school board is directed to make provision to have the subject taught. Frequently the responsibility for enforcement of the law is placed upon the state superintendent of public instruction or upon the state board of education. There may be a time specification that the subject be taught for a minimum number of minutes or periods per week. The pupil may be required to pass an examination in the subject in order to be eligible for promotion or to receive a diploma. It may be necessary to adopt an approved textbook. The teacher may be required to pass an examination in this particular subject before being given a certificate. Normal schools may be required to give special training in this subject. The teacher may be required to include in her monthly report a statement that she has complied with the provisions of the law regarding the subject; the principal may be required to certify that she has done so; the superintendent may be required to report regarding each of the teachers under his charge to the state department showing whether or not the law has been complied with. Refusal or neglect on the part of any one of these to comply with the law may be made a misdemeanor punishable by loss of salary or by revocation of license or by a fine or by imprisonment. Sometimes the school district forfeits all claim to any part of the public funds.

Implication is not intended that it would be common for all of these provisions to be found with any one law or that any considerable number of them would be found with all laws of recent enactment or that none of them would be found in the prescriptions in force twenty years ago. The fact which it is desired to bring out is that provisions such as those given above are very much more common now than they were at the earlier period when they were most frequently found in connection with Stimulants and Narcotics.

GENERAL OBSERVATIONS

Each of the forty-eight states is aware of its authority to legislate regarding the content of the elementary curriculum. To some extent every one of the states is exercising this authority and throughout the period covered by this study has exercised such authority. There is a wide variation in practice among the different states; some have enacted a long list of prescriptions, others very few; some have delegated large discretionary authority to the state board of education, others have left the control of the schools and of the curriculum almost entirely to local boards; in some states the voters of a district may prescribe additional subjects to the curriculum; some states have been reluctant to delegate any authority. There is no state where some discretion as to the subjects to be taught is not left to educational authorities and in every state there is abundant freedom to select the subdivisions which shall be included in a given subject. There is no single subject which, by direct mandate, is uniformly required throughout the common schools of the country.

CHAPTER XI

CONCLUSION

The implications of the findings which have been presented in the foregoing chapters are far-reaching. Reflection upon them will cause us to challenge current practice in many matters of prime importance. We shall be forced anew to realize the need of an adequate basic philosophy not only for education but for all of our political and social relationships. To what extent should the state, through its legislative body attempt to determine the curriculum of the elementary schools? In other words, to what extent should it attempt to dictate what children shall study, what shall be the activities of the school, and what shall be the methods employed in the process of instruction? In so far as such dictation is indulged in, and realizes its aim, just so far are the habits, ideas, and ideals of the prospective citizen determined by legislative groups. The question involved includes a consideration of the proper function of the supreme legislative authority of the commonwealth. It will be seen that this, in turn, involves the whole question of the relation of the state to education and the proper means for best fulfilling its educational functions. In guaranteeing an educational opportunity to every child in the commonwealth should the state, through its elected legislative body, attempt to guarantee what this minimum of opportunity shall include? Are there knowledges and skills so important for the common welfare and so universally necessary and desirable that the state is justified in requiring that they be taught and in prescribing the extent, manner, and means of such instruction? What reason is there for assuming that the objective will or can be attained in accordance with the legal mandate?

Two opposed tendencies are apparent; one to delegate more and more authority to the state educational boards, the other to enact more and more legislation directing that a particular subject be included in the curriculum. These opposed tendencies are going on at the same time and frequently in the same state. The first has not yet progressed, in any state, to a point where it would meet the present standard of many of our leaders in educational thought. Along with such an increase in authority there would probably need to go a change in the method of selecting those who are to exercise the authority as well as a change in the qualifications demanded of them. As regards the opposed tendency, while the increase in the number of prescriptions during the twenty-year period is marked, and especially so during the last ten years, the demands of such legislation at the present time are not so exacting as might at first appear. After all, a law which merely provides that a particular subject shall be taught, without specifying the length of time it shall be taught or what shall be included in it, need work no great hardship upon school authorities. The majority of laws are of this type. Every requirement, even of those states which are most mandatory, might be fully met and there still remain wide latitude for enrichment and differentiation of the curriculum. Teachers who find their course of study so prescribed and inflexible that they cannot use the problem method or other more individual methods of instruction nor introduce topics of local interest must seek for the explanation elsewhere than in State legislative enactments. State-wide uniformity in the use of textbooks, for example, wherever enforced, is immensely more cramping than the sum-total of the legal prescriptions regarding the subject matter of instruction at present to be found in any of our states.

While it is true that, as yet, these legislative prescriptions need not seriously cripple the initiative and judgment of school people, it must be recognized that our legislators are pursuing a course which, if persisted in, will eventually deprive pupils of the advantages of professional leadership in this field. If we continue to increase the number of subjects required and to hedge them about with detailed specifications, it is only a question of time when the legislature will have assumed entire responsibility for the course of study. Curriculum-making is regarded, at least within the profession, as an expert undertaking sufficiently difficult in its nature to call for the coöperation of all those involved in the education of the child. Entire books have been published devoted to the theory and practice of curriculum reconstruction. A long list of books and another long list of surveys devote generous portions of their space to a consideration of this problem. Universities are supporting research departments expressly to investigate in this field. Practically every school of education is offering courses to prepare teachers and school administrators to modify the school curriculum in terms of local and individual needs. At meetings of teachers' associations the country over, including those of the National Education Association, a part of the program is commonly given over to a consideration of questions dealing with the formation of the course of study. These efforts will prove of little avail if the actual school program is to be dictated by the members of our state legislatures. Some may object that we are looking a long way ahead for trouble; some may contend that the period covered by this study is not long enough to give a reliable indication of trends; some may feel that an exhaustive study, not only of the historical development of our entire educational program but of concurrent social and political forces, would be necessary before valid conclusions could be drawn. These objections must be fully recognized. Other investigations should be made to supply needed additional information. If we had data, similar to those presented in the foregoing pages, at intervals of ten years extending back to the formation of our Union there would be a total of fourteen such intervals, stopping with the year 1793. This study has covered three separate periods, or somewhat better than one out of five of the total number. Moreover, to secure the information for the year 1903 it was necessary in a number of states to examine the law for several years earlier. It is probably safe to say that it is generally more difficult to get a law repealed than to get it enacted. The writer feels that it is very unlikely that the findings of this study represent merely a temporary and exceptional condition. Until we have positive evidence to the contrary we shall probably do well to accept the tendencies here revealed as trustworthy. Quite regardless of earlier conditions, the facts here given show the situation as it now exists and as it has been developing during the past generation. Not only is every new mandate an additional encroachment upon the sphere which many thoughtful citizens feel may best be left to professional school men but, what is more important, it may be and frequently is, a definite curtailment of possible service to the child and to society.

There are agencies, entirely apart from the government and therefore not subject to popular control, which are definitely working to induce legislatures to enact specific laws directing that certain subjects be taught. One cannot read the laws of the several states without being impressed by the frequent recurrence of the same phraseology. Laws to accomplish a given purpose are similarly worded; identical provisions are very common; identical sections are not infrequent, while whole laws are sometimes verbatim reproductions. This is not particularly surprising nor is it necessarily unwholesome. For one state to copy from another a law, or part of a law, which has worked well may be commendable if conditions in the two states are sufficiently alike to warrant the expectation that the law will be equally effective in both. For the identical nature of many of our laws, however, there is another explanation which demands more careful consideration. Reference is had to those laws which are placed upon the statute books at the insistence of small but determined and resourceful minorities. There are a number of organizations, national in scope, which are interested in promoting definite programs and have adopted the policy of using the public schools as a means of accomplishing their purpose. The crusade of the Woman's Christian Temperance Union to put into schools the compulsory teaching of the evil effects of alcoholic stimulants and narcotics is probably one of the earliest as it is by far the most successful effort along this line. No one knows how many organizations are attempting similar action. It is safe to say that the number has been increasing in recent years and that there is no assurance that these attempts are all in the real interest of public welfare. It is time to inquire as to the wisdom of allowing our public educational institutions to be used as agencies of propaganda, even when that propaganda is promoted by the highest motives. The problem here suggested is one which calls for an investigation beyond the scope of the present study.

A number of "model laws" have been prepared and are being promoted by citizens who doubtless believe that what they are doing is for the best interest of the child and the community. There are, for example, several organizations which are active in a concerted effort to make the teaching of the Constitution of the United States a legal requirement. There was such a law in nine states in 1903 and in nine states in 1913. In 1923 the number of these states had increased to twenty-three. A printed circular put out by one organization backing this movement says they will continue their campaign until the law is placed upon the statute books of every State in the Union. The same circular has this statement:

> Occasionally we have met opposition from the educational authorities in States where our Bill has been introduced, on the ground of objection to mandatory legislative control of education, but we are glad to say that State legislators generally, representative of the public will, have not agreed with these gentlemen and their arguments and have looked upon knowledge of the Constitution as an essential in citizen making.

Before they persist with this program they should carefully consider the following: Upon whom should responsibility for the formation of the curriculum be placed? Does the making of a curriculum demand special qualifications? What effect does the teaching of a subject like the Constitution of the United States have upon an immature mind? Does it have the desired effect when one is forced to study it? What does it mean "to teach" the Constitution? Has it been adequately taught when the child is able "to recite" specific facts about it? Whose rights are at stake? Those of the teacher? The child? His parents? The community? The next generation? Should a law be enacted for the purpose of bringing about a reform or should it embody only that which is already generally approved? Will the ends of good government, justice, and human welfare be more surely and fully realized when interested groups bring to bear upon legislators, in behalf of a particular measure, such pressure as they can command or would it better for such groups to plead their cause before the bar of public opinion? How may a layman most effectively express his individual preference? Do we need some additional device for ascertaining the popular will as a guide to legislators? Should opinions, in a democracy, always be counted or are there times when they may be "weighed"? What is the proper place of the expert?

Many educational leaders contend that the educative process, rather than previously chosen subject matter of instruction, should determine the school program. They would have the child engage in activities which conform to his present interest, need, and ability and which at the same time make for present and future development; they would have the subject matter grow out of such activities. In the event that further observation and controlled experimentation shall substantiate the correctness of the position held by these educators there will need to be sweeping readjustments of school procedure. Legislative prescriptions regarding the curriculum may impede or actually prevent readjustments which have been determined as desirable by professional teachers. It has not yet been shown that we can teach a child how to think and at the same time control what he shall think. Even if we could do this we do not know that it would be desirable.

The legal right of the state to determine what shall be taught in the public schools is fully recognized. The question is one of advisability. To what extent should this authority be exercised? Answers vary widely even among educational leaders. Many say the legislature should not stipulate any subjects at all. Some want only the mandate that no sectarian doctrine shall be taught; some want the added provision that all instruction shall be in English. Some feel that there is a common core of subject matter necessary for intelligent American citizenship irrespective of one's place of abode and that this should be required by law to be included in the common school curriculum. Difficulty arises at this point because no agreement has yet been reached as to what constitutes the common core. There are some who take the position that the citizens of a state, through their representatives, may properly prescribe the teaching of any and all subjects they choose, provided they leave the teacher unhampered to devise the means and processes. Even this extreme position has been exceeded in many of our states by laws now upon the statute books. Every time-specification may well operate to cripple the initiative of the teacher; and there are numerous instances of other prescriptions which restrict the flexibility of the program and limit the teacher's choice as to method of instruction. A few examples will illustrate this. In both Delaware and New Jersey we find the requirement not only that at least five verses from the Bible shall be read daily but this must be done "at the opening of the school day." It is difficult to see what useful purpose is served by thus restricting the flexibility of the school program. In Nebraska each County Superintendent must hold an annual exhibit of school work; he must also "offer and award premiums intended to stimulate the interest in school affairs." The wisdom of using rewards and premiums to stimulate school activity is very doubtful. In Montana teachers must give "oral and blackboard instructions" using data and statements supplied by the state board of health concerning the causes and prevention of communicable diseases. In North Dakota, in the teaching of hygiene, pupils in the lowest three primary grades are to be instructed "orally" by teachers using textbooks; above the third grade the instruction is to be given from textbooks "in the hands of the pupils." This provision limits the teacher to the use of a method the efficacy of which is open to question. In Montana the duty of preparing a book dealing with fire-dangers is placed upon the Commissioners of Insurance; the book to be conveniently arranged in lessons and "one of such lessons to be read by the teachers" each week. In this case the entire content of the course, including the arrangement of the material and the choice of language in which it is to be presented, may be determined without even consulting an educational authority; while the method of instruction, which is extremely poor, is prescribed by law. Of course such laws as these are exceptional as compared with the total number of laws; nevertheless they do not stand alone; many more could be cited equally restrictive. Few who are genuinely interested in the welfare of our public schools will attempt to justify such legislative interference in the professional aspects of education. The educative process is too delicate a matter for legislative bungling. Teachers should not be forced to choose between obeying the law and serving the child.

Doubtless many of the conditions here set forth are due to forces which had their origin during the World War. While they are not sufficiently extensive to constitute a menace, they are not self-corrective. There is, at least as far as this study goes, no evidence of their abatement. The tendency, as already stated, is in the opposite direction. True friends of education are confronted, as are public-minded citizens in general, by an extremely difficult problem which may prove momentous in its consequences. Granted that it is desirable for legislatures to curtail their activities, how can this be brought about? To maintain, as some do, that nothing can be done, that the forces here operating are uncontrollable, is tantamount to an accusation that men, in their group relationships, are unable to learn. Democracy is with us; there is no likelihood of returning to a condition where the people will have any less control over their own government. Either we must devise a way for men in the mass to profit by experience and by conscious thought processes or the nations of the world are doomed to a mediocre existence, subject only to intermittent progress of the happy-chance variety.

Through the centuries man has been groping and struggling for freedom; for the right to order his own life. Are we to believe that he is finally to be barred from the fruits of victory because, having no one to restrain him, he is either unable or unwilling to restrain himself? A man's response to this question is a test of his faith in humanity. There must be a way by which an organized group, acting as a group, can acquire sufficient skill and wisdom to enable it to choose the means of pursuing a given end which will not defeat the very end pursued.

APPENDIX

I

REFERENCES TO LEGISLATIVE ENACTMENTS IN THE FORTY-EIGHT STATES REGARDING SUBJECT MATTER OF INSTRUCTION IN THE PUBLIC ELEMENTARY SCHOOL

Arranged in serial order of occurrence under each state for the three years 1903, 1913, and 1923. The terminology is the same as that used throughout this study for the purposes of classification.

ALABAMA

1903

Code of 1896, Vol. I,

p. 998, sec. 3546,

subsec. 3: physiology and hygiene, stimulants and narcotics.

subsec. 4: constitution of the state, constitution of the United States.

p. 1007, sec. 3578: stimulants and narcotics.

General Laws 1903,

p. 167, no. 164: arithmetic, English, geography, history of the state, history of the United States, penmanship, reading, spelling, sectarian doctrine.

p. 537, no. 560: agriculture.

1913

Code of 1907, Vol. I,

p. 741, sec. 1685,

subsec. 3: physiology and hygiene, stimulants and narcotics.

subsec. 4: constitution of the state, constitution of the United States.

p. 759, sec. 1746: stimulants and narcotics, tobacco.

p. 759, sec. 1747: agriculture.

p. 775, secs. 1808-1810: arithmetic, English, geography, history of the state, history of the United States, penmanship, reading, spelling.

p. 775, sec. 1811: sectarian doctrine.

General Laws 1909 (Special Session), p. 27, no. 40: placards.

1923

General Laws 1919,

p. 571, no. 442, art. 3, sec. 7: agriculture, all instruction in English, arithmetic, citizenship, elementary science, English, foreign language, geography, history of the state, history of the United States, penmanship, personal hygiene, physical education, reading, sanitation, spelling.

p. 634, no. 442, art. 23, sec. 6: sectarian doctrine.
p. 676, no. 442, art. 43: stimulants and narcotics, tobacco.
p. 701, no. 459: Bible reading.
p. 1002, no. 695: humane treatment and protection of animals and birds, importance of animals and birds, animal experimentation.
p. 1020, no. 701, sec. 13: fire drill.
p. 1045, no. 722: stimulants and narcotics.

General Laws 1920 (Special Session), p. 149, no. 101: physical education, physical examination.

General Laws 1923
p. 87, no. 109: constitution of the United States.
p. 590, no. 444: flag display (state and United States).

Arizona

1903

U. S. Statutes At Large, Vol. XXIV, p. 69, ch. 362 (Forty-ninth Congress, 1885–1887, session I): physiology and hygiene, stimulants and narcotics.

Revised Statutes 1901 (Territory of Arizona),
p. 174, secs. 310–313: day of special observance (Arbor).
p. 602, sec. 2213: all instruction in English.
p. 602, sec. 2214: arithmetic, bookkeeping, drawing, English, geography, history of the United States, penmanship, physiology and hygiene, reading, spelling, stimulants and narcotics.
p. 602, sec. 2215: manners, morals.
p. 602, sec. 2217: sectarian doctrine.
p. 608, sec. 2243: social and ethical outcomes.

Acts of 1903, p. 25, no. 19: days of special observance (Flag, Lincoln, Memorial, Washington), flag display, flag exercises.

1913

Constitution, Art. XI, sec. 7: sectarian doctrine.

Revised Statutes, Civil Code, 1913,
p. 932, sec. 2769: all instruction in English.
p. 942, sec. 2808: sectarian doctrine.
p. 951, secs. 2837–2840: day of special observance (Arbor).
p. 952, sec. 2843: flag display.
p. 952, secs. 2844–2846: days of special observance (Flag, Lincoln, Memorial, Washington), flag exercises.

1923

Constitution, Art. XI, sec. 7: sectarian doctrine.

Revised Statutes, Civil Code, 1913,
p. 932, sec. 2769: all instruction in English.
p. 942, sec. 2808: sectarian doctrine.
p. 951, secs. 2837–2840: day of special observance (Arbor).
p. 952, sec. 2843: flag display.
p. 952, secs. 2844–2846: days of special observance (Flag, Lincoln, Memorial, Washington), flag exercises.

Arkansas

1903

Kirby's Digest of the Statutes, 1904,

p. 1549, secs. 7575, 7576: land designation.

p. 1558, sec. 7622: physiology and hygiene, stimulants and narcotics.

p. 1563, sec. 7654: sectarian doctrine.

1913

Kirby's Digest of the Statutes, 1904,

p. 1549, secs. 7575, 7576: land designation.

p. 1558, sec. 7622: physiology and hygiene, stimulants and narcotics.

p. 1563, sec. 7654: sectarian doctrine.

Supplement to Kirby's Digest, 1911,

p. 642, secs. 7622*a*–7622*c:* day of special observance (Lee's Birthday).

p. 642, secs. 7622*d*–7622*h:* agriculture.

1923

Digest of the Statutes, 1919,

p. 1593, sec. 5955: fire drill.

p. 2322, sec. 9028: sectarian doctrine.

p. 2329, sec. 9062: all instruction in English.

p. 2338, secs. 9093–9095: day of special observance (Lee's Birthday).

General Acts, 1921,

p. 328, Act 285, sec. 2: agriculture, algebra, arithmetic, dictionary, English, geography, government of the state, government of the United States, history of the state, history of the United States, household arts, penmanship, physiology and hygiene, reading, spelling.

General Acts, 1923,

p. 370, Act 397: social and ethical outcomes.

p. 497, Act 614: flag display, history of the United States, patriotism.

California

1903

Political Code, 1903,

p. 349, sec. 1664: all instruction in English.

p. 349, sec. 1665: arithmetic, bookkeeping, civil government, drawing, elementary science, English, geography, history of the United States, humane treatment and protection of animals and birds, music, penmanship, physiology and hygiene, reading, spelling, stimulants and narcotics.

p. 349, sec. 1667: manners, morals, stimulants and narcotics.

p. 350, sec. 1668: physical education.

p. 370, sec. 1672: sectarian doctrine.

p. 386, sec. 1702: social and ethical outcomes.

1913

Political Code, 1909,

p. 401, sec. 1617*a:* flag display.

p. 410, sec. 1664: all instruction in English.

p. 410, sec. 1665: arithmetic, bookkeeping, civil government, drawing, elementary science, English, geography, history of the United States, humane treatment and protection of animals and birds, manners, morals, music, penmanship, physical education, physiology and hygiene, reading, spelling, stimulants and narcotics, tobacco.
p. 412, sec. 1667: manners, morals, stimulants and narcotics.
p. 412, sec. 1668: physical education.
p. 413, sec. 1672: sectarian doctrine.
p. 428, sec. 1702: social and ethical outcomes.

1923

Constitution, Art. IX, sec. 8: sectarian doctrine.

General Laws 1915,

p. 84, Act 348*a* (*Statutes 1915*, p. 777, ch. 471): day of special observance (Conservation, Bird and Arbor).

Consolidated Supplement 1917–1921,

p. 1936, Act 3586*i* (*Statutes 1917*, p. 1176, ch. 668 as amended *Statutes 1921*, p. 1195, ch. 702): physical education.
p. 1947, Act 3586*r* (*Statutes 1921*, p. 89, ch. 93): fire prevention.

Political Code 1923,

p. 5, sec. 10: days of special observance (Armistice, Columbus, Labor, Lincoln, Washington).
p. 393, sec. 1519*a*, ninth; physical education.
p. 439, sec. 1607: sectarian doctrine.
p. 449, sec. 1614: flag display.
p. 466, sec. 1664: all instruction in English.
p. 466, sec. 1665: arithmetic, bookkeeping, citizenship, civil government, drawing, elementary science, English, geography, history of the state, history of the United States, household arts, humane treatment and protection of animals and birds, industrial arts, manners, morals, music, penmanship, physical education, physiology and hygiene, reading, spelling, stimulants and narcotics, thrift, tobacco.
p. 468, sec. 1667: manners, morals, stimulants and narcotics.
p. 468, sec. 1668: physical education.
p. 469, sec. 1672: sectarian doctrine.
p. 476, sec. 1702: social and ethical outcomes.

Statutes 1923, p. 418, ch. 176: constitution of the United States.

Colorado

1903

Constitution, Art. IX, sec. 8: sectarian doctrine.

Mills' Annotated Statutes 1891,

Vol. I,
p. 1300, secs. 2129–2131: day of special observance (Arbor).
Vol. II,
p. 2125, secs. 4046, 4047: physiology and hygiene, stimulants and narcotics.

Laws of 1901, p. 362, ch. 96: foreign language, German, humane treatment and protection of animals and birds.

Laws of 1901, p. 362, ch. 96 and *Laws of 1903*, p. 421, ch. 165; arithmetic, civil government, constitution of the state, constitution of the United States, English, geography, history of the United States, penmanship, reading, spelling.

Laws of 1903, p. 418, ch. 164: arithmetic, English, geography, penmanship, reading, spelling.

1913

Constitution, Art. IX, sec. 8: sectarian doctrine.

Mills' Annotated Statutes 1912,

Vol. I,

p. 297, sec. 639: arithmetic, English, geography, penmanship, reading, spelling.

p. 1480, secs. 3369, 3370: day of special observance (Arbor).

Vol. II,

p. 2740, secs. 6501, 6502: day of special observance (Good Roads).

p. 2836, sec. 6755 }
p. 2848, sec. 6778 }: arithmetic, civil government, constitution of the state, constitution of the United States, English, geography, history of the United States, penmanship, physiology and hygiene, reading, spelling, stimulants and narcotics.

p. 2842, sec. 6761: physical examination.

p. 2848, sec. 6778: foreign language (Spanish), German, humane treatment and protection of animals and birds.

p. 2849, sec. 6779: physiology and hygiene, stimulants and narcotics.

1923

Constitution, Art. IX, sec. 8: sectarian doctrine.

Compiled Laws 1921,

p. 1119, secs. 3804, 3805: day of special observance (Arbor).

p. 1120, secs. 3814, 3815: day of special observance (Good Roads).

p. 2173, sec. 8468: arithmetic, English, geography, penmanship, reading, spelling.

p. 2179, sec. 8497: all instruction in English, foreign language.

p. 2179, secs. 8498, 8499: government of the state, history of the state.

p. 2180, secs. 8500, 8501: physiology and hygiene, stimulants and narcotics.

p. 2181, secs. 8506, 8507: physical examination.

Session Laws 1923, p. 550, ch. 104: flag exercises.

Connecticut

1903

General Statutes, Revision of 1902,

p. 561, sec. 2130: arithmetic, English, geography, history of the United States, penmanship, reading, spelling.

p. 562, sec. 2139 }
p. 563, sec. 2141 }: flag display.

p. 562, sec. 2140: day of special observance (Flag).

p. 567, sec. 2162: physiology and hygiene, stimulants and narcotics.

p. 586, sec. 2251: physical examination.
p. 1067, sec. 4438: day of special observance (Arbor and Bird).
Public Acts 1903, p. 65, ch. 96: citizenship.

1913
General Statutes, Revision of 1902,
p. 561, sec. 2130: arithmetic, English, geography, history of the United States, penmanship, reading, spelling.
p. 562, sec. 2139; p. 563, sec. 2141: flag display.
p. 562, sec. 2140: day of special observance (Flag).
p. 567, sec. 2162: physiology and hygiene, stimulants and narcotics.
p. 586, sec. 2251: physical examination.
p. 1067, sec. 4438: day of special observance (Arbor and Bird).
Public Acts 1903, p. 65, ch. 96: citizenship.

1923
General Statutes, Revision of 1918, Vol. I,
p. 312, sec. 851: arithmetic, English, geography, history of the United States, penmanship, reading, spelling.
p. 314, secs. 860, 861: flag display.
p. 314, sec, 862: day of special observance (Flag).
p. 315, sec. 863: day of special observance (Arbor and Bird).
p. 315, sec. 864: day of special observance (Fire Prevention).
p. 321, sec. 889: physiology and hygiene, stimulants and narcotics.
p. 326, secs. 912–915: physical examination.
Public Acts 1921, p. 3420, ch. 399: personal hygiene, physical education.
Public Acts 1923,
p. 3581, ch. 148: citizenship, civil government.
p. 3591, ch. 166: all instruction in English, foreign language.
p. 3627, ch. 195: physical examination.
p. 3712, ch. 256: days of special observance (Armistice, Maine Memorial).

Delaware

1903
Constitution, Art. X, sec. 3: sectarian doctrine.
Laws of 1898–1899, p. 185, ch. 67, sec. 16: flag display, physiology and hygiene, stimulants and narcotics.

1913
Constitution, Art. X, sec. 3: sectarian doctrine.
Revised Statutes of 1915,
p. 1100, sec. 2288: constitution of the state, flag display, physiology and hygiene, stimulants and narcotics.
p. 1102, sec. 2289: animal experimentation, humane treatment and protection of animals and birds, importance of animals and birds, social and ethical outcomes.

1923

Constitution, Art. X, sec. 3: sectarian doctrine.

Session Laws of 1921, p. 482, ch. 160, sec. 8, subsec. 5: all instruction in English.

Session Laws of 1923,

p. 551, ch. 182: Bible reading.

p. 552, ch. 183: constitution of the state, constitution of the United States.

p. 553, ch. 184: flag display.

FLORIDA

1903

Constitution, Art. XII, sec. 13: sectarian doctrine.

Revised Statutes 1892

p. 181, sec. 242 (tenth): physiology and hygiene, stimulants and narcotics.

p. 184, sec. 253; social and ethical outcomes.

Acts 1903, p. 179, ch. 5206: arithmetic, elementary science, English, geography, government of the state, government of the United States, history of the state, history of the United States, penmanship, physiology and hygiene, reading, spelling.

1913

Constitution, Art. XII, sec. 13: sectarian doctrine.

Compiled Laws 1914, Vol. I,

p. 129, sec. 347 (tenth): physiology and hygiene, stimulants and narcotics.

p. 133, sec. 352*f*: fire drill.

p. 133, sec. 352*h*: agriculture, civil government.

p. 139, sec. 379: social and ethical outcomes.

p. 139, secs. 379*a*, 379*b*: day of special observance (Mother's).

p. 141, secs. 389–391: arithmetic, elementary science, English, geography, government of the state, government of the United States, history of the state, history of the United States, penmanship, physiology and hygiene, reading, spelling.

1923

Constitution, Art. XII, sec. 13: sectarian doctrine.

Revised General Statutes 1919, Vol. I,

p. 444, sec. 454 (tenth): physiology and hygiene, stimulants and narcotics.

p. 450, secs. 471, 472: fire drill.

p. 451, secs. 475, 487: agriculture, civil government.

p. 451, secs. 479–484: stimulants and narcotics.

p. 463, sec. 523: social and ethical outcomes.

p. 464, sec. 524: day of special observance (Mother's).

p. 466, secs. 533–535: arithmetic, elementary science, English, geography, government of the state, government of the United States, history of the state, history of the United States, penmanship, physiology and hygiene, reading, spelling.

p. 759, secs. 1206, 1207: flag display.

p. 1077, sec. 2020: physical examination.

Acts and Resolutions 1923,

p. 139, ch. 9142: humane treatment and protection of animals and birds, importance of animals and birds.

p. 420, ch. 9335 (no. 217): day of special observance (Temperance and Health).

Georgia

1903

Code of 1895, Vol. I,

p. 376, secs. 1365: Bible reading, sectarian doctrine.

p. 386, secs. 1395, 1396: day of special observance (Arbor).

Acts of 1901, p. 54, no. 367: physiology and hygiene, stimulants and narcotics.

Acts of 1903, p. 64, no. 385: agriculture, civil government.

1913

Code of 1910, Vol. I,

p. 367, sec. 1439: arithmetic, constitution of the state, constitution of the United States, English, geography, history of the state, history of the United States, penmanship, physiology and hygiene, reading, sectarian doctrine, spelling.

p. 376, secs. 1464, 1465: agriculture, civil government.

p. 395, secs. 1526, 1527: day of special observance (Arbor).

p. 395, sec. 1528: day of special observance (Georgia).

1923

Park's Annotated Code 1914, Vol. V, p. 4587, sec. 6551 (Constitution, Art. VII, sec. I): all instruction in English.

Supplement 1923 to Park's Annotated Code, Vol. VIII,

p. 295, sec. 1432*a:* all instruction in English.

p. 301, sec. 1434*a:* arithmetic, constitution of the state, constitution of the United States, English, geography, history of the state, history of the United States, penmanship, reading, sectarian doctrine, spelling.

p. 301, secs. 1434*a*, 1434*b:* agriculture, civil government.

p. 302, sec. 1434*b:* Bible reading, physiology and hygiene, stimulants and narcotics.

p. 360, sec. 1443*a:* physical education.

Acts of 1922, p. 183, no. 507: day of special observance (Temperance).

Acts of 1923, p. 130, no. 9: constitution of the state, constitution of the United States.

Idaho

1903

Constitution, Art. IX, sec. 6: sectarian doctrine.

Political Code 1901, (Vol. 1)

p. 329, sec. 1067: social and ethical outcomes.

p. 339, sec. 1092: sectarian doctrine.

General Laws 1903,

p. 215, H.B. no. 133: day of special observance (Arbor).

p. 289, H.B. no. 174, sec. 2: flag display.

1913

Constitution, Art. IX, sec. 6: sectarian doctrine.

General Laws 1911, ch. 159,

p. 508, sec. 59: flag display.

p. 518, sec. 86*b*: social and ethical outcomes.

p. 545, sec. 160: arithmetic, English, geography, penmanship, reading, spelling.

p. 554, sec. 186: sectarian doctrine.

p. 555, sec. 188: day of special observance (Arbor).

p. 556, sec. 190: physiology and hygiene, stimulants and narcotics.

1923

Constitution, Art. IX, sec. 6: sectarian doctrine.

Compiled Statutes, 1919,

Vol. I,

p. 229, sec. 803, subsec. 16: physical education, physical examination.

p. 269, sec. 944: social and ethical outcomes.

p. 280, sec. 985: all instruction in English, foreign language.

p. 289, sec. 1018: arithmetic, English, geography, penmanship, reading, spelling.

p. 297, sec. 1046: sectarian doctrine.

p. 298, sec. 1048: day of special observance (Arbor).

p. 298, sec. 1050: physiology and hygiene, stimulants and narcotics.

p. 789, sec. 2769: importance of animals and birds.

Vol. II,

p. 2587, sec. 9450 and *General Laws 1921*, p. 454, ch. 215, sec. 49½: days of special observance (Columbus, Labor, Pioneer, Washington).

General Laws 1921, p. 449, ch. 215, sec. 46, subsec. 17: flag display.

General Laws 1923, p. 28, ch. 26: constitution of the United States.

Illinois

1903

Constitution, Art. VIII, sec. 3: sectarian doctrine.

Hurd's Revised Statutes 1903,

p. 991, ch. 56*a*: flag display.

p. 1683, ch. 122, secs. 187 and 190: arithmetic, English, geography, history of the United States, penmanship, physiology and hygiene, reading, spelling.

p. 1715, ch. 122, sec. 362: physiology and hygiene, stimulants and narcotics.

1913

Constitution, Art. VIII, sec. 3: sectarian doctrine.

J. and A., Annotated Statutes 1913, Vol. V,

p. 5912, secs. 10216, 10217: arithmetic, civil government, English, geography, history of the state, history of the United States, penmanship, reading, spelling.

p. 5938, sec. 10301: sectarian doctrine.

p. 5940, sec. 10311: physiology and hygiene, stimulants and narcotics.

p. 5967, sec. 10405: social and ethical outcomes.
p. 5968, sec. 10406: humane treatment and protection of animals and birds, importance of animals and birds.
p. 5968, sec. 10407: animal experimentation.
p. 5969, sec. 10412: flag display.

1923
Constitution, Art. VIII, sec. 3: sectarian doctrine.
Cahill's Revised Statutes 1923,
p. 1772, ch. 56*a*, sec. 3: flag display.
Ch. 122,
p. 3144, sec. 397: physiology and hygiene, stimulants and narcotics.
p. 3148, sec. 401: all instruction in English.
p. 3177, secs. 548–550: civil government, patriotism.
p. 3178, sec. 551: social and ethical outcomes.
p. 3178, sec. 552: humane treatment and protection of animals and birds, importance of animals and birds.
p. 3178, sec. 553: animal experimentation.
p. 3178, secs. 556, 557: physical education.

Indiana

1903
Horner's Revised Statutes 1901, Vol. I,
sec. 4422*s:* sectarian doctrine.
sec. 4444*g:* physiology and hygiene, stimulants and narcotics.
sec. 4493: Bible reading.
sec. 4497: all instruction in English, arithmetic, English, foreign language, German, geography, history of the United States, manners, penmanship, physiology and hygiene, reading, spelling.

1913
Burns' Annotated Statutes 1914, Vol. III,
p. 246, sec. 6320: sectarian doctrine.
p. 384, sec. 6578: Bible reading.
p. 384, sec. 6582: all instruction in English, arithmetic, English, foreign language, German, geography, history of the United States, manners, penmanship, physiology and hygiene, reading, spelling.
p. 385, sec. 6582*a:* patriotic songs.
p. 388, sec. 6586: physiology and hygiene, stimulants and narcotics,
p. 403, sec. 6616*c:* communicable diseases, personal hygiene, sanitation.
p. 416, sec. 6641*e:* agriculture, household arts, industrial arts.
p. 695, sec. 7441*n:* fire drill.
p. 701, secs. 7461*a*, 7461*c:* day of special observance (Arbor).
p. 798, sec. 7648*j:* communicable diseases, tobacco.

1923
Burns' Annotated Statutes 1914, Vol. III,
p. 246, sec. 6320: sectarian doctrine.
p. 384, sec. 6578: Bible reading.
p. 385, sec. 6582*a:* patriotic songs.

p. 388, sec. 6586: physiology and hygiene, stimulants and narcotics,
p. 403, sec. 6616*c:* communicable diseases, personal hygiene, sanitation.
p. 416, sec. 6641*e:* agriculture, household arts, industrial arts.
p. 695, sec. 7441*n:* fire drill.
p. 701, secs. 7461*a*, 7461*c:* day of special observance (Arbor).
p. 798, sec. 7648*j:* communicable diseases, tobacco.

Burns' Annotated Statutes Supplement 1921, Vol. V.
p. 881, sec. 6581*a:* all instruction in English, arithmetic, English, German, geography, history of the United States, manners, penmanship, physiology and hygiene, reading, spelling.

Iowa

1903

Annotated Code 1897,
p. 933, sec. 2749, subsec. 3: all instruction in English, foreign language.
p. 942, sec. 2775: physiology and hygiene, stimulants and narcotics.
p. 955, sec. 2805: Bible reading.

Supplement, 1902, to the Code,
p. 325, sec. 2823*a:* arithmetic, English, geography, history of the United States, penmanship, physiology and hygiene, reading, spelling.
p. 329, sec. 2823*s:* music.

1913

Annotated Code 1897,
p. 933, sec. 2749: all instruction in English, foreign language.
p. 942, sec. 2775: physiology and hygiene, stimulants and narcotics.
p. 955, sec. 2805: Bible reading.

Supplement, 1913, to the Code,
p. 931, sec. 2468*k:* fire drill, fire prevention.
p. 1171, sec. 2775*a:* agriculture, household arts, industrial arts.
p. 1184, secs. 2804*a*, 2804*c:* flag display.
p. 1192, sec. 2823*a:* arithmetic, English, geography, history of the United States, penmanship, physiology and hygiene, reading, spelling.
p. 1196, sec. 2823*s:* music.

1923

Code, 1919,
p. 329, sec. 1048: fire drill, fire prevention.
p. 690, secs. 2263, 2264: all instruction in English.
p. 693, secs. 2271, 2272: citizenship.
p. 780, sec. 2555: physiology and hygiene, stimulants and narcotics.
p. 780, sec. 2557: agriculture, household arts, industrial arts.
p. 780, sec. 2558: music.
p. 784, sec. 2573: flag display.
p. 785, sec. 2575: Bible reading.
p. 799, sec. 2628: flag exercises.
p. 809, sec. 2663: arithmetic, English, geography, history of the United States, penmanship, physiology and hygiene, reading, spelling.

Supplement, 1923, to the Compiled Code,

p. 251, secs. 2274*a*1, 2274*a*2: constitution of the state, constitution of the United States.

p. 295, sec. 2693*a*1: day of special observance (Bird).

Kansas

1903

Constitution, Art. VI, sec. 8: sectarian doctrine.

General Statutes of 1901,

p. 1247, sec. 6235: physiology and hygiene, stimulants and narcotics.

p. 1257, sec. 6284}
p. 1264, sec. 6318}: Bible reading, sectarian doctrine.

p. 1294, sec. 6460: sectarian doctrine.

Session Laws 1903, p. 672, ch. 435: all instruction in English, arithmetic, English, geography, history of the state, history of the United States, penmanship, reading, spelling.

1913

Constitution, Art. VI, sec. 8: sectarian doctrine.

General Statutes of 1909,

p. 1614, sec. 7478: all instruction in English, arithmetic, English, geography, history of the state, history of the United States, penmanship, reading, spelling.

p. 1622, sec. 7519: physiology and hygiene, stimulants and narcotics.

p. 1632, sec. 7578: Bible reading, sectarian doctrine.

p. 1640, sec. 7613: Bible reading.

p. 1672, secs. 7748, 7749; flag display.

p. 1672, secs. 7750, 7751: days of special observance (Flag, Lincoln, Memorial, Washington), flag exercises.

p. 1684, sec. 7813: sectarian doctrine.

p. 1694, secs. 7856, 7857: fire drill.

Laws 1913, p. 537, ch. 312, sec. 15: fire drill, fire prevention.

1923

Constitution, Art. VI, sec. 8: sectarian doctrine.

Revised Statutes (annotated) 1923,

p. 556, par. 31–208: fire drill, fire prevention.

p. 1170, par. 72–1101: all instruction in English, arithmetic, English, geography, history of the state, history of the United States, penmanship reading, spelling.

p. 1170, par. 72–1102: all instruction in English.

p. 1170, par. 72–1103 to 72–1105: citizenship, civil government, history of the United States, patriotism.

p. 1174, par. 72–1327: physiology and hygiene, stimulants and narcotics.

p. 1181, par. 72–1722}
p. 1185, par. 72–1819}: Bible reading, sectarian doctrine.

p. 1215, par. 72–4606: fire drill.

p. 1219, par. 72–5304, 72–5305: flag display.

p. 1219, par. 72–5308: days of special observance (Flag, Lincoln, Memorial, Washington).

p. 1219, par. 72–5308 }
p. 1220, par. 72–5309 }: flag exercises.

p. 1220, par. 72–5310: day of special observance (Temperance).

Kentucky

1903

Constitution, sec. 189: sectarian doctrine.

Carroll's Statutes of 1903,

p. 1525, sec. 4368: sectarian doctrine.

p. 1530, sec. 4383: arithmetic, civil government, English, geography, history of the state, history of the United States, penmanship, physiology and hygiene, reading, spelling, stimulants and narcotics.

1913

Constitution, sec. 189: sectarian doctrine.

Carroll's Statutes of 1909,

p. 1746, sec. 4368: sectarian doctrine.

p. 1751, sec. 4383: arithmetic, civil government, English, geography, history of the state, history of the United States, penmanship, physiology and hygiene, reading, spelling, stimulants and narcotics.

1923

Constitution, sec. 189: sectarian doctrine.

Carroll's Statutes of 1922,

p. 371, sec. 762*b*–7 (*f*): fire drill, fire prevention.

p. 2075, sec. 4368: sectarian doctrine.

p. 2075, sec. 4369*b*–1: agriculture.

p. 2076, secs. 4369*c*–1, 4369*c*–2: day of special observance (Temperance).

p. 2076, secs. 4369*d*–1, 4369*d*–2: thrift.

p. 2076, sec. 4369*d*–2: placards.

p. 2076, sec. 4369*e*–1: physical education.

p. 2077, sec. 4369*f*: humane treatment and protection of animals and birds, importance of animals and birds.

p. 2081, sec. 4383: arithmetic, civil government, English, geography, history of the state, history of the United States, penmanship, physiology and hygiene, reading, spelling, stimulants and narcotics.

p. 2106, sec. 4421*b*–10: sectarian doctrine.

Acts of 1922, p. 102, ch. 27: patriotic songs.

Louisiana

1903

Constitution,

Art. 53 and Art. 253: sectarian doctrine.

Art. 251: foreign language.

Wolff's Revised Laws of 1904, Vol. I,

p. 612, sec. 23 (Acts of 1902, p. 412, no. 214, sec. 23): arithmetic, drawing, English, foreign language, geography, history of the United States, penmanship, physiology and hygiene, reading, spelling, stimulants and narcotics.

p. 633 (Act 40, 1888, p. 29): physiology and hygiene, stimulants and narcotics.

1913

Constitution,

Art. 53 and Art. 253: sectarian doctrine.

Art. 251: foreign language.

Wolff's Revised Laws of 1904, Vol. I,

p. 633 (Act 40, 1888, p. 29): physiology and hygiene, stimulants and narcotics.

Supplement to Wolff's Revised Laws 1904–1908,

p. 229 (Act 292, 1908, p. 432): physical examination.

p. 300 (Act 198, 1906, p. 351, sec. 14): day of special observance (Bird).

Acts of 1910,

p. 92, no. 56: day of special observance (Columbus).

p. 451, no. 261, sec. 16: day of special observance (Arbor), forestry.

p. 523, no. 306: agriculture.

Acts of 1912, p. 469, no. 214, sec. 16: arithmetic, drawing, English, foreign language, geography, history of the United States, penmanship, physiology and hygiene, reading, spelling, stimulants and narcotics.

1923

Constitution of 1921, Art. XII,

sec. 3: citizenship, civil government.

sec. 12: all instruction in English.

sec. 13: sectarian doctrine.

Wolff's Statutes of 1920,

Vol. I,

p. 575 (Act 306 of 1910, p. 523): agriculture.

p. 576 (Act 292 of 1908, p. 432): physical examination.

p. 577 (Act 56 of 1910, p. 92): day of special observance (Columbus).

Vol. II,

p. 1388 (Act 261 of 1910, p. 446, sec. 16): day of special observance (Arbor).

p. 1426 (Act 83 of 1918, p. 121, sec. 11): day of special observance (Bird).

Acts of 1922, p. 221, no. 100, sec. 60: arithmetic, drawing, English, geography, history of the United States, penmanship, physiology and hygiene, reading, spelling, stimulants and narcotics.

Maine

1903

Revised Statutes 1903, Ch. 15,

p. 209, sec. 35 (III): physiology and hygiene, stimulants and narcotics.

p. 220, sec. 86: humane treatment and protection of animals and birds, social and ethical outcomes.

1913

Revised Statutes 1903, Ch. 15,

p. 209, sec. 35 (III): physiology and hygiene, stimulants and narcotics.

p. 220, sec. 86: humane treatment and protection of animals and birds, social and ethical outcomes.

Acts of 1907, p. 199, ch. 182: flay display, patriotism.

Acts of 1909, p. 79, ch. 73: physical examination.

Acts of 1913, p. 240, ch. 195: day of special observance (Lincoln).

1923

Revised Statutes 1916, Ch. 16,

p. 359, sec. 38 (II): physiology and hygiene, stimulants and narcotics.

p. 361, sec. 45: physical examination.

p. 363, sec. 52: flag display, patriotism.

p. 379, sec. 108: social and ethical outcomes.

p. 379, sec. 109: day of special observance (Lincoln).

Laws 1917, p. 263, ch. 228: humane treatment and protection of animals and birds.

Laws of 1919,

p. 68, ch. 73: personal hygiene, physical education, sanitation.

p. 261, ch. 208: animal experimentation.

p. 147, ch. 146 and *Laws 1921*, p. 27, ch. 25: civil government, foreign language, history of the United States.

Laws 1921,

p. 27, ch. 25: all instruction in English.

p. 123, ch. 109: day of special observance (Temperance).

Laws 1923,

p. 44, ch. 50: day of special observance (Lincoln).

p. 255, ch. 166: Bible reading.

Maryland

1903

Code of 1888, Vol. II, Art. 77,

p. 1175, sec. 40: physiology and hygiene, stimulants and narcotics.

p. 1179, sec. 58: sectarian doctrine.

Laws of 1898,

p. 738, ch. 221: algebra, arithmetic, bookkeeping, constitution of the state, constitution of the United States, drawing, English, geography, German, history of the State, history of the United States, household arts, manners, music, penmanship, personal hygiene, physiology and hygiene, reading, spelling.

p. 1201, ch. 520: civil government.

1913

Bagby's Annotated Code 1910, Vol. II, Art. 77,

p. 1728, sec. 44: arithmetic, civil government, constitution of the state, constitution of the United States, drawing, English, geography, history of the state, history of the United States, household arts, manners,

music, penmanship, personal hygiene, physiology and hygiene, reading, spelling.
p. 1728, sec. 45: physiology and hygiene, stimulants and narcotics.
p. 1730, sec. 52: days of special observance (Maryland, Washington).
p. 1734, sec. 67: sectarian doctrine.

1923
Bagby's Annotated Code 1910, Vol. II, Art. 77,
p. 1728, sec. 45: physiology and hygiene, stimulants and narcotics.
p. 1734, sec. 67: sectarian doctrine.
Laws of 1916, ch. 506,
p. 1023, sec. 44: arithmetic, citizenship, English, geography, history of the state, history of the United States, manners, penmanship, personal hygiene, reading, sanitation, spelling.
p. 1024, sec. 49: exhibition.
Laws of 1918,
p. 121, ch. 75: flag display, flag exercises, patriotism.
p. 650, ch. 269: physical education.
Laws of 1920, p. 665, ch. 381: patriotic songs.
Laws of 1922, p. 552, ch. 239: days of special observance (Arbor, Armistice, Maryland, Memorial, Washington).

Massachusetts

1903
Constitution, Art. XVIII of amendments: sectarian doctrine.
Revised Laws 1902, Vol. I, ch. 42,
p. 466, sec. 1: arithmetic, drawing, English, foreign language, geography, history of the United States, manners, penmanship, physiology and hygiene, reading, spelling, stimulants and narcotics.
p. 468, sec. 9: industrial arts.
p. 469, sec. 18: social and ethical outcomes.
p. 469, sec. 19: Bible reading, sectarian doctrine.
p. 469, sec. 20: day of special observance (Memorial).
p. 469, sec. 21: animal experimentation.
p. 474, sec. 50: flag display.

1913
Constitution, Art. XVIII of amendments: sectarian doctrine.
Revised Laws 1902, Vol. I, Ch. 42,
p. 466, sec. 1: arithmetic, drawing, English, foreign language, geography, history of the United States, manners, penmanship, physiology and hygiene, reading, spelling, stimulants and narcotics.
p. 468, sec. 9: industrial arts.
p. 469, sec. 18: social and ethical outcomes.
p. 469, sec. 19: Bible reading, sectarian doctrine.
p. 469, sec. 20: day of special observance (Memorial).
p. 469, sec. 21: animal experimentation.
p. 474, sec. 50: flag display.
Acts 1906, p. 681, ch. 502, secs. 5, 6: physical examination.
Acts 1908, p. 133, ch. 181: communicable diseases.

1923

Constitution, Art. XLVI of amendments: sectarian doctrine.

General Laws 1921, Vol. I, ch. 71,

p. 701, sec. 1: arithmetic, communicable diseases, drawing, English, geography, history of the United States, manners, penmanship, physiology and hygiene, reading, spelling, stimulants and narcotics.

p. 702, sec. 2: citizenship, history of the United States.

p. 705, sec. 17: household arts, industrial arts.

p. 707, sec. 30: social and ethical outcomes.

p. 707, sec. 31: Bible reading, sectarian doctrine.

p. 707, sec. 32: day of special observance (Memorial).

p. 707, sec. 33: animal experimentation.

p. 711, sec. 57: physical examination.

p. 713, sec. 69: flag display.

Acts of 1921, p. 389, ch. 360: physical education.

Acts of 1923, p. 217, ch. 222: constitution of the United States.

MICHIGAN

1903

Constitution, Art. XIII, sec. 4: all instruction in English.

The Compiled Laws 1897, Vol. II,

p. 1475, sec. 4676: sectarian doctrine.

p. 1477, sec. 4680: physiology and hygiene, stimulants and narcotics.

p. 1508, sec. 4781: sectarian doctrine.

p. 1513, sec. 4796: communicable diseases.

p. 1514, sec. 4802: flag display.

1913

Constitution, Art. XI, sec. 9: all instruction in English.

Howell's Annotated Statutes, Second Edition, 1913,

Vol. III, p. 3206, sec. 7891: fire drill.

Vol. IV,

p. 3909, sec. 9766: physical education.

p. 3955, sec. 9897: sectarian doctrine.

p. 3957, sec. 9901: physiology and hygiene, stimulants and narcotics.

p. 4021, sec. 10033: days of special observance (Columbus, Lincoln, Washington).

p. 4045, sec. 10067: flag display.

p. 4056, sec. 10108: communicable diseases.

Public Acts of 1913, p. 444, no. 227: humane treatment and protection of animals and birds, importance of animals and birds.

1923

Constitution, Art. XI, sec. 9: all instruction in English.

Compiled Laws 1915, Vol. II,

p. 2142, sec. 5678: sectarian doctrine.

p. 2145, sec. 5682: physiology and hygiene, stimulants and narcotics.

p. 2193, sec. 5807: communicable diseases.

p. 2194, sec. 5811: flag display.

p. 2198, sec. 5823: days of special observance (Columbus, Lincoln, Washington).

p. 2209, secs. 5871–5873: humane treatment and protection of animals and birds, importance of animals and birds.

p. 3312, sec. 9116: fire drill.

Supplement 1922 to Compiled Laws,

p. 567, sec. 5641: all instruction in English.

p. 585, sec. 5806 (1): constitution of the state, constitution of the United States.

p. 585, sec. 5806 (3): physical education.

p. 589, sec. 5823: days of special observance (Armistice, Roosevelt, September Seventeenth).

p. 589, sec. 5824 (1): day of special observance (Carleton).

Minnesota

1903

Constitution, Art. VIII, sec. 3: sectarian doctrine.

General Statutes 1894, Vol. I,

p. 1010, sec. 3697: foreign language.

p. 1054, secs. 3892–3896: physiology and hygiene, stimulants and narcotics.

1913

Constitution, Art. VIII, sec. 3: sectarian doctrine.

General Statutes 1913,

p. 629, sec. 2797: foreign language.

p. 630, secs. 2806, 2807: day of special observance (State).

p. 637, sec. 2835: morals, physiology and hygiene, stimulants and narcotics.

p. 1127, sec. 5156: fire drill.

1923

Constitution, Art. VIII, sec. 3: sectarian doctrine.

General Statutes 1913,

p. 629, sec. 2797: foreign language.

p. 630, secs, 2806, 2807: day of special observance (State).

p. 637, sec. 2835: morals, physiology and hygiene, stimulants and narcotics.

p. 1127, sec. 5156: fire drill.

Session Laws 1917,

p. 135, ch. 108: patriotism.

p. 450, ch. 313: flag display.

Session Laws 1919, p. 337, ch. 320: all instruction in English, foreign language.

Session Laws 1923,

p. 388, ch. 291: constitution of the United States, Declaration of Independence.

p. 464, ch. 323: personal hygiene, physical education.

Mississippi

1903

Constitution,

sec. 18: Bible reading.

sec. 208: sectarian doctrine.

Annotated Code 1892,

p. 886, sec. 4006 (*e*): sectarian doctrine.

p. 889, secs. 4019, 4022, 4023: arithmetic, English, geography, history of the United States, physiology and hygiene, reading, spelling, stimulants and narcotics.

1913

Constitution,

sec. 18: Bible reading.

sec. 208: sectarian doctrine.

Code of 1906,

p. 1231, sec. 4525(*e*): sectarian doctrine.

p. 1235, secs. 4540, 4543, 4544: arithmetic, English, geography, history of the United States, physiology and hygiene, reading, spelling, stimulants and narcotics.

p. 1246, sec. 4595: foreign language, penmanship.

Laws of 1910, p. 113, ch. 123: placards.

1923

Constitution,

sec. 18: Bible reading.

sec. 208: sectarian doctrine.

Hemingway's Annotated Code 1917, Vol. II,

p. 2983, secs. 7327, 7328: placards.

p. 3116, sec. 7798: agriculture, algebra, arithmetic, civil government, elementary science, English, geography, history of the state, history of the United States, physiology and hygiene, reading, sanitation, spelling, stimulants and narcotics.

p. 3127, sec. 7838: foreign language, penmanship.

Supplement of 1921 to Annotated Code,

p. 715, sec. 7413*i:* flag display.

Laws of 1922, p. 272, ch. 205: manners, morals, sectarian doctrine.

Missouri

1903

Constitution, Art. XI, sec. 11: sectarian doctrine.

Revised Statutes 1899, Vol. II, p. 2277, sec. 9799: physiology and hygiene, stimulants and narcotics.

1913

Constitution, Art. XI, sec. 11: sectarian doctrine.

Revised Statutes 1909, Vol. III, p. 3353, sec. 10806: communicable diseases, physiology and hygiene, stimulants and narcotics.

1923

Constitution, Art. XI, sec. 11: sectarian doctrine.

Revised Statutes 1919,

Vol. II, p. 1841, sec, 5852: day of special observance (State).

Vol. III,

p. 3498, sec. 11162: communicable diseases, physiology and hygiene, stimulants and narcotics.

p. 3499, sec. 11163: day of special observance (Temperance).

Laws of 1921,

p. 639; personal hygiene.

p. 641: physical education.

MONTANA

1903

Constitution, Art. XI, sec. 9: sectarian doctrine.

Codes and Statutes 1895,

p. 153, secs. 1807–1809: flag display.

p. 157, sec. 1845: social and ethical outcomes.

p. 171, secs. 1990–1992: day of special observance (Arbor).

Laws of 1903,

p. 33, ch. 23: all instruction in English, arithmetic, English, geography, history of the state, history of the United States, humane treatment and protection of animals and birds, penmanship, physiology and hygiene, reading, spelling, social and ethical outcomes, stimulants and narcotics.

p. 161, ch. 88: day of special observance (State).

1913

Constitution, Art. XI, sec. 9: sectarian doctrine.

Laws of 1913, Ch. 76, pp. 196–306.

p. 233, sec. 508, subsec. 21: flag display.

p. 237, sec. 601: all instruction in English, arithmetic, civil government, English, geography, history of the state, history of the United States, penmanship, physiology and hygiene, reading, spelling, stimulants and narcotics.

p. 239, sec. 609: sectarian doctrine.

p. 239, sec. 610: fire drill.

p. 240, sec. 611: fire prevention.

p. 240, sec. 612: communicable diseases.

p. 245, sec. 803, subsec. 4: social and ethical outcomes.

p. 263, sec. 1400: day of special observance (State).

p. 264, sec. 1401: day of special observance (Arbor).

1923

Constitution, Art. XI, sec. 9: sectarian doctrine.

Revised Codes of 1921, Vol. I,

p. 519, sec. 1015, subsec. 11: physical examination.

p. 520, sec. 1015, subsec. 21: flag display.

p. 540, sec. 1054: agriculture, all instruction in English, arithmetic, civil government, English, geography, history of the state, history of the United States, penmanship, physiology and hygiene, reading, spelling, stimulants and narcotics.

p. 542, sec. 1062: days of special observance (Arbor, Armistice, Columbus, Flag, Lincoln, State, Washington).

p. 543, secs. 1063–1067: day of special observance (State).

p. 543, secs. 1068–1070: day of special observance (Arbor).

p. 544, sec. 1071: fire drill.

p. 545, sec. 1072: fire prevention.

p. 545, sec. 1073: communicable diseases.

p. 548, sec. 1079: social and ethical outcomes.

Nebraska

1903

Constitution, Art. VIII, sec. 11: sectarian doctrine.

Compiled Statutes 1901, p. 1072, sec. 4760: physiology and hygiene, stimulants and narcotics.

1913

Constitution, Art. VIII, sec. 11: sectarian doctrine.

Revised Statutes 1913,

p. 1911, sec. 6850: day of special observance (State Fire Day).

p. 1911, sec. 6851: fire prevention.

p. 1919, sec. 6878: physiology and hygiene, stimulants and narcotics.

p. 1934, sec. 6941: foreign language.

1923

Constitution of 1920, Art. VII, sec. 11: sectarian doctrine.

Compiled Statutes 1922,

p. 2002, sec. 6324
p. 2019, sec. 6385 }: agriculture, arithmetic, bookkeeping, drawing, English, geography, penmanship, reading, spelling.

p. 2032, sec. 6421: day of special observance (State Fire Day).

p. 2032, sec. 6422: fire prevention.

p. 2043, sec. 6446: physiology and hygiene, stimulants and narcotics.

p. 2045, secs. 6457–6462: all instruction in English.

p. 2045, sec. 6459: foreign language.

p. 2057, sec. 6508, subsec. *j:* civil government, history of the United States.

p. 2065, secs. 6530–6535: flag display.

p. 2065, sec. 6531: days of special observance (Flag, Lincoln, Memorial, Washington), flag exercises.

p. 2066, secs. 6536–6541: physical examination.

p. 2066, secs. 6543–6545: exhibition.

Nevada

1903

Constitution, Art. XI, sec. 9: sectarian doctrine.

Compiled Laws 1900,

p. 317, sec. 1346: stimulants and narcotics.

p. 319, sec. 1350: foreign language.
p. 979, sec. 5055: day of special observance (Arbor).

Statutes 1901

p. 50, ch. 39: arithmetic, drawing, English, geography, history of the United States, penmanship, physiology and hygiene, reading, spelling.
p. 56, ch. 47: importance of animals and birds.

1913

Constitution, Art. XI, sec. 9: sectarian doctrine.

Revised Laws 1912, Vol. I

p. 966, sec. 3344: sectarian doctrine.
p. 966, sec. 3346: physiology and hygiene, stimulants and narcotics.
p. 967, secs. 3347, 3348: importance of animals and birds.
p. 967, secs. 3349, 3350: day of special observance (Arbor).
p. 967, sec. 3351: days of special observance (Arbor, Lincoln, State, Washington).
p. 967, sec. 3352: flag display.
p. 981, sec. 3401; p. 982, sec. 3403; p. 984, sec. 3410: arithmetic, drawing, English, geography, history of the United States, music, penmanship, reading, physiology and hygiene, spelling.

Statutes 1913, p. 103, ch. 80: bookkeeping, industrial arts.

1923

Constitution, Art. XI, sec. 9: sectarian doctrine.

Revised Laws 1912, Vol. I,

p. 966, sec. 3344: sectarian doctrine.
p. 966, sec. 3346: physiology and hygiene, stimulants and narcotics.
p. 967, sec. 3347: importance of animals and birds.
p. 967, secs. 3349, 3350: day of special observance (Arbor).
p. 967, sec. 3351: days of special observance (Arbor, Lincoln, State, Washington).
p. 967, sec. 3352: flag display.
Vol. III, (*Supplement 1919*),
p. 2918, sec. 3242 (*Statutes 1913*, p. 103, ch. 80): bookkeeping, industrial arts.
p. 2938 (*Statutes 1919*, p. 247, ch. 133): all instruction in English, foreign language.
p. 2939 (*Statutes 1919*, p. 61, ch. 47): day of special observance (Temperance).

Statutes 1921,

p. 28. ch. 25: civil government, flag display, history of the state, history of the United States, patriotism.
p. 255, ch. 168: thrift.
p. 306, ch. 208, secs. 14, 15: arithmetic, drawing, English, geography, history of the United States, music, penmanship, physiology and hygiene, reading, spelling.

Statutes 1923,

p. 13, ch. 14: fire drill.

p. 323, ch. 182: constitution of the state, constitution of the United States.

New Hampshire

1903

Public Statutes 1901, Ch. 92.

p. 298, sec. 5 (Laws 1895, p. 357, ch. 13 as amended 1897, p. 16, ch. 14): day of special observance (Memorial).

p. 299, sec. 6: physiology and hygiene, stimulants and narcotics.

p. 299, sec. 9: sectarian doctrine.

Laws of 1903,

p. 25, ch. 31: constitution of the state, constitution of the United States.

p. 32, ch. 39: flag display.

1913

Public Statutes 1901, Ch. 92,

p. 298, sec. 5: day of special observance (Memorial).

p. 299, sec. 6: physiology and hygiene, stimulants and narcotics.

p. 299, sec. 9: sectarian doctrine.

Supplement 1913 to the Public Statutes,

p. 172 (P.S. ch. 92 sec. 6 as amended 1903 p. 25 ch. 31, 1909 p. 359 ch. 49 and 1911 p. 155 ch. 136): constitution of the state, constitution of the United States, humane treatment and protection of animals and birds, physiology and hygiene, stimulants and narcotics.

p. 172 (P. S. ch. 92 sec. 8 as amended 1903 p. 32 ch. 39): flag display.

1923

Laws of 1921, Ch. 85, pp. 107–154,

p. 123, Part II, sec. 2: physiology and hygiene, stimulants and narcotics.

p. 125, Part II, sec. 9: flag display.

p. 125, Part II, sec. 10: all instruction in English, foreign language.

p. 125, Part II, sec. 13: sectarian doctrine.

p. 127, Part II, sec. 23: day of special observance (Memorial).

Laws of 1923, p. 57, ch. 47: constitution of the state, constitution of the United States, physiology and hygiene, stimulants and narcotics.

New Jersey

1903

Acts of 1903 (Second Special Session) Chap. I,

p. 45, sec. 114: Bible reading.

p. 91, sec. 230: flag display.

p. 92, sec. 233: stimulants and narcotics.

p. 92, sec. 235: day of special observance (Arbor).

p. 93, sec. 236: days of special observance (Lincoln, Memorial, Thanksgiving, Washington).

1913

Compiled Statutes 1910,

Vol. II, p. 2561 (Acts 1907, p. 165, ch. 84): day of special observance (Flag).

Vol. IV (Schools).

p. 4765, sec. 114: Bible reading.

p. 4775, secs. 153, 154: arithmetic, English, geography, penmanship, reading, spelling.

p. 4803, sec. 229: physical examination.

p. 4803, sec. 230: flag display.

p. 4804, sec. 233: stimulants and narcotics.

p. 4804, sec. 235: day of special observance (Arbor).

p. 4804, sec. 236: days of special observance (Lincoln, Memorial, Thanksgiving, Washington).

Acts of 1913, p. 407, ch. 222, and p. 508, ch. 269: accident prevention.

1923

Compiled Statutes 1910,

Vol. II, p. 2561 (Acts 1907 p. 165 ch. 84): day of special observance (Flag).

Vol. IV (Schools),

p. 4765, sec. 114: Bible reading.

p. 4803, sec. 229: physical examination.

p. 4803, sec. 230: flag display.

p. 4804, sec. 233: stimulants and narcotics.

p. 4804, sec. 235: day of special observance (Arbor).

p. 4804, sec. 236: days of special observance (Lincoln, Memorial, Thanksgiving, Washington).

Supplement to Compiled Statutes, 1911–1915, p. 1459 (Schools), secs. 220–223: accident prevention.

Acts of 1916, p. 553, ch. 263: Bible reading.

Acts of 1917, p. 221, ch. 107: accident prevention, citizenship, personal hygiene, physical education.

Acts of 1919

p. 71, ch. 35: all instruction in English, arithmetic, English, geography, penmanship, reading, spelling.

p. 304, ch. 135: citizenship, geography (of N. J.), history of the state.

p. 341, ch. 154: fire drill.

Acts of 1920, p. 253, ch. 118: fire prevention.

Acts of 1923, p. 43, ch. 17: constitution of the United States.

New Mexico

1903

U. S. Statutes At Large, Vol. XXIV, p. 69, ch. 362, (Forty-ninth Congress, 1885–1887, session I): physiology and hygiene, stimulants and narcotics.

Compiled Laws 1897 (Territory of New Mexico),

p. 425, sec. 1529: arithmetic, English, geography, history of the United States, penmanship, reading, spelling.

p. 436, sec. 1582: sectarian doctrine.

p. 444, sec. 1625*a*: day of special observance (Arbor).

1913

Statutes 1915 (codification including 1913),

p. 801, sec. 2726: day of special observance (Arbor).

p. 1403, sec. 4843: arithmetic, English, geography, history of the United States, penmanship, reading, spelling.

p. 1407, secs, 4860, 4861: flag display.

p. 1407, sec. 4862: day of special observance (Lincoln).

p. 1407, sec. 4863: physiology and hygiene, stimulants and narcotics.

p. 1413, sec. 4894: sectarian doctrine.

p. 1429, secs. 4957–4959: government of the state, government of the United States, history of the state, history of the United States.

1923

Statutes 1915 (codification including 1913), p. 801, sec. 2726: day of special observance (Arbor).

Laws of 1923, pp. 290–328, ch. 148 (New School Code),

p. 315, sec. 1102: sectarian doctrine.

p. 325, sec. 1416: flag display.

p. 325, sec. 1418: arithmetic, bookkeeping, civil government, constitution of the state, constitution of the United States, Declaration of Independence, drawing, English, foreign language, geography, history of the state, history of the United States, household arts, industrial arts, manners, morals, music, penmanship, personal hygiene, physical education, physiology and hygiene, reading, social and ethical outcomes, spelling.

New York

1903

Constitution, Art. IX, sec. 4: sectarian doctrine.

Revised Statutes 1901 (Birdseye Third Edition), Vol. I, The Consolidated School Law, pp. 559–654,

p. 576, sec. 68*a:* flag display.

p. 592, sec. 131, subsec. 11: physiology and hygiene, stimulants and narcotics.

p. 633, sec. 278: physiology and hygiene, stimulants and narcotics.

p. 639, secs. 303–306: day of special observance (Arbor).

p. 644, sec. 314: arithmetic, English, geography, penmanship, reading, spelling.

p. 653, secs. 355, 356: flag display.

p. 653, secs. 357–359: days of special observance (Flag, Lincoln, Memorial, Washington), flag exercises.

p. 653, secs. 360–362: fire drill.

1913

Constitution, Art. IX, sec. 4: sectarian doctrine.

Consolidated Education Law 1910,

p. 67, sec. 275, subsec. 10: physiology and hygiene, stimulants and narcotics.

p. 81, sec. 310, subsec. 5: physiology and hygiene, stimulants and narcotics.

p. 158, sec. 620: all instruction in English, arithmetic, English, geography, penmanship, reading, spelling.
p. 172, secs. 690, 691: physiology and hygiene, stimulants and narcotics.
p. 176, secs. 710, 711: flag display
p. 176, secs. 712, 713: days of special observance (Flag, Lincoln, Memorial, Washington), flag exercises.
p. 177, secs. 730–732: fire drill.
p. 178, secs. 750–752: day of special observance (Arbor).
Laws of 1913, Vol. III, p. 1675, ch. 627: physical examination.

1923
Constitution, Art. IX, sec. 4: sectarian doctrine.
Consolidated Laws 1917, Vol. II,
Education Law pp. 2007–2389,
p. 2107, sec. 275, subsec. 10: physiology and hygiene, stimulants and narcotics.
p. 2221, secs. 570–577: physical examination.
p. 2251, sec. 690: physiology and hygiene, stimulants and narcotics.
p. 2256, sec. 700: humane treatment and protection of animals and birds, importance of animals and birds.
p. 2256, secs. 710, 711: flag display.
p. 2257, secs. 712, 713: days of special observance (Flag, Lincoln, Memorial, Washington), flag exercises.
p. 2257, secs. 730–732: fire drill.
p. 2258, secs. 750–752: day of special observance (Arbor).
Laws of 1918, Vol. II, p. 886, ch. 241: citizenship, patriotism.
Laws of 1921, Vol. II,
p. 1211, ch. 386, sec. 1; all instruction in English, arithmetic, civil government, English, geography, history of the United States, penmanship, reading, spelling.
p. 1226, ch. 389: physical education.
Laws of 1923, p. 635, ch. 397: fire prevention.

North Carolina

1903
Public Laws 1901,
p. 3, ch. 1, sec. 2: reading, sectarian doctrine.
p. 57, ch. 4, sec. 37: agriculture, arithmetic, civil government, constitution of the state, constitution of the United States, drawing, English, geography, history of the state, history of the United States, penmanship, physiology and hygiene, spelling, stimulants and narcotics.
p. 63, ch. 4, sec. 63: social and ethical outcomes.

1913
Pell's Revisal of 1908, Vol. II,
p. 2049, sec. 4060: sectarian doctrine.
p. 2060, sec. 4087: agriculture, arithmetic, civil government, constitution of the state, constitution of the United States, drawing, English, geography, history of the state, history of the United States, penman-

ship, physiology and hygiene, reading, spelling, stimulants and narcotics.

p. 2094, sec. 4166: social and ethical outcomes.

p. 2101, secs. 4167*v*, 4167*w*, 4167*x*, 4167*y*: stimulants and narcotics.

1923

Consolidated Statutes 1919, Vol. II,

p. 276, secs. 5543–5545: day of special observance (Arbor).

Public Laws 1923,

p. 233, ch. 49: constitution of the state, constitution of the United States, patriotism.

p. 321, ch. 136, sec. 39: agriculture, all instruction in English, arithmetic, drawing, English, fire prevention, geography, history of the state, history of the United States, penmanship, physiology and hygiene, reading, spelling, stimulants and narcotics.

p. 354, ch. 136, sec. 165: music, social and ethical outcomes.

p. 356, ch. 136, sec. 170: physical examination.

p. 424, ch. 136, sec. 368: day of special observance (Temperance).

p. 425, ch. 136, sec. 369: day of special observance (Arbor).

North Dakota

1903

Constitution,

secs. 147 and 152: sectarian doctrine.

sec. 149: social and ethical outcomes.

Revised Codes 1899,

p. 216, sec. 709: all instruction in English.

p. 228, sec. 750: arithmetic, civil government, English, geography, history of the United States, penmanship, physiology and hygiene, reading, spelling, stimulants and narcotics.

p. 229, sec. 754: Bible reading, social and ethical outcomes.

p. 229, sec. 754*a*: physical education.

p. 255, sec. 865: flag display.

1913

Constitution,

secs. 147 and 152: sectarian doctrine.

sec. 149: social and ethical outcomes.

Compiled Laws 1913, Vol. I,

p. 290, sec. 1199: all instruction in English.

p. 332, sec. 1382: days of special observance (Lincoln, Memorial, Washington).

p. 332, sec. 1383: agriculture, arithmetic, civil government, communicable diseases, elementary science, English, geography, history of the United States, penmanship, physiology and hygiene, reading, spelling, stimulants and narcotics.

p. 332, sec. 1384: humane treatment and protection of animals and birds.

p. 333, sec. 1388: Bible reading.

p. 333, sec. 1389: social and ethical outcomes.

p. 334, sec. 1390: physical education.
p. 336, sec. 1400: flag display.
p. 351, sec. 1451: penmanship.

1923
Constitution,
secs. 147 and 152: sectarian doctrine.
sec. 149: social and ethical outcomes.
Compiled Laws 1913, Vol. I,
p. 290, sec. 1199: all instruction in English.
p. 332, sec. 1383: agriculture, arithmetic, civil government, communicable diseases, elementary science, English, geography, history of the United States, penmanship, physiology and hygiene, reading, spelling, stimulants and narcotics.
p. 332, sec. 1384: humane treatment and protection of animals and birds.
p. 333, sec. 1388: Bible reading.
p. 333, sec. 1389: social and ethical outcomes.
p. 334, sec. 1390: physical education.
p. 336, sec. 1400: flag display.
p. 351, sec. 1451: penmanship.
Laws of 1915, p. 174, ch. 137: fire drill.
Laws of 1917, p. 340, ch. 234: day of special observance (Temperance).
Laws of 1923, p. 402, ch. 282 (sec. 1382): days of special observance (Armistice, Columbus, Labor, Lincoln, Washington).

Ohio

1903
Constitution, Art. VI, sec. 2: sectarian doctrine.
Revised Statutes 1902, Vol. II,
p. 2197, sec. 3986–1: flag display.
p. 2235, sec. 4020–17: physical education.
p. 2236, sec. 4020–23: physiology and hygiene, stimulants and narcotics.
p. 2237, sec. 4021: German.
p. 2238, sec. 4022–1 and *General Acts 1902*, p. 115, (secs. 4007, 4007–1): arithmetic, English, geography, penmanship, reading, spelling.
General Acts 1902 (Vol. 95),
p. 38, day of special observance (Arbor).
p. 115 (secs. 4007, 4007–1): civil government, history of the United States, physiology and hygiene.

1913
Constitution, Art. VI, sec. 2: sectarian doctrine.
General Code 1910,
Vol. II,
p. 1615, sec. 7621: flag display.
p. 1621, sec. 7644
p. 1622, secs. 7645, 7648 }: civil government, history of the United States, physiology and hygiene.
p. 1621, sec. 7644
p. 1622, secs. 7645, 7648
p. 1643, sec. 7762 }: arithmetic, English, geography, penmanship, reading, spelling.

p. 1628, sec. 7688: day of special observance (Arbor).
p. 1635, sec. 7721: physical education.
p. 1635, secs. 7723, 7724: physiology and hygiene, stimulants and narcotics.
p. 1636, sec. 7729: all instruction in English, German.
Vol. III,
p. 2742, sec. 12900: fire drill.
p. 2742, secs. 12901, 12902: fire prevention.
Legislative Acts 1911 (Vol. 102) p. 38: agriculture.
Legislative Acts 1913 (Vol. 103) p. 134: accident prevention.

1923
Constitution, Art. VI, sec. 2: sectarian doctrine.
General Code 1920,
Vol. II,
p. 3511, sec. 7621: flag display.
p. 3522, secs. 7644, 7645
p. 3523, sec. 7648
p. 3558, sec. 7762
Vol. III, p. 5071, sec. 12974
}: arithmetic, citizenship, civil government, English, geography, history of the United States, penmanship, reading, spelling.
p. 3522, sec. 7645
p. 3523, sec. 7648
}: physiology and hygiene.
p. 3522, sec. 7645: thrift.
p. 3534, sec. 7688: day of special observance (Arbor).
p. 3545, secs. 7723, 7724: physiology and hygiene, stimulants and narcotics.
p. 3545, secs. 7724–1, 7724–2: accident prevention.
p. 3557, sec. 7761–1: agriculture.
p. 3558, sec. 7762–1: all instruction in English, German.
Legislative Acts 1921 (Vol. 109),
p. 253 (secs. 12900–12902): fire drill, fire prevention.
p. 587 (sec. 7688–1): day of special observance (Temperance).
Legislative Acts 1923 (Vol. 110),
p. 18 (secs. 7721 and 7721–1 to 7721–7): physical education, physical examination.
p. 411 (sec. 7645–1): constitution of the state, constitution of the United States.

Oklahoma

1903
U. S. Statutes At Large, Vol. XXIV, p. 69, ch. 362 (Forty-ninth Congress, 1885–1887, session I): physiology and hygiene, stimulants and narcotics.
Wilson's Statutes of 1903 (Territory of Oklahoma),
Vol. I, p. 143, secs. 17, 18: day of special observance (Arbor).
Vol. II,
p. 1387, sec. 6189: Bible reading, sectarian doctrine.
p. 1389, sec. 6199: all instruction in English, arithmetic, English, geography, penmanship, reading, spelling.

1913

Constitution,

Art. 1, sec. 5: all instruction in English.

Art. XIII, sec. 7: agriculture, household arts.

Revised Laws 1910, Vol. II,

p. 2084, secs. 7667, 7668: agriculture, household arts.

p. 2116, sec. 7775: all instruction in English, arithmetic, English, geography, penmanship, reading, spelling.

p. 2158, sec. 7939: flag display.

p. 2158, sec. 7940: Bible reading, sectarian doctrine.

p. 2158, sec. 7941: social and ethical outcomes.

p. 2159, sec. 7942: humane treatment and protection of animals and birds, importance of animals and birds.

p. 2159, sec. 7942: animal experimentation.

p. 2160, secs. 7952, 7953: day of special observance (Arbor).

1923

Constitution,

Art. 1, sec. 5: all instruction in English.

Art. XIII, sec. 7: agriculture, household arts.

Compiled Statutes 1921, Vol. II,

p. 1654, secs. 3875–3880: exhibitions.

p. 3403, sec. 10334: all instruction in English, agriculture, arithmetic, civil government, English, geography, history of the United States, penmanship, physiology and hygiene, reading, spelling.

p. 3450, secs. 10504–10512: agriculture, household arts.

p. 3478, sec. 10614: flag display.

p. 3478, secs. 10615, 10616: flag exercises.

p. 3478, sec. 10618: Bible reading, sectarian doctrine.

p. 3479, sec. 10621: social and ethical outcomes.

p. 3479, sec. 10622: humane treatment and protection of animals and birds, importance of animals and birds.

p. 3479, sec. 10623: animal experimentation.

p. 3480, sec. 10627: day of special observance (Arbor).

p. 3480, sec. 10630: physiology and hygiene, stimulants and narcotics.

p. 3481, secs. 10635, 10636: foreign language.

p. 3481, sec. 10638: history of the United States, patriotism.

Laws of 1923, p. 296, ch. 175, sec. 12: Darwinism.

Oregon

1903

Codes and Statutes 1901, Vol. II,

p. 1166, sec. 3396, subsec. 3: physiology and hygiene, social and ethical outcomes, stimulants and narcotics.

p. 1167, sec. 3396, subsecs. 5 and 8: physical education.

p. 1171, sec. 3408, subsec. 10: foreign language.

p. 1174, secs. 3426, 3427: day of special observance (Arbor).

1913

Lord's Oregon Laws 1909, Vol. II,

p. 1604, secs. 4057, 4058: flag display.

p. 1615, sec. 4102, subsec. 10: foreign language.

p. 1617, sec. 4117, subsec. 3: physiology and hygiene, social and ethical outcomes, stimulants and narcotics.

p. 1618, sec. 4117, subsecs. 5 and 8: physical education.

p. 1625, secs. 4135, 4136: day of special observance (Arbor).

General Laws 1913,

p. 158, ch. 94: days of special observance (Columbus, Lincoln, Washington).

p. 317, ch. 177: fire drill, fire prevention.

1923

Olson's Laws 1920,

Vol. I, p. 1274, sec. 2223–3: all instruction in English, foreign language.

Vol. II,

p. 2162, secs. 5073, 5074: flag display.

p. 2184, sec. 5175: days of special observance (Columbus, Labor, Lincoln, Washington).

p. 2203, sec. 5255, subsec. 3: physiology and hygiene, social and ethical outcomes, stimulants and narcotics.

p. 2203, sec. 5255, subsecs. 5 and 8: physical education.

p. 2205, secs. 5257, 5258: fire drill, fire prevention.

p. 2210, secs. 5275, 5276: physical education.

p. 2237, secs. 5390, 5391: day of special observance (Arbor).

p. 2237, sec. 5392: day of special observance (Temperance).

Laws of 1921, p. 805, ch. 410: humane treatment and protection of animals and birds, importance of animals and birds.

Laws of 1923, p. 17, ch. 7: constitution of the United States.

Pennsylvania

1903

Constitution, Art. X, sec. 2: sectarian doctrine.

Purdon's Digest, 1903, Vol. I,

Common Schools, pp. 638–718,

p. 660, sec. 109: arithmetic, English, geography, penmanship, reading, spelling.

p. 709, secs. 408, 409: physiology and hygiene, stimulants and narcotics.

p. 709, secs. 413, 414: physical education.

1913

Constitution, Art. X, sec. 2: sectarian doctrine.

Laws of 1911,

p. 294 (An Act to require fire drills in public schools): fire drill.

An act to establish a public school system, pp. 309–461,

p. 352, sec. 629: flag display.

p. 391, sec. 1501 to p. 392, sec. 1505: physical examination.

p. 394, sec. 1607: all instruction in English, arithmetic, civil government, English, geography, history of the state, history of the United States, humane treatment and protection of animals and birds, penmanship, physical education, physiology and hygiene, reading, spelling.

p. 394, sec. 1609: communicable diseases, physiology and hygiene, stimulants and narcotics.

p. 395, sec. 1610: animal experimentation, humane treatment and protection of animals and birds.

Laws of 1913, p. 226, no. 159: Bible reading.

1923

Constitution, Art. X, sec. 2: sectarian doctrine.

Digest of Statute Law 1920,

p. 468, secs. 5071–5073 and *Supplement 1924 to Digest of Statute Law*, p. 142, secs. 5070, 5074 (Laws of 1921, p. 939, no. 329): physical examination.

p. 470, sec. 5091: communicable diseases, physiology and hygiene, stimulants and narcotics.

p. 470, sec. 5092: animal experimentation, humane treatment and protection of animals and birds.

p. 470, secs. 5093, 5094: Bible reading.

p. 494, sec. 5401: fire drill.

p. 1068, sec. 10935: fire prevention.

p. 1161, secs. 11866, 11867: day of special observance (Bird).

Supplement 1924 to Digest of Statute Law,

p. 134, sec. 4854: flag display.

p. 143, sec. 5089 (Laws of 1921, p. 980, no. 351): accident prevention, all instruction in English, arithmetic, art, civil government, English, foreign language, geography, history of the state, history of the United States, humane treatment and protection of animals and birds, music, personal hygiene, physical education, penmanship, reading, spelling.

p. 143, secs. 5094*a*1, 5094*a*2, (Laws of 1923, p. 351, no. 223): constitution of the United States.

Rhode Island

1903

General Laws 1896,

p. 211, ch. 60, sec. 7: physiology and hygiene, stimulants and narcotics.

p. 215, ch. 61, sec. 7: morals.

Public Laws 1901, p. 168, or *Acts and Resolves 1901*, (January Session) p. 55, ch. 818: day of special observance (Lincoln), flag display, flag exercises.

1913

General Laws, Revision of 1909,

p. 267, ch. 64, sec. 7: flag exercises.

p. 274, ch. 67, sec. 4: physiology and hygiene, stimulants and narcotics.

p. 275, ch. 67, secs. 14, 15: flag display.

p. 275, ch. 67, sec. 16: day of sepcial observance (Lincoln).

p. 277, ch. 68, sec. 8: morals.

Public Laws 1908, p. 277, or *Acts and Resolves 1908*, p. 277, } ch. 1591: day of special observance (State).

Public Laws 1911, p. 143 or *Acts and Resolves 1911*, p. 143, } ch. 725: physical examination.

Public Laws 1912, p. 121, or *Acts and Resolves 1912*, p. 121, } ch. 797: fire drill.

1923

General Laws, 1923 Revision,

p. 335, secs. 936–938: fire prevention.

p. 335, sec. 941: flag exercises.

p. 336, secs. 942–945: day of special observance (State).

p. 346, sec. 985: physiology and hygiene, stimulants and narcotics.

p. 348, secs. 995, 996: flag display.

p. 349, sec. 998: civil government, government of the state, history of the state.

p. 350, sec. 1006: morals.

p. 350, sec. 1007 and p. 351, secs. 1008, 1009: fire drill.

p. 356, sec. 1033: days of special observance (Arbor, Lincoln).

p. 362, sec. 1054: physical examination.

p. 363, sec. 1058: physical education.

South Carolina

1903

Constitution, Art. XI, sec. 9: sectarian doctrine.

Code of Laws 1902, Vol. I,

p. 452, sec. 1175: sectarian doctrine.

p. 462, sec. 1201: agriculture, algebra, arithmetic, constitution of the state, constitution of the United States, English, geography, history of the state, history of the United States, manners, morals, penmanship, physiology and hygiene, reading, spelling, stimulants and narcotics.

p. 476, sec. 1242: day of special observance (Arbor).

1913

Constitution, Art. XI, sec. 9: sectarian doctrine.

Code of Laws 1912, Vol. I,

p. 472, sec. 1699: sectarian doctrine.

p. 480, sec. 1731: agriculture, algebra, arithmetic, constitution of the state, constitution of the United States, English, geography, history of the state, history of the United States, manners, morals, penmanship, physiology and hygiene, reading, spelling, stimulants and narcotics.

p. 480, secs. 1732, 1734: physiology and hygiene, stimulants and narcotics.

p. 496, sec. 1809: day of special observance (Arbor).

p. 496, sec. 1810: day of special observance (State).

1923

Constitution, Art. XI, sec. 9: sectarian doctrine.

Code of Laws 1922, Vol. III,

p. 746, sec. 2533: sectarian doctrine.

p. 761, sec. 2589: agriculture, algebra, arithmetic, constitution of the state, constitution of the United States, English, geography, history of the state, history of the United States, manners, morals, penmanship, physiology and hygiene, reading, spelling, stimulants and narcotics.

p. 762, secs. 2590–2592: physiology and hygiene, stimulants and narcotics.

p. 792, sec. 2696: day of special observance (Arbor).

p. 793, sec. 2697: day of special observance (State).

p. 793, sec. 2698: day of special observance (Temperance).

Acts of 1923,

p. 44, ch. 21: fire prevention.

p. 180, ch. 131, physical examination.

South Dakota

1903

Constitution, Art. VIII, sec. 16: sectarian doctrine.

Revised Codes 1903,

p. 427, sec. 2349: all instruction in English.

p. 429, sec. 2358: social and ethical outcomes.

p. 432, sec. 2378: arithmetic, civil government, English, geography, history of the United States, penmanship, physiology and hygiene, reading, spelling, stimulants and narcotics.

p. 441, sec. 2423: Bible reading, sectarian doctrine.

p. 447, secs. 2457, 2458: humane treatment and protection of animals and birds.

p. 447, sec. 2458: animal experimentation.

1913

Constitution, Art. VIII, sec. 16: sectarian doctrine.

Compiled Law 1913, Vol. I,

p. 588, sec. 131: all instruction in English.

p. 590*a*, sec. 138: arithmetic, civil government, drawing, English, geography, history of the state, history of the United States, music, penmanship, physiology and hygiene, reading, spelling, stimulants and narcotics.

p. 591, sec. 143: social and ethical outcomes.

p. 591, sec. 144: humane treatment and protection of animals and birds, animal experimentation.

p. 609, sec. 203: Bible reading, sectarian doctrine.

Laws of 1913, p. 234, ch. 189: flag display.

1923

Constitution, Art. VIII, sec. 16: sectarian doctrine.

Revised Code 1919, Vol. II,

p. 1878, sec. 7511: all instruction in English, arithmetic, civil government, drawing, English, geography, history of the state, history of the United

States, penmanship, physiology and hygiene, reading, spelling, stimulants and narcotics.

p. 1910, sec. 7631: social and ethical outcomes.

p. 1910, sec. 7632: music.

p. 1911, sec. 7637: humane treatment and protection of animals and birds.

p. 1911, sec. 7638: animal experimentation.

p. 1917, sec. 7659: Bible reading, sectarian doctrine.

p. 1917, sec. 7660: patriotism.

p. 1917, sec. 7661: flag display.

p. 1917, sec. 7662: day of special observance (Temperance).

Laws of 1923, p. 148, ch. 171: constitution of the state, constitution of the United States.

TENNESSEE

1903

Shannon's Code of 1896,

p. 413, sec. 1416, subsec. 10: day of special observance (Arbor).

p. 420, secs. 1452–1454: agriculture, algebra, arithmetic, bookkeeping, civil government, constitution of the United States, English, geography, history of the state, history of the United States, penmanship, physiology and hygiene, reading, spelling.

p. 420, sec. 1455: physiology and hygiene, stimulants and narcotics, tobacco.

Supplement 1904,

p. 244 (1899, p. 424, ch. 205, sec. 1): sectarian doctrine.

p. 269, sec. 1453 (1899, p. 38, ch. 28): constitution of the state.

1913

Shannon's Code of 1896,

p. 413, sec. 1416, subsec. 10: day of special observance (Arbor).

p. 420, secs. 1452–1454: agriculture, algebra, arithmetic, bookkeeping, civil government, constitution of the United States, English, geography, history of the state, history of the United States, penmanship, physiology and hygiene, reading, spelling.

p. 420, sec. 1455: physiology and hygiene, stimulants and narcotics, tobacco.

Supplement 1904

p. 244: sectarian doctrine.

p. 269, sec. 1453: constitution of the state.

1923

Compilation of the Statutes 1917, Vol. I,

p. 974, sec. 1447*a*2: Bible reading.

p. 984, sec. 1455: physiology and hygiene, stimulants and narcotics, tobacco.

p. 984, sec. 1456*a*1: day of special observance (Temperance).

p. 993, sec. 1461*a*24: sectarian doctrine.

Vol. II, p. 2185, sec. 3079*a*295: fire drill.

Vol. V, p. 6540, sec. 1453*b*1 (1917, p. 258, ch. 80): arithmetic, constitution of the state, constitution of the United States, English, geography, history of the state, history of the United States, music, penmanship, physiology and hygiene, reading, spelling.

Public Acts 1919,

p. 43, ch. 15: day of special observance (Arbor).

p. 579, ch. 153: flag display.

Public Acts 1921, p. 408, ch. 157: forestry and plant life.

Public Acts 1923,

p. 78, ch. 17: constitution of the United States.

p. 159, ch. 61: physical education.

Texas

1903

Constitution, Art. VII, sec. 5: sectarian doctrine.

Sayles' Civil Statutes 1897, Vol. II, p. 1421, sec. 3976*d*: all instruction in English, foreign language.

General Laws 1903, p. 229, ch. 140: arithmetic, civil government, English, geography, history of the state, history of the United States, humane treatment and protection of animals and birds, penmanship, physiology and hygiene, reading, spelling, stimulants and narcotics.

General Laws 1903 (First Called Session), p. 22, ch. 12, sec. 1: sectarian doctrine.

1913

Constitution, Art. VII, sec. 5: sectarian doctrine.

Vernon's Sayles' Civil Statutes 1914, Vol. II,

p. 1997, art. 2782: all instruction in English, foreign language.

p. 1998, art. 2783: agriculture, arithmetic, civil government, English, geography, history of the state, history of the United States, humane treatment and protection of animals and birds, penmanship, physiology and hygiene, reading, spelling, stimulants and narcotics.

p. 2040, art. 2896: sectarian doctrine.

p. 2046, art. 2909*bb:* sectarian doctrine.

General Laws 1913, p. 129, ch. 70: cotton grading.

1923

Constitution, Art. VII, sec. 5: sectarian doctrine.

Complete Statutes 1920,

p. 467, art. 2782: all instruction in English.

p. 467, art. 2783: agriculture, arithmetic, civil government, cotton grading, English, geography, history of the state, history of the United States, humane treatment and protection of animals and birds, penmanship, physiology and hygiene, reading, spelling, stimulants and narcotics.

p. 491, arts. 2903*a*, 2903*b:* history of the state.

p. 492, art. 2904*aa:* patriotism.

p. 492, arts. 2904*aaa*, 2904*aaaa:* flag display.

p. 492, art. 2904*aaaaa:* all instruction in English.

p. 298, art. 2909*bb:* sectarian doctrine.

Utah

1903

Constitution,

Art. III (Fourth) and Art. X, sec. 1: sectarian doctrine.

Art. X, sec. 11: metric system.

Revised Statutes 1898,

p. 438, sec. 1829: physiology and hygiene, stimulants and narcotics.

p. 441, sec. 1848: sectarian doctrine, social and ethical outcomes.

p. 441, sec. 1850: all instruction in English.

1913

Constitution,

Art. III (Fourth) and Art. X, sec. 1: sectarian doctrine.

Art. X, sec. 11: metric system.

Compiled Laws 1907,

p. 700, sec. 1829: physiology and hygiene, stimulants and narcotics.

p. 700, sec. 1829*x:* communicable diseases, sanitation.

p. 704, sec. 1848: sectarian doctrine, social and ethical outcomes.

p. 704, sec. 1850: all instruction in English.

p. 742, sec. 1965*x:* flag display.

Laws of 1911, p. 285, ch. 140: physical examination.

Laws of 1913, p. 93, ch. 60: day of special observance (Bird).

1923

Constitution,

Art. III (Fourth) and Art. X, sec. 1: sectarian doctrine.

Art. X, sec. 11: metric system.

Compiled Laws 1917,

p. 920, sec. 4533: day of special observance (Bird).

p. 920, sec. 4534: physiology and hygiene, stimulants and narcotics.

p. 921, sec. 4535: communicable diseases, sanitation.

p. 922, secs. 4546–4550: physical examination.

p. 957, sec. 4744: flag display.

Laws of 1921, p. 284, ch. 95: sectarian doctrine.

Laws of 1923, p. 4, ch. 4: constitution of the United States.

Vermont

1903

Statutes 1894,

p. 187, sec. 683 }
p. 208, sec. 812 }: arithmetic, constitution of the state, constitution of the United States, drawing, English, geography, government of the state, history of the state, history of the United States, manners, penmanship, physiology and hygiene, reading, spelling, stimulants and narcotics.

p. 188, sec. 684: day of special observance (Memorial).

p. 209, sec. 826: foreign language.

1913

Public Statutes 1906,

p. 274, sec. 1003: arithmetic, constitution of the state, constitution of the United States, drawing, English, geography, government of the state, history of the state, history of the United States, manners, penmanship, physiology and hygiene, reading, spelling, stimulants and narcotics.

p. 275, sec. 1005: day of special observance (Memorial).

p. 303, secs. 1160–1162: fire drill.

p. 303, sec. 1164: physical examination.

Acts of 1910, p. 77, ch. 67: flag display.

1923

General Laws 1917,

p. 295, sec. 1240: day of special observance (Memorial).

p. 295, sec. 1241: day of special observance (Lincoln).

p. 308, sec. 1319: physical examination.

p. 309, secs. 1322–1324: fire drill.

p. 310, sec. 1326: flag display.

Acts of 1923, p. 56, no. 35 (sec. 1237): arithmetic, citizenship, constitution of the state, constitution of the United States, drawing, English, geography, government of the state, history of the state, history of the United States, manners, penmanship, physiology and hygiene, reading, spelling, stimulants and narcotics.

Virginia

1903

Acts of 1903, p. 817, ch. 509 (pp. 798–823), sec. 1497: arithmetic, civil government, drawing, English, geography, history of the state, history of the United States, penmanship, physiology and hygiene, reading, spelling, stimulants and narcotics.

1913

Acts of 1906, p. 443, ch. 248, sec. 1497: arithmetic, civil government, drawing, English, geography, history of the state, history of the United States, morals, penmanship, physiology and hygiene, reading, spelling, stimulants and narcotics.

Acts of 1908, p. 661, ch. 377: physical examination.

1923

General Laws 1923,

p. 189, sec. 702: accident prevention, arithmetic, citizenship, civil government, drawing, English, fire prevention, geography, history of the state, history of the United States, morals, penmanship, physiology and hygiene. reading, spelling, stimulants and narcotics.

p. 190, sec. 702*a:* personal hygiene, physical education, physical examination.

p. 193, sec. 724: physical examination.

WASHINGTON

1903

Constitution, Art. IX, sec. 4: sectarian doctrine.

Ballinger's Codes and Statutes 1897, Vol. I,

p. 605, sec. 2329: social and ethical outcomes.

p. 607, sec. 2335: all instruction in English, arithmetic, English, geography, history of the United States, humane treatment and protection of animals and birds, penmanship, physiology and hygiene, reading, social and ethical outcomes, spelling, stimulants and narcotics.

p. 646, sec. 2464: animal experimentation.

p. 646, sec. 2466: flag display.

Mahan's Supplement 1899–1903, p. 228, sec. 2311 (Tenth): sectarian doctrine.

1913

Constitution, Art. IX, sec. 4: sectarian doctrine.

Remington and Ballinger's Code 1910, Vol. II,

p. 451, sec. 4407: all instruction in English, arithmetic, English, geography, history of the United States, humane treatment and protection of animals and birds, penmanship, physiology and hygiene, reading, social and ethical outcomes, spelling, stimulants and narcotics.

p. 453, sec. 4414: sectarian doctrine.

p. 471, sec. 4481 (ninth): sectarian doctrine.

p. 472, sec. 4482: flag display.

p. 490, sec. 4550: social and ethical outcomes.

p. 533, sec. 4703: animal experimentation.

p. 544, sec. 4748: fire drill.

1923

Constitution, Art. IX, sec. 4: sectarian doctrine.

Remington's Compiled Statutes 1922, Vol. II,

p. 698, sec. 4681: all instruction in English, arithmetic, English, geography, history of the United States, humane treatment and protection of animals and birds, penmanship, physiology and hygiene, reading, social and ethical outcomes, spelling, stimulants and narcotics.

p. 698, sec. 4682: physical education.

p. 727, secs. 4777, 4778: flag display, flag exercises.

p. 751, sec. 4855: social and ethical outcomes.

p. 762, sec. 4899: day of special observance (Armistice).

p. 814, sec. 5061: animal experimentation.

p. 827, sec. 5106: fire drill.

Laws of 1923, p. 236, ch. 76: day of special observance (Temperance). (*Supplement 1923*, p. 257, sec. 4901–1).

WEST VIRGINIA

1903

Warth's Code 1899, Ch. 45 (pp. 385–455),

p. 392, sec. 11: arithmetic, bookkeeping, civil government, English, geography, history of the state, history of the United States, penmanship, physiology and hygiene, reading, spelling.

p. 392, sec. 11*a:* physiology and hygiene, stimulants and narcotics.
p. 406, sec. 32: social and ethical outcomes.

1913
Hogg's Code 1913, Vol. I,
p. 278, sec. 712: days of special observance (Columbus, Lincoln).
p. 880, secs. 2125–2129: physical examination.
p. 883, sec. 2131: agriculture, arithmetic, bookkeeping, civil government, English, geography, history of the state, history of the United States, penmanship, physiology and hygiene, reading, spelling, stimulants and narcotics.

1923
Barnes' Code 1923,
p. 318, ch. 15*q:* days of special observance (Columbus, Lincoln).
p. 823, ch. 45, sec. 9: all instruction in English.
p. 829, ch. 45, sec. 27: fire prevention.
p. 845, ch. 45, sec. 57: day of special observance (Washington).
Acts of 1923
p. 37, ch. 7: flag display.
p. 39, ch. 10: civil government, constitution of the state, constitution of the United States, history of the United States.

WISCONSIN

1903
Constitution, Art. X, sec. 3: sectarian doctrine.
Statutes of 1898, Vol. I,
p. 357, sec. 436*a:* flag display.
p. 363, sec. 447: all instruction in English, arithmetic, constitution of the state, constitution of the United States, English, foreign language, geography, history of the United States, penmanship, reading, spelling.
p. 364, sec. 447*a:* physiology and hygiene, stimulants and narcotics.

1913
Constitution, Art. X, sec. 3: sectarian doctrine.
Statutes 1913,
p. 251, sec. 436*a:* flag display.
p. 258, sec. 447: agriculture, all instruction in English, arithmetic, English, foreign language, geography, government of the state, government of the United States, history of the state, history of the United States, penmanship, reading, spelling.
p. 258, sec. 447*a:* physiology and hygiene, stimulants and narcotics.
p. 258, sec. 447*g:* accident prevention.
p. 314, sec. 553*a:* physical education.
p. 314, sec. 553*a*–1: humane treatment and protection of animals and birds, importance of animals and birds, social and ethical outcomes.

1923
Constitution, Art. X, sec. 3: sectarian doctrine.
Statutes 1923, Vol. I,

p. 422, sec. 40.27, subsec. 3: flag display.
p. 424, sec. 40.28, subsec. 3: days of special observance (Lincoln, Washington).
p. 425, sec. 40.30, subsec. 1: agriculture, all instruction in English, arithmetic, citizenship, English, foreign language, geography, government of the state, government of the United States, history of the state, history of the United States, penmanship, reading, spelling.
p. 425, sec. 40.30, subsec. 2: communicable diseases, personal hygiene, physiology and hygiene, sanitation, stimulants and narcotics.
p. 426, sec. 40.30, subsec. 3: physical education.
p. 426, sec. 40.30, subsec. 4: accident prevention.
p. 426, sec. 40.30, subsec. 5: humane treatment and protection of animals and birds, importance of animals and birds, social and ethical outcomes.
p. 426, sec. 40.30, subsec. 6: fire drill.
p. 427, sec. 40.30, subsec. 7: importance of animals and birds.
p. 427, sec. 40.30, subsec. 7*a:* fire prevention.
p. 448, sec. 40.67: sectarian doctrine.

WYOMING

1903
Constitution, Art. VII, sec. 12: sectarian doctrine.
Revised Statutes 1899,
p. 225, sec. 612: physiology and hygiene, stimulants and narcotics.
p. 729, sec. 2697: day of special observance (Arbor).
Session Laws of 1901, p. 7, ch. 8: humane treatment and protection of animals and birds.
Session Laws of 1903, p. 114, ch. 83: flag display.

1913
Constitution, Art. VII, sec. 12: sectarian doctrine.
Compiled Statutes 1910,
p. 544, sec. 1976: humane treatment and protection of animals and birds.
p. 547, sec. 1991: flag display.
p. 877, sec. 3582: day of special observance (Arbor).
Session Laws of 1913, p. 45, ch. 53: agriculture, arithmetic, elementary science, English, geography, government of the state, history of the state, history of the United States, humane treatment and protection of animals and birds, penmanship, physiology and hygiene, reading, spelling, stimulants and narcotics.

1923
Constitution, Art. VII, sec. 12: sectarian doctrine.
Compiled Statutes, 1920,
p. 479, sec. 2267: agriculture, arithmetic, elementary science, English, geography, government of the state, history of the state, history of the United States, humane treatment and protection of animals and birds, penmanship, physiology and hygiene, reading, spelling, stimulants and narcotics.

p. 481, sec. 2282: humane treatment and protection of animals and birds.
p. 481, secs. 2283–2287: physical examination.
p. 484, sec. 2302: flag display.
p. 831, sec. 4523: day of special observance (Arbor).

II

BIBLIOGRAPHY

GENERAL

"Facts on the Public School Curriculum" in *Research Bulletin of the National Education Association,* volume I, no. 5 (1924), containing Statutory and State Board of Education Requirements Relative to Elementary School Curricula, based upon information obtained from the Superintendents of the Forty-eight States; containing, also, a Selected and Annotated Bibliography.

The Statutes at Large of the United States of America. Edited, printed and published by authority of Congress under the direction of the Secretary of State. Washington, Government Printing Office (as cited).

Barnes' Federal Code, containing all Federal Statutes of General and Public Nature now in force. Edited by Uriah Barnes, Indianapolis, Bobbs-Merrill, 1919.

Supplement, 1923, to *Barnes' Federal Code,* containing all Federal Statutes of General and Public Nature enacted during the years 1919–1922. Edited by Uriah Barnes, Indianapolis, Bobbs-Merrill.

The Federal and State Constitutions, Colonial Charters, and other Organic Laws of the States, Territories and Colonies now or heretofore forming the United States of America, compiled and edited by Francis Newton Thorpe. 7 vol. Washington, Government Printing Office, 1909.

The State Constitution and the Federal Constitution and Organic Laws of the Territories and other Colonial Dependencies of the United States of America, compiled and edited by Charles Kettleborough. Indianapolis, B. F. Bowen & Co., 1918.

Index Digest of the State Constitutions, prepared by the Legislative Drafting Research Fund of Columbia University. The New York State Constitutional Convention Commission, 1915.

Note. A copy of the state constitution is included almost invariably in each compilation.

REFERENCES TO STATE LAWS

ALABAMA

Code of 1896, approved February 16, 1897, 2 vol.

Code of 1907, approved July 27, 1907, 3 vol.

General Laws and Joint Resolutions of the Legislature of Alabama, 1898–1923 (as cited).

ARIZONA

The Revised Statutes of Arizona Territory, 1901.

The Revised Statutes, Civil Code, 1913.
Acts, Resolutions and Memorials of the Legislature of Arizona, 1903–1923 (as cited).

ARKANSAS

A Digest of the Statutes in Force 1903, compiled by W. F. Kirby (cited as Kirby's Digest of the Statutes, 1904).
Supplement to Kirby's Digest of the Statutes in Force 1911, compiled by J. T. Castle.
A Digest of the Statutes in Force 1919, compiled by Crawford and Moses.
General Acts and Joint Concurrent Resolutions of the General Assembly, 1913–1923 (as cited).

CALIFORNIA

The Political Code, as amended to and including 1903.
The Political Code, as amended to and including 1909.
Consolidated Supplement to the Codes and General Laws, showing changes for 1911 and 1913.
General Laws of 1915, as amended to end of extra session 1916.
Consolidated Supplement to the Codes and General Laws, showing changes for 1917, 1919 and 1921.
The Political Code, as amended to and including 1923.
Statutes, 1923, including General Laws, Amendments to Codes, Resolutions, passed at session of Legislature 1923; Measures submitted to electors 1922.
The Constitution with Amendments to and including November 7, 1922, edited by E. F. Treadwell. Fifth Edition, 1923.
Index to the Laws, 1850–1920, including Statutes, Codes, and Constitution with Amendments, prepared by Legislative Counsel.

COLORADO

Mills' Annotated Statutes,
Volumes I and II, Embracing the General Statutes of 1883 and subsequent General Laws in force January 1, 1891.
Volume III, embracing subsequent General Laws to January 1, 1897.
Mills' Annotated Statutes, Revised Edition, 1912. 2 vol.
The Compiled Laws, 1921.
Laws passed at sessions of the General Assembly, 1897–1923 (as cited).

CONNECTICUT

The General Statutes, Revision of 1902.
The General Statutes, Revision of 1918, 3 vol.
Public Acts passed by the General Assembly, 1903–1923 (as cited).

DELAWARE

The Revised Statutes of 1852, as amended to and including 1893.
Revised Statutes, 1915 (including General Laws in force in 1913).
Laws of the State of Delaware passed at sessions of the General Assembly, 1895–1923 (as cited).

FLORIDA

The Revised Statutes, 1892.

The Compiled Laws, 1914 (including General Laws in force in 1913. Annotated), 3 vol.

The Revised General Statutes, 1919, 3 vol.

Acts and Resolutions adopted by the Legislature, 1893–1923 (as cited).

GEORGIA

The Code of 1895, adopted December 15, 1895, 3 vol.

Supplement to the Code of 1895, prepared by Howard Van Epps. 1901.

The Code of 1910, adopted August 15, 1910, prepared by John L. Hopkins. 2 vol.

Park's Annotated Code, 1914, embracing amendments and additions to Code of 1910 to and including 1914. 7 vol.

Supplement to Park's Annotated Code, 1922, embracing amendments and additions 1915–1921 inclusive, prepared by H. B. Skillman. 4 vol. (issued as Volumes VIII, IX, X and XI).

Acts and Resolutions of the General Assembly, 1901-1923 (as cited).

IDAHO

Political, Civil, Civil Procedure and Penal Codes, 1901 (annotated). 4 vol.

The Revised Codes, 1908, prepared by John F. McLane. 2 vol.

The Compiled Statutes of 1919. 3 vol.

General Laws passed at sessions of the State Legislature, 1903–1923, (as cited).

ILLINOIS

The Revised Statutes of 1903, containing the *General Statutes in Force January 1, 1904,* compiled by H. B. Hurd.

Annotated Statutes in Force January 1, 1913, edited by Jones and Addington. 6 vol. (Cited as J. and A., Annotated Statutes, 1913.)

Revised Statutes, embracing all general laws in force July 1, 1923, compiled by J. C. Cahill.

Laws enacted at sessions of the General Assembly 1903–1923 (as cited).

INDIANA

The Revised Statutes, embracing General Laws in force October 1, 1901 (annotated), compiled by F. A. Horner. 2 vol.

Burns' Annotated Statutes, showing General Statutes in force January 1, 1914. 4 vol.

A General Index to Burns' Annotated Statutes of 1914.

Burns' Annotated Statutes, Supplement of 1921, containing the General Statutes enacted at Legislative sessions 1915–1921, prepared by Burns and Gifford. 2 vol.

Laws passed at sessions of the General Assembly 1903–1923 (as cited).

IOWA

Annotated Code of 1897, containing all laws of a general nature to July 2, 1897.
Supplement, 1902, to the Code, containing general and permanent laws enacted by General Assemblies 27–29.
Supplement, 1913, to the Code, containing general and permanent laws enacted by General Assemblies 27–35.
Code, 1919, containing all general laws, compiled by Trewin, Mabry and Whitney, Code Commissioners.
Supplement, 1923, to the Compiled Code, containing all general laws enacted. by 39th and 40th General Assemblies.
Acts and Joint Resolutions passed at sessions of General Assembly (as cited).

KANSAS

General Statutes 1901, including the Session Laws of 1901.
General Statutes 1909, including the Session Laws of 1909 (annotated).
Revised Statutes 1923 (annotated), containing all laws of a general nature in force, including acts passed at the regular and special sessions of 1923.
Session Laws 1903–1923 (as cited).

KENTUCKY

The Statutes of 1903, containing all general laws, prepared by J. D. Carroll (cited as Carroll's Statutes 1903).
The Statutes of 1909, containing all general laws, prepared by J. D. Carroll (cited as Carroll's Statutes 1909).
The Statutes of 1922, containing all general laws. Sixth Edition, revised to January 1922 (cited as Carroll's Statutes 1922).
Acts of the General Assembly 1910–1922 (as cited).

LOUISIANA

Constitution and Revised Laws, compiled by Solomon Wolff.
Volumes I and II, to and including 1902.
Volume III (supplemental), containing General Statutes, 1904-1908.
Constitution and Statutes, as Amended to January 1920, compiled by Solomon Wolff. 3 vol.
Constitution adopted June 18, 1921.
Acts passed by the General Assembly 1910–1922 (as cited).

MAINE

The Revised Statutes, 1903, passed September 1, 1903.
The Revised Statutes, Sixth Edition, passed September 29, 1916.
Acts and Resolves of the Legislature 1905-1923 (as cited).

MARYLAND

The Code of 1888, public general laws codified by J. P. Poe, adopted March 14, 1888. 2 vol.
Supplement to the Code of 1888, containing the general public laws passed at sessions of the General Assembly 1890–1898.

The Annotated Code of the Public Civil Laws, including the general laws of 1910, edited by G. P. Bagby. 2 vol.

The Annotated Code of the Public General Laws, including 1914, edited by G. P. Bagby (volume III).

Laws made and passed at sessions of the General Assembly 1900–1922 (as cited).

MASSACHUSETTS

The Revised Laws, 1902, enacted November 21, 1901, to take effect January 1, 1902. 2 vol.

The Index of the Revised Laws, 1902.

Supplement to the Revised Laws, containing the general laws enacted 1902–1908.

The General Laws, 1921, enacted December 22, 1920. 2 vol.

The Index to the General Laws of 1921.

Acts and Resolves passed by the General Court 1902–1908 (as cited).

MICHIGAN

The Compiled Laws, 1897, compiled by L. M. Miller. 3 vol.

Index to the Compiled Laws of 1897, by L. M. Miller.

Howell's Annotated Statutes, Second Edition, 1913, compiled by C. P. Campbell, including the acts of the second extra session of 1912. 6 vol.

The Compiled Laws, 1915. 5 vol.

Annotated Supplement, 1922, to the Compiled Laws of 1915, prepared by J. C. Cahill.

Public Acts of the Legislature 1898–1923 (as cited).

MINNESOTA

The General Statutes, 1894, including all general laws in force December 31, 1894. 2 vol.

General Statutes, 1913.

Supplement, 1917, to the General Statutes, including General Laws of 1917.

General Laws passed at sessions of the Legislature 1895–1913 (as cited).

Session Laws passed by Legislature 1915–1923 (as cited).

MISSISSIPPI

The Annotated Code of the General Statute Law, adopted at regular Legislative session in 1892.

The Code of 1896 of the Public Statute Law.

The Annotated Code, showing general statutes in force August 1, 1917, prepared by William Hemingway. 2 vol.

Supplement of 1921 to the Annotated Code, including General Statutes of 1920.

Laws passed at sessions of Legislature 1892–1922 (as cited).

MISSOURI

The Revised Statutes, 1899, revised and promulgated by the Fortieth General Assembly. 2 vol.

The Revised Statutes, 1909, revised and promulgated by the Forty-fifth General Assembly. 3 vol.

The Revised Statutes, 1919, revised and promulgated by the Fiftieth General Assembly. 3 vol.

Laws passed at sessions of the General Assembly 1901–1923 (as cited).

MONTANA

The Complete Codes and Statutes in Force July 1, 1895, edited by W. F. Sanders.

The Revised Codes of 1907, containing all general laws in force at close of Tenth Legislative Assembly. 2 vol.

The Revised Codes of 1921, containing the permanent laws in force 1921. 4 vol.

Laws, Resolutions and Memorials passed at sessions of the Legislative Assembly 1897–1923 (as cited).

NEBRASKA

The Compiled Statutes, 1881, with Amendments, 1882 to 1901, comprising all general laws in force July 1, 1901 (cited as Compiled Statutes 1901).

The Revised Statutes, 1913, containing all general laws in force January 1, 1914.

Compiled Statutes, 1922, comprising all statutory laws of a general character in force July 1, 1922.

Laws, Resolutions and Memorials passed by the Legislatures 1903–1923 (as cited).

NEVADA

The Compiled Laws in Force 1861–1900, compiled by H. C. Cutting (cited as Compiled Laws 1900).

Revised Laws, 1912, containing general statutes from 1861, revised to 1912. 2 vol.

Revised Laws, Supplement 1919, containing statutes of a general nature from 1913 to 1919 (Volume III).

Statutes passed at sessions of the Legislature 1901–1923 (as cited).

NEW HAMPSHIRE

The Public Statutes and General Laws in force January 1, 1901, compiled by Chase and Chase.

Supplement to the Public Statutes, giving all amendments to and including 1913.

Laws passed at sessions of the Legislature 1901–1923 (as cited).

NEW JERSEY

General Statutes 1896. 3 vol.

Compiled Statutes 1910. 5 vol.

First Supplement to the Compiled Statutes (1911–1915).

Acts of the Legislature 1896–1923 (as cited).

New Mexico

Compiled Laws (Territory of New Mexico), approved March 16, 1897.

Statutes Annotated, 1915, containing the Codification passed at the second session of the State Legislature.

Acts of the Territorial Legislative Assembly 1899–1903 (as cited).

Laws passed by sessions of the State Legislature 1915–1923 (as cited).

New York

The Revised Statutes, Codes and General Laws in force January 1, 1902. Third Edition, compiled by C. F. Birdseye. 3 vol.

The Consolidated Laws, 1909, edited by F. E. Wadhams, Secretary of the Board of Statutory Consolidation. 7 vol.

The Consolidated Laws as amended by the Legislature of 1910 (*Laws 1910,* Chapter 140), Volume VIII (cited as *Consolidated Education Law 1910*).

Annotated Consolidated Laws, Second Edition, as amended to January 1, 1918, edited by Cummings and Gilbert. 9 vol.

Cumulative Supplement to Annotated Consolidated Laws, Second Edition, with amendments and other general statutes to and including 1920. 2 vol.

Cumulative Supplement to Annotated Consolidated Laws, Second Edition, with amendments and other general statutes to and including 1923. 2 vol. Edited by Cummings and Gilbert.

Laws passed at sessions of the Legislature 1902–1923 (as cited).

North Carolina

Code of 1899.

Revisal of 1908, prepared by G. P. Pell, including public laws of 1908. 2 vol.

Supplement to Pell's Revisal, edited by E. C. Gregory, containing General Laws of 1913 (cited as Gregory's Supplement, 1913).

Consolidated Statutes, 1919, prepared by L. P. McGehee (annotated). 2 vol.

Public Laws and Resolutions passed by the General Assembly at sessions 1899–1923 (as cited).

North Dakota

The Revised Codes, 1899.

The Compiled Laws, 1913. 2 vol.

Laws passed at sessions of the Legislative Assembly 1901–1923 (as cited).

Ohio

The Annotated Revised Statutes, including all general laws in force January 1, 1902, compiled by Clement Bates, Third Edition. 3 vol.

The General Code, 1910, approved February 15, 1910. 4 vol.

The General Code, Revised Compact Edition, including all laws of a general nature in force January 1, 1921. Revised by W. H. Page.

General and Local Acts and Joint Resolutions adopted by General Assemblies 1902–1908 (as cited).

Legislative Acts and Joint Resolutions adopted by General Assemblies 1909–1923 (as cited).

Oklahoma

Annotated Statutes of the Indian Territory, 1899, embracing all laws of general and permanent character in force at close of second session of Fifty-fifth Congress, prepared by Dorset Carter.

Revised and Annotated Statutes, 1903 (Territory of Oklahoma), prepared by W. F. Wilson. 2 vol. (cited as Wilson's Statutes of 1903).

Revised Laws of Oklahoma, 1910, prepared by Harris and Day, edited by C. O. Bunn. 2 vol.

Compiled Statutes, 1921, annotated by C. O. Bunn. 2 vol.

Session Laws passed at sessions of Legislative Assembly of Territory 1903–1905 (as cited).

Session Laws passed at sessions of the State Legislature 1907–1923 (as cited).

Oregon

The Codes and Statutes, including general laws in force 1901, compiled by Bellinger and Cotton. 2 vol.

Lord's Laws, including general laws in force 1909, 3 vol.

Laws, including general laws in force 1920, compiled by C. P. Olson. 2 vol.

General Laws and Joint Resolutions and Memorials adopted at sessions of Legislative Assembly 1903–1923 (as cited).

Pennsylvania

A Digest of the Statute Law from 1700 to 1903. Originally compiled in 1811 by John Purdon. Thirteenth Edition, compiled by Ardemas Stewart. 4 vol.

Supplement to Stewart's Purdon's Digest. A Digest of the Statute Law for the years 1905–1909.

Cumulative Supplement to Purdon's Digest, A Digest of the Statute Law for the year 1911.

Digest of the Statute Law, 1920, containing all the General Statutes of the Commonwealth down to 1920.

Supplement, 1924, to Digest of Statute Law, containing general statutes of 1921 and 1923.

Laws of the General Assembly passed at sessions 1903–1923 (as cited).

Rhode Island

General Laws of the State of Rhode Island and Providence Plantations, 1896.

General Laws, Revision of 1909.

Index to General Laws, Revision of 1909.

General Laws, Revision of 1923.

Index to General Laws, Revision of 1923.

Public Laws of the State of Rhode Island and Providence Plantations passed at sessions for the General Assembly 1896–1923 (as cited).

Acts and Resolves passed by the General Assembly of the State of Rhode Island and Providence Plantations at sessions 1896–1923 (as cited).

South Carolina

Code of Laws, 1902, 2 vol.

Code of Laws, 1912, 2 vol.
Code of Laws, 1922, 3 vol.
Acts and Joint Resolutions passed at sessions of the General Assembly 1902–1923 (as cited).

South Dakota

The Revised Codes, 1903, Official State Edition.
The Compiled Law, 1913.
The Revised Code, 1919. 2 vol.
Laws passed at sessions of the Legislature 1903–1923 (as cited).

Tennessee

Annotated Code, 1896, including public and permanent statutes of a general nature, compiled by R. T. Shannon (cited as Shannon's Code of 1896).
Supplement, 1904, to Shannon's Code, including general laws of 1903.
A Compilation of the Statutes of a general public nature in force January 1, 1917. Annotated by R. T. Shannon. 4 vol.
A Compilation of the Statutes of a general nature in force on January 1, 1919, by including acts of 1917 in body of work and in a supplement. (Vol. V).
Index to Shannon's Code, prepared by R. T. Shannon.
Public Acts passed by the General Assembly 1903–1923 (as cited).

Texas

Annotated Civil Statutes, 1897, compiled by Sayles and Sayles. 2 vol. (cited as *Sayles' Civil Statutes 1897*).
Revised Civil Statutes, 1911, adopted at regular session of Thirty-second Legislature.
Vernon's Sayles' Annotated Civil Statutes, 1914, embracing Revised Statutes of 1911, with amendments to close of Legislature 1913. 5 vol.
Complete Statutes, 1920, including general statutes to and including Thirty-sixth Legislature.
General Laws passed at sessions of Legislature 1897–1923 (as cited).

Utah

The Revised Statutes in Force January 1, 1898, revised by Young, Smith and Lee.
The Compiled Laws, 1907, compiled by Hammond and Smith.
The Compiled Laws, 1917, compiled by Sanford and Thurman.
Laws passed at sessions of the Legislature 1899–1923 (as cited).

Vermont

The Statutes, 1894, including the public acts of 1894.
The Public Statutes, 1906, including the public acts of 1906.
The General Laws, 1917, including the public acts of 1917.
Acts and Resolves passed by the General Assembly at sessions 1896–1923 (as cited).

VIRGINIA

The Code, 1887.

Supplement to the Code, containing acts of general and permanent nature, 1898.

Code as amended to adjournment of General Assembly 1904 (annotated). Edited by J. G. Pollard. 2 vol.

Pollard's Supplement to the Code, containing general statutes passed 1906–1910.

General Laws, as in Force July, 1 1923, edited by C. H. Morrissett.

Acts and Joint Resolutions passed by General Assembly, sessions 1899–1923 (as cited).

WASHINGTON

Annotated Codes and Statutes, showing all statutes in force 1897, prepared by R. A. Ballinger. 2 vol.

Supplement to Ballinger's Codes and Statutes, containing general statutes and code amendments, 1899–1903, compiled by J. H. Mahan.

Annotated Codes and Statutes, showing statutes in force 1909, prepared by R. C. Ballinger and Arthur Remington. 2 vol. (cited as Remington and Ballinger's Code 1910).

Index to Remington and Ballinger's Annotated Code, prepared by E. G. Kreider, 1910.

Supplement to Remington and Ballinger's Annotated Codes and Statutes, showing general statutes 1911 and 1913 (Volume III) prepared by Arthur Remington.

Compiled Statutes, showing all statutes in force to and including 1921, prepared by Arthur Remington. 3 vol.

Supplement, 1923, to Remington's Compiled Statutes (including 1923).

WEST VIRGINIA

The Code (Fourth Edition), containing the code as amended to and including 1899 with an appendix containing all other general statutes in force, compiled by J. A. Warth.

Code Annotated, containing the code as amended to and including 1913, edited by C. E. Hoggs. 3 vol.

Code, 1923, containing all statutes of a general nature now in force, edited by Uriah Barnes.

Acts of the Legislature at sessions 1901–1923 (as cited).

WISCONSIN

Statutes of 1898, approved August 20, 1897, edited by Sanborn and Berryman. 2 vol.

Statutes, 1913, embracing all general laws in force at the close of the General Session of 1913, consolidated and revised by Nash and Belitz.

Statutes, 1923, edited by E. E. Brossard. 2 vol.

The Laws, Joint Resolutions and Memorials passed at sessions of the Legislature 1899–1903 (as cited).

WYOMING

Revised Statutes in force December 1, 1899, revised by Van Orsdel and Chatterton.

Compiled Statutes, Annotated, 1910, including permanent laws in force on March 10, 1909. Compiled by W. E. Mullen.

Compiled Statutes, Annotated, 1920, including permanent laws in force on March 10, 1919, compiled by Mullen and Swainson.

Session Laws passed by Legislatures 1901–1923 (as cited).

INDEX